WHOLE WIDE WORLD
EASTER ISLAND

by Kristine Spanier, MLIS

Ideas for Parents and Teachers

Pogo Books let children practice reading informational text while introducing them to nonfiction features such as headings, labels, sidebars, maps, and diagrams, as well as a table of contents, glossary, and index.

Carefully leveled text with a strong photo match offers early fluent readers the support they need to succeed.

Before Reading

- "Walk" through the book and point out the various nonfiction features. Ask the student what purpose each feature serves.
- Look at the glossary together. Read and discuss the words.

Read the Book

- Have the child read the book independently.
- Invite him or her to list questions that arise from reading.

After Reading

- Discuss the child's questions. Talk about how he or she might find answers to those questions.
- Prompt the child to think more. Ask: Did you know about Easter Island before reading this book? What more would you like to learn about it?

Pogo Books are published by Jump!
5357 Penn Avenue South
Minneapolis, MN 55419
www.jumplibrary.com

Library of Congress Cataloging-in-Publication Data

Names: Spanier, Kristine, author.
Title: Easter Island / by Kristine Spanier, MLIS.
Description: Minneapolis, MN: Jump!, Inc., [2022]
Series: Whole wide world
Includes index. | Audience: Ages 7-10
Identifiers: LCCN 2021025759 (print)
LCCN 2021025760 (ebook)
ISBN 9781636903071 (hardcover)
ISBN 9781636903088 (paperback)
ISBN 9781636903095 (ebook)
Subjects: LCSH: Easter Island—History—Juvenile literature.
Classification: LCC F3169 .S63 2022 (print)
LCC F3169 (ebook) | DDC 996.18—dc23
LC record available at https://lccn.loc.gov/2021025759
LC ebook record available at https://lccn.loc.gov/2021025760

Editor: Jenna Gleisner
Designer: Molly Ballanger

Photo Credits: Vladimir Krupenkin/Shutterstock, cover; yakthai/Shutterstock, 1; Sergey-73/Shutterstock, 3, 9; Fotografia Torino/Shutterstock, 4; Ricardojara/Dreamstime, 5; Bryan Busovicki/Shutterstock, 6-7; mdulieu/iStock, 8; abriendomundo/Shutterstock, 10-11; Adrian Wojcik/iStock, 12-13; Rosanne Tackaberry/Alamy, 14; daboost/iStock, 15; Alberto Loyo/Shutterstock, 16-17; GybasDigiPhoto/Shutterstock, 18-19; Hemis/Alamy, 20-21; IVAN VIEITO GARCIA/Shutterstock, 23.

Printed in the United States of America at Corporate Graphics in North Mankato, Minnesota.

TABLE OF CONTENTS

CHAPTER 1

ISLAND OF STATUES

Travel across the Pacific Ocean to a **remote** island. Here, you will see great stone faces rising from the ground. This is Easter Island!

Easter Island

This island is about 2,300 miles (3,700 kilometers) west of Chile. Less than 10,000 people live here.

There are 887 **monoliths** spread across the island. These stone statues were made more than 500 years ago! They were made to look like humans. Some are kneeling. Some have carvings on their backs.

DID YOU KNOW?

Settlers first arrived on the island around 1200. They called it Te Pito o Te Henua. In 1722, Dutch sailors named it Easter Island. Why? They arrived on Easter Sunday. Today, **locals** call it Rapa Nui.

CHAPTER 2

CARVED STONES

The first people to come to the island were Polynesians. They made stone **altars** called ahu. Marriages and other **ceremonies** took place near them.

ahu ···· ▶

Families made statues to **honor** their **ancestors**. They called the statues moai. They made them big. Why? It showed that a family was powerful. They placed the moai on the ahu.

moai

The moai were carved from a soft stone called tuff. It is volcanic ash that has hardened. It came from Rano Raraku. This is an **extinct** volcano on the island.

Rano Raraku

unfinished
moai

 **Groups**

Groups

Planning and Leadership Skills

BETSY J. PAGE

Kent State University

MARTIN J. JENCIUS

Kent State University

Lahaska Press
Houghton Mifflin Company
Boston ▪ New York

Publisher, Lahaska Press: Barry Fetterolf
Senior Editor, Lahaska Press: Mary Falcon
Senior Marketing Manager, Lahaska Press: Barbara LeBuhn
Senior Project Editor: Margaret Park Bridges
Cover Design Manager: Anne S. Katzeff
Senior Composition Buyer: Chuck Dutton
New Title Project Manager: Susan Brooks-Peltier
Editorial Assistant: Stephanie VanCamp

Cover Image: © Bob Commander/Images.com

For instructors who want more information about Lahaska Press books and teaching aids, contact the Houghton Mifflin Faculty Services Center at
Tel: 800-733-1717, x4034
Fax: 800-733-1810
Or visit us on the Web at **www.lahaskapress.com**.

Lahaska Press, established as an imprint of Houghton Mifflin Company in 1999, is dedicated to publishing textbooks and instructional media for counseling and the helping professions. Its editorial offices are located in the small town of Lahaska, Pennsylvania. *Lahaska* is a Native American Lenape word meaning "source of much writing."

Printed in the U.S.A.

Library of Congress Control Number: 2007931283

ISBN-10: 0-618-63943-8
ISBN-13: 978-0-618-63943-4

123456789-VHO-12 11 10 09 08

CONTENTS

CHAPTER EIGHT | **Working with Cultural Complexities and Differences 159**

CHAPTER NINE | **Interventions for Critical Incidents 187**

CHAPTER TEN   **Leading Psychotherapy Groups**   **221**

CHAPTER ELEVEN   **Moving Toward Professional Practice**   **243**

PREFACE

The goal of this book is to help students who are preparing for careers in counseling, social work, human services, clinical psychology, and other helping professions develop their skills for planning and leading groups.

A group is a living organism composed of members and a leader or coleaders. Groups exist in environments that both promote and define them. The interconnection of a group's members, leaders, and the environment all impact upon the nature and quality of the group; however, the single factor most critical to the quality of the group experience for the members is the skillfulness of the group's leaders. We will use an analogy of growing a sunflower to illustrate the connections and interactions among the various planning and leadership skills presented in this book. Your knowledge base and understanding of human development, counseling theory, and group theory is analogous to the soil in which the sunflower grows. Any work you do to improve your knowledge in these areas will increase the nutrients in the soil.

As the roots and stem of the sunflower, we have identified ethics and Yalom's Therapeutic Factors, which are discussed in Chapter 1 and emphasized throughout the text. Chapter 2 focuses on starting groups and on the pregroup skills of developing a group proposal and screening and selecting members. The flower itself is circular with a large central core and multiple petals. From our perspective, the group leader skills presented in Chapters 6 and 7 on mastering group leadership skills are the core of the flower and the core of the skills you will use in leading groups. The petals of the flower include applying individual counseling skills in groups (Chapters 3 and 4), planning and structuring groups (Chapter 5), skills for working with cultural complexities and differences (Chapter 8), skills for intervening in critical incidents (Chapter 9), skills for leading psychotherapy groups (Chapter 10), and ideas for carrying your professional growth into the future (Chapter 11).

Features of the Book

- *Learning Objectives* Each chapter starts with learning objectives to help you as a student understand what you should be learning in the chapter.
- *Ethics Pointers* Ethics pointers embedded in each chapter help you apply the American Counseling Association code of ethics to the aspects of leadership discussed in the chapter.

- *Yalom's Therapeutic Factor Reminders* Throughout the book, examples of leader interventions intended to activate specific therapeutic factors are called to your attention with YTF Reminders.
- *Case Examples* Case examples throughout the text illustrate the use of leadership skills in the context of a real-life group.
- *Integrative Case Examples* Longer examples are provided toward the end of chapters to illustrate the use of multiple skills in the context of leading a specific group.
- *Exercises for Active Learning* Placed after each skill discussion, hands-on exercises give you the opportunity to think about what you have learned and test your understanding.
- *Key Concepts* Key concepts are listed at the end of each chapter, and the page on which the concept appears is identified.
- *Study Questions* Study questions at the end of each chapter ask you to explain the skills and concepts taught in the chapter.

Words of Thanks

We would like to thank our editor, Mary Falcon, for her encouragement with this book. Her creative ideas and careful editing contributed greatly to the quality and organization of the book.

Thank you also to the following academic reviewers for their thoughtful critiques of the manuscript:

Maria Bartlett, Humboldt State University
Ann Bauer, Cleveland State University
Terry Bordan, CW Post/Long Island University
Teddi Cunningham, Valdosta State University
Matt Englar-Carlson, California State University, Fullerton
Darcy Haag Granello, The Ohio State University
Robbin Lee, University of Tennessee, Chatanooga
Sylvia Marotta, George Washington University
Daniel T. Sciarra, Hofstra University
Abby K. Smith, Edmonds Community College
Robert Wilson, University of Cincinnati

And finally, we would like to thank our families who provided support and encouragement throughout the process of writing the book.

CHAPTER 1

Introduction to Group Planning and Leadership

LEARNING OBJECTIVES

After reading this chapter you should be able to

- Discuss the importance of group work.
- List and define Yalom's therapeutic factors.
- Discuss the importance of ethics as the foundation of group work.
- Define the core values of the helping professions, and discuss how they impact the ethical codes and standards of practice.
- Describe the two ethical decision-making models outlined in this chapter, and discuss their impact on the ethical codes and standards of practice.

INTRODUCTION: THE IMPORTANCE OF GROUP WORK

The role of the helping professional in both individual and group counseling is to respond to human need. To begin to understand the kinds of needs people bring to a group counseling setting, consider the four case examples that follow. These three individuals and one group of friends have not yet entered group counseling, but they will all ultimately do so to help them with their unique situations.

Alexa

Alexa is a 24-year-old single mother with a 3-year-old daughter. Alexa finds single parenting a struggle. She and her daughter live in a tiny, two-room apartment. Alexa has a full-time job that she likes, but she is unhappy with the poor quality of the day care she has arranged for her daughter. The company she works for has offered her a different job at its downtown office, which will pay a little better and is only a block away from a good day care center. However, the day care center is not only expensive but it is also strict about parents being on time to pick up their children by 6:00 PM sharp. The center charges a dollar for every minute a parent is late. Alexa doesn't think she would like the new job as much as her present job, but she is willing to make the job change to get her daughter into a better day care environment. However, she is concerned about what the real cost of day care will be, as the new job might often involve working 15–30 minutes overtime, and she would only be making slightly more money than in her current job.

Nathan

Nathan is a 10-year-old boy who has a little sister in kindergarten. This year his mother has given him the responsibility of babysitting his sister from the time he and his sister get home from school to the time their mother gets home from work. Nathan is participating in a group on new responsibilities. Yesterday, Nathan's sister left the yard and went to visit her friend next door without talking to Nathan first. Nathan was worried that his sister might be lost and frightened that he would be blamed. He followed the emergency plan outlined by his mother and quickly retrieved his sister. Nevertheless, his mother was furious with him when she discovered what had happened.

The Ice Fishing Friends

In a small town in Wisconsin, a group of seven friends had been ice fishing together on the same lake twice every winter for 14 years. They were always careful about surveying the thickness of the ice over the fishing area before proceeding. However, this time the truck in which two of the men was riding broke through a thin spot in the ice and plunged them into the freezing water. In their frenzied rescue attempt the friends managed to save one of the men. However, the other man drowned. The six friends, including the man who was rescued, are all filled with grief over the loss of their friend and believe that their friend's wife and children blame them for his death.

Frank

Frank is a 35-year-old man who has recently been diagnosed with lymphoma, a form of cancer. His wife, Alice, has a history of severe depression that has been

under control for years but which has resurfaced since Frank's diagnosis. Shortly after Frank's diagnosis, Alice may have attempted suicide by overdosing on pills, as she tried years ago, though the overdose may have been accidental. Not only is Frank worried about having cancer but he is also frightened that Alice may not be able to cope while he is undergoing treatment and unable to devote the constant support and care with which he usually provides her.

As counselors we are challenged to respond to people's needs, whether the people in need are individuals like Alexa, Nathan, and Frank, who might benefit from either an individual or group counseling setting, or groups of people, such as the ice fishing friends, who also might benefit from either individual or group counseling. Alexa would probably do well in individual counseling, but she might benefit even more from joining a group for single parents who face similar struggles in their everyday lives. Nathan's school counselor might counsel him about new responsibilities or include him in a group with other children with similar issues. One of the first responders to the ice fishing incident might suggest to the surviving friends that they get together with a grief counselor at the local mental health clinic a few times to help one another cope with their shared traumatic experience. Finally, Frank might be encouraged by his oncologist to join the support group of cancer survivors who meet weekly at the hospital. We will continue with each of these cases later in this book.

FOUNDATIONS OF GROUP WORK

Group counseling began to take form during the late nineteenth and early twentieth centuries via such innovators as Jane Adams, whose Hull House settlement in Chicago served the urban poor and incorporated group counseling into its programs to assist patrons in matters of medical care, child care, and legal advice, and Joseph Pratt, whose tuberculosis group in Boston helped patients with chronic ailments come to terms with their illness (Gladding, 2003). Today, it is common for people with problems to participate in a wide variety of groups, from substance-abuse groups, grief groups, and parenting groups, to groups designed simply to help members negotiate their similar everyday life difficulties and roadblocks. The research base supporting the effectiveness of group counseling has developed slowly over the course of time. Recently, Barlow, Fuhriman, and Burlingame have written, "The efficacy of group psychotherapy has been undeniably established in research literature" (Barlow, Fuhriman, & Burlingame, 2004, p. 5).

Part of the research base focuses on therapeutic factors. These factors evolved from Corsini and Rosenberg's (1955) study of member reports of what was helpful in groups. After the publication of *The Theory and Practice of Group Psychotherapy* (Yalom, 1970), it became common to refer to the factors as Yalom's therapeutic factors. Now in its fifth edition (Yalom, 2005), the book has been translated into many languages and is widely considered one of the foremost textbooks on group psychotherapy.

Yalom's Therapeutic Factors

Yalom's therapeutic factors (Yalom, 1970, 1995) represent a theory of group process that emphasizes interpersonal learning growing out of the interactions among members. In our opinion the members of the groups you lead will be well served if you are constantly mindful of promoting Yalom's factors (Yalom, 1995):

1. ***Instillation of hope*** is when group members observe that others with similar problems have improved and come to the understanding that they too will improve with the group's help.
2. ***Universality*** occurs when group members realize that other group members have had similar problems and/or thoughts.
3. ***Imparting of information*** (or ***guidance***) is the passing of beneficial information about the problem and/or the solution on to group members by either the group leader(s) or other group members.
4. ***Altruism*** is the idea that members benefit from helping one another.
5. ***The corrective recapitulation of the primary family experience*** (or ***family reenactment)*** refers to the way in which being part of a group enables group members to free themselves from old family roles and test new behaviors in the safety of the group setting.
6. ***Self-understanding*** refers to members "discovering and accepting previously unknown or unacceptable parts" of themselves (Yalom, 1995, Table 4.1).
7. ***Imitative behavior*** (or ***identification***) is the concept that group members may model themselves after other group members or group leader(s). According to Yalom, group members who report imitative behavior as therapeutic are not simply imitating others; more pointedly, they are adopting strategies or personality traits that have been effective for others.
8. ***Interpersonal learning input*** is members learning how they come across to others and what others think of them.
9. ***Interpersonal learning output*** is members "feeling more trustful of groups" and learning how to relate to the other members (Yalom, 1995, Table 4.1).
10. ***Group cohesiveness*** (or ***cohesion)*** is the sense of belonging to the group and being understood and accepted.
11. ***Catharsis*** is the expression of feelings both positive and negative.
12. ***Existential factors*** refer to those aspects of group therapy related to themes of existential therapy: "death, freedom, isolation, and life purpose" (Yalom, 1995, p. 90). The most prominent of these themes is that members learn to take responsibility for the way they live their lives.

Yalom's therapeutic factors may operate at the *intrapersonal level* (within the individual), the *interpersonal level* (between individuals), or the *group level* (among all members of the group). Group leaders may use specific skills, interventions, or activities to promote the activation of these therapeutic factors. Throughout this book we have provided reminders of Yalom's therapeutic factors (YTF) at work. The reminders appear in brackets like this: [**YTF Reminder:** This is an example of the therapeutic factor *catharsis*]. Because Yalom's therapeutic factors are integral to this book's focus, in various case examples we will also highlight situations in which leaders act to promote Yalom's specific therapeutic factors.

Ethics as a Foundation for Group Work

The goal of this book is to help you build your group leadership and planning skills—individual skills as applied to groups (group-specific skills); co-leadership skills (setting up, planning, and structuring groups); working with diverse members, and more. However, we want to be clear at the outset that your mastery of all these skills and tasks will be meaningless if your leadership is not built upon a foundation of ethical practice.

When most group leaders in training hear the word *ethics*, they tend to immediately think of the dos and don'ts of the ethical codes and standards of practice endorsed by the professional associations, such as the American Counseling Association (ACA), the American Psychological Association (APA), the National Association of Social Workers (NASW), the National Organization for Human Services (NOHS), and—more specific to group work—the American Group Psychotherapy Association (AGPA) (2002) and the Association for Specialists in Group Work (ASGW). It is essential that beginning group leaders learn these codes and standards of practice. However, they don't simply exist as documents for you to memorize; they must be incorporated into everything you do as a group leader.

To help you internalize the codes and standards of practice, we will first talk about the core values upon which they are based—core values that all caring human beings would agree are fundamental to human interaction. Once you have learned the core values and the codes and standards of practice, you then need to learn how to apply the codes and standards. In order to do that, you need to have an understanding of ethical decision-making models. In short, core values, the ethics codes and standards of practice, and ethical decision-making models all work together to facilitate ethical practice in group work, as illustrated in Figure 1-1.

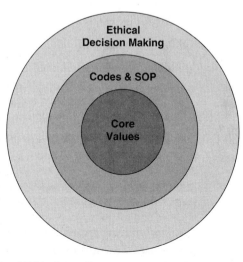

Figure 1-1   Fields of Ethical Practice

Core Values of Ethical Practice

According to Hayes (1991), in order to understand and act upon the ethical codes and standards of practice, a counselor must first understand the core values that underpin the codes and standards. The two primary core values for helping professionals to understand and internalize are *beneficence* and *nonmaleficence* (Kitchener, 1984).

***Definition of* beneficence**   Doing your work in a way that benefits your clients.

***Definition of* nonmaleficence**   Refraining from intentionally or unintentionally harming your clients.

In groups, **beneficence** means keeping the focus of the group's work on how it benefits members as well as the group as a whole and making sure that the action you perform as leader in the planning, leading, and processing of the group are for the good of each member and the greater good of the group as a whole. **Nonmaleficence** means refraining from doing anything that is intentionally or unintentionally harmful to members or the group as a whole. These core values of beneficence and nonmaleficence coexist in the ethical foundation of the effective leader, occasionally in conflict but more often in unison. An effective leader simultaneously gauges each action or decision by the group and its members based on assessing its likelihood of it doing good for others (beneficence) but also on the action or decision of doing no harm to others (nonmaleficence).

While beneficence and nonmaleficence are the two primary core values of ethical practice, the additional core values of *justice, autonomy, veracity,* and *fidelity* are also germane to both individual and group counseling (Kitchener, 1984; Meara, Schmidt, and Day, 1996).

***Definition of* justice**   Treating all people with equity and fairness.

***Definition of* autonomy**   Respecting clients' independence, freedom of choice, and self-determination.

***Definition of* veracity**   Always being truthful.

***Definition of* fidelity**   Being responsible, honorable, and trustworthy.

In groups, **justice** means treating all members with equity and fairness. This value promotes multicultural ethical considerations that impact underrepresented and underserved populations. **Autonomy** means respecting all group members' personal independence to choose their own direction. Leadership involves working with members to promote a sense of personal autonomy but also engaging the group as a whole in a way that promotes the group's autonomy from experiences outside of the group. Members should have a sense of personal freedom, and the group should recognize their freedom, which is protected in the group by the leader. For both leaders and members, **veracity** means not only being honest in one's disclosure and feedback to other members, it also means being open to *receiving* honest disclosure and feedback from other members. **Fidelity** means being responsible, honorable, and trustworthy. By modeling fidelity a leader can build the trust and loyalty of members and encourage members to also practice fidelity. Leaders model

a commitment to the group and elicit the commitment of members to do the necessary work agreed upon by the group.

Effective leaders should not only internalize and practice these core values, but they should also model the core values in group sessions, thereby encouraging members to incorporate these values into their own behavior patterns. Each of the core values practiced by members contributes to an overall pattern of ethical behavior in the group, behavior that avoids pitfalls such as the marginalization of individual members, lack of truthful information with which to base healing, and lack of progress due to the subsuming of individual identities within the group. When leaders incorporate core values as a foundation for group process, they establish the unique growth-producing experience that we call group counseling.

Exercise for Active Learning
Exploring the Core Values of Ethical Practice
In the previous section we introduced six core values: beneficence, nonmaleficence, justice, autonomy, veracity, *and* fidelity. *Reflect on the last year of your life, and try to identify situations in which these values influenced your decisions. Make notes of your thoughts on the lines below.*

Beneficence

_____

_____

Nonmaleficence

_____

_____

Justice

_____

_____

Autonomy

_____

_____

Veracity

_____

_____

Fidelity

_____

_____

Ethical Codes and Standards of Practice

Each helping profession has established its own codes of ethics and standards of practice that serve as the foundation of their profession. The American Counseling Association (ACA), the American Psychological Association (APA), the National Association of Social Workers (NASW), and the National Organization for Human Services (NOHS) have their ethical guidelines available for practitioners and the public at their organizational websites. We encourage you to thoroughly review your own professional organization's guidelines. When we discuss ethics in this book, we will focus on the ACA Ethics Code, which can be downloaded from the Internet (**www.counseling.org/Resources/CodeOfEthics/TP/Home/CT2.aspx**).

In addition to the ACA Ethics Code, the ASGW has produced several documents that provide supplemental information on appropriate group practice: Best Practice Guidelines (ASGW, 1998a) (**www.asgw.org/best.htm**), Principles for Diversity-Competent Group Workers (ASGW, 1998b) (**www.asgw.org/diversity.htm**), and Professional Standards for the Training of Group Workers (ASGW, 2000) (**www.asgw.org/training_standards.htm**).

Exercise For Active Learning
Recognizing the Core Values Within Your Professional Ethics Code

Print out the Ethics Code of your professional organization (URLs have been provided). Mark on the printout with a yellow highlighter where you see sections that are related to the values of beneficence, nonmaleficence, justice, autonomy, veracity, *and* fidelity.

The Ethical Decision-Making Process

Although the ethics codes are important guides, learning the codes is only the first step toward ethical practice. Because leaders often face ethical challenges during group sessions, they must learn how to make ethical decisions in the moment. Various authors have proposed ethical decision-making models that help group leaders make decisions about ethical dilemmas as they happen.

Numerous ethical decision-making models have been devised over the years. One of the easiest models to work with is the Sileo and Kopala (1993) model, which involves an easy-to-remember anagram. Their A-B-C-D-E model provides leaders with five considerations to keep in mind when making ethical decisions.

The A stands for *assessment.* A leader must first assess the ethical situation and consider its impact on all of the parties involved, including the members, the group as a whole, and the leader. The B stands for *benefit.* The leader needs to consider which course of action among various choices is likely to lead to the best benefit for all parties involved. In other words, the leader must keep the core value of beneficence in mind.

The C stands for both *consequences* and *consultation.* The leader needs to consider what possible consequences or outcomes could occur as a result of his actions as group leader and choose the action that will lead to the best possible ethical outcome. In addition to considering consequences, leaders are encouraged to consult with colleagues regarding ethical decisions whenever possible. Consultation may

not be an option in an immediate ethical situation; however, leaders are encouraged to improve their understanding of ethical practice by regularly discussing the ethical situations they have experienced with colleagues and supervisors.

The D stands for *duty*. The leader needs to consider that she has a duty to take action in an ethical manner, protecting individual members and the group as a whole from potential harm. Ethical decisions should be based on how to best protect group members from harm. Finally, the E stands for *education*. Leaders need to not only educate themselves about ethics but to also educate members regarding ethical practice. Leaders can do this by establishing rules and by planning and structuring the group based on best practice principles.

Incorporating the five considerations of the Sileo and Kopala (1993) A-B-C-D-E model into your group skills will help you deal with ethical dilemmas as they arise during group sessions. These considerations will also help you to prevent ethical dilemmas from arising if you keep them in mind during the planning of the group. Hindsight may be easier than foresight when it comes to ethical decision making, but foresight can prevent a great deal of problems. The more work you put into addressing potential ethical concerns during the planning process, the less likely it is that you will be faced with problems when leading the group. In Chapter 2 we will address planning issues, such as selecting members for the group and screening out inappropriate candidates. Having ethical safeguards in place prior to starting the group minimizes potential ethical issues from arising during group sessions, when your mind is focused more on the immediacy of group process and less on ethical implications.

Whereas the A-B-C-D-E model will help you think and act ethically at all times, the American Counseling Association Ethical Decision Making Model (Forester-Miller & Davis, 1996, Forester-Miller, 2002) provides a simple seven-stage process that counselors can apply when facing a specific ethical problem:

1. *Identify* the problem.
2. Apply the *ACA Code of Ethics*. If the code provides a clear-cut way to resolve the problem, follow the recommended course of action. If a resolution to the problem is not readily apparent, then the problem may be viewed as a true ethical dilemma, and you need to proceed with ethical decision-making steps 3–7.
3. Determine the *nature and extent* of the dilemma.
4. Generate *potential actions* to take.
5. Consider all the *consequences* that could occur from pursuing each course of action and then *select* a course of action.
6. *Evaluate* the course of action you select.
7. *Implement* the action.

Exercise for Active Learning
The Ethics Complaint Committee

You were appointed to the ethics compliant committee for your state's clinical and school counselor licensure board. Cases are referred to your committee when clients, state agencies, or counseling professionals file a complaint.

The complaint procedure.   The complaining party writes a letter describing the nature of the complaint. Then the counselor whom the complaint is about responds to the complaint with any information he thinks is relevant to the complaint. The chairperson of the board reads the complaint and the counselor's response and either dismisses the complaint or sends it to the investigator employed by the licensure board. The investigator gathers information and files a report to the licensure board. The licensure board reviews information, makes a decision, and recommends an action to be taken. The complaint may be dismissed or deemed justified. If the complaint is deemed justified, the board may mandate specific training or a period of clinical supervision in which the counselor must engage, or the license of the counselor may be suspended or permanently revoked.

Your assignment.   As a member of the ethics compliant committee, your assignment is to review the case that follows and write an opinion on the case including the action the board should take on the case. Your opinion should address ethical issues related to the counselors in the case as well as the agency that employs them. Support your opinion by citing specific points from the ACA Ethics Code.

The case.   The counseling agency for which they worked assigned Carol and Myra to lead a "support" group held in the social hall of a church. The purpose of the group was to help the members live a better life free from drinking. The group was advertised within the church and in the local newspaper as a support group. The cost of the group was $10 per session per member in advance. About half the members paid cash, and the other half used their insurance, which was billed through the agency by which Carol and Myra were employed. This money went entirely to pay Carol and Myra for leading the group. The church made an agreement with the counseling agency that it would provide the space to hold the group free of charge, with the proviso that the group would be open to all church members. Therefore, Carol and Myra did not do any screening.

The drinking behaviors of the members ranged from infrequent social drinking to drinking steadily for years. In the first session some members set goals to stop drinking. One member, George, said that he wanted to stop drinking totally within a few days. Carol and Myra advised against this because of George's long-term drinking history. They encouraged George to undergo formal substance abuse assessment that would probably result in a brief inpatient stay for detoxification. George nodded in agreement. However, as Carol and Myra later learned, since George did not want to miss any days of work, he had no intention of going for assessment.

Twenty-four hours before the second group session, George stopped drinking without telling anyone. George passed out in the front seat of his car in the parking lot of the church prior to the group session. One of the other members found him and called the ambulance.

George's health insurance company complained to the licensure board that the group endangered George. The company wants either Carol and Myra, or their counseling agency, or the church to pay the $500 for the ambulance and emergency care.

Summary of the investigator's report.   Carol is licensed as a school counselor and as a clinical counselor. She has seven years experience—much of it is in substance abuse counseling. Myra is a graduate student working part time for the agency to help support her graduate study. Her job title with the agency is "case manager." Carol is respected in the community as a skilled substance abuse counselor, and there have been no previous complaints filed against either Carol or Myra. The counselors failed to conduct any screening or to have medical screening done for substance use. Further, no records at all were kept of the group.

Your report to the ethics committee

_____

_____

_____

_____

_____

PREPARING TO BE AN EFFECTIVE GROUP LEADER

Most of you are reading this book as part of a course on group counseling. The course will provide you with a broad background on groups and a good set of leader skills. You will learn leadership skills and know how and when to use these skills. You will practice group leadership under close supervision until you lead with skill, confidence, and effectiveness. Above and beyond what you learn in this class, you should do some personal preparation for each and every group you lead. Some of the things you can do as preparation include the following:

■ *Consider your designated scope of practice.* Counselor licensure laws of your state probably specify the scope of practice for each type and level of licensure. Your clinical supervisor would be the best person with whom to discuss your personal scope of practice. For the safety of your members, your safety, and your credibility, you should counsel within your designated scope of practice.

Ethics Pointer

ACA Ethics Code C.2.a requires counselors to practice within the boundaries of their competence (American Counseling Association, 2005, p. 9).

■ *Consider your experience and expertise.* Before making the commitment to lead a group, you should honestly evaluate your expertise on the topic that is the focus of the group as well as on your experience leading such a group. All of us have to start somewhere building our experience. If you don't have experience or expertise, colead a group with a counselor more experienced in the type of group you wish to lead.

■ *Secure clinical supervision.* As a beginning counselor and group leader, clinical supervision is particularly important. At a minimum, you should choose a supervisor who has more clinical experience than you do and who meets state requirements as a counseling supervisor. A supervisor who is experienced leading groups should be able to help you gain insight in understanding what is happening in the group and how to lead safely and effectively. The umbrella of your supervisor's experience and license shelters you to a degree while you learn. When an administrator without counseling training attempts to supervise your counseling, it is an undesirable situation. Such an administrator probably has only a minimal pool of knowledge from which to provide instruction and has less ability to provide even a semi-sheltered learning environment.

■ *Read.* Take some time to read up on the topic of the group. If this is the first time you have led a group on the topic, try to find a current book that describes the topic and what approaches are usually effective in working with members on the topic. If this is the type of group you have run before, try to find a book chapter, a journal article, or a credible Internet site that adds to what you already know.

Evaluating Your Potential for Effectiveness

The other part of your preparation for leading groups is personal. At this point in your training, you should take time for self-reflection. Here are some questions you might wish to consider:

■   What are my motivations for wanting to be a counselor? A group leader?
■   How can I use these motivations to develop my strengths as a counselor and group leader?

Your answers to these questions can be important for you since they can help you connect with or increase your commitment to your training as a professional counselor. Here are two other important questions to your development as a group leader:

■   What are my strengths when I interact with people in groups (e.g., in my family, at school, at work, and in my recreational activities)?
■   What aspects of interacting with people in groups do I find difficult or challenging?

Your answers to these questions can help you set goals for your own learning, perhaps in collaboration with the instructor of your group counseling course. We would advise a dual approach of using your strengths and working toward gradual improvement in areas that are challenging for you.

STUDY QUESTIONS

1. Discuss the importance of group work.
2. List the 12 therapeutic factors described by Yalom.
3. Define each of the therapeutic factors listed in question 2.
4. Distinguish between ethical codes and standards of practice.

5. Describe the core values of ethics. How do these core values influence the ethics codes?
6. Explain the five considerations of the Sileo and Kopala ethical decision-making model.
7. Describe the seven steps of the American Counseling Association Ethical Decision Making Model.

KEY CONCEPTS

altruism p. 4
autonomy p. 6
beneficence p. 6
catharsis p. 4
cohesion p. 4
guidance p. 4
existential factors p. 4
family reenactment p. 4
fidelity p. 6
identification p. 4

instillation of hope p. 4
interpersonal learning—input p. 4
interpersonal learning—output p. 4
justice p. 6
nonmaleficence p. 6
self-understanding p. 4
universality p. 4
veracity p. 6
Yalom's therapeutic factors p. 4

REFERENCES

American Counseling Association. (2005). *ACA code of ethics.* Alexandria, VA: Author.

American Counseling Association. (2005). *ACA code of ethics.* Retrieved April 4, 2007, from ACA website: www.counseling.org/Resources/CodeOfEthics/TP/Home/CT2.aspx.

American Group Psychotherapy Association (AGPA). (2002). *AGPA and NRCGP Guidelines for Ethics.* Retrieved July 28, 2006, from AGPA website: www.agpa.org/group/ethicalguide .html.

Association for Specialists in Group Work (ASGW). (1998). *Association for Specialists in Group Work Best Practice Guidelines.* Retrieved July 20, 2006, from ASGW website: www.asgw .org/best.htm.

Association for Specialists in Group Work (ASGW). (1998). *Association for Specialists in Group Work Principles for Diversity-Competent Group Workers.* Retrieved July 20, 2006, from ASGW website: www.asgw.org/diversity.htm.

Association for Specialists in Group Work (ASGW). (2000). *Professional Standards for the Training of Group Workers.* Retrieved July 20, 2006, from ASGW website: www.asgw.org/training_ standards.htm.

Barlow, S. H., Fuhriman, A. J., & Burlingame, G.W. (2004). The history of group counseling and psychotherapy. In J. L. DeLucia-Waack, D. A. Gerrity, C. R. Kalodner & M. T. Riva (Eds.), *Handbook of group counseling and psychotherapy.* Thousand Oaks, CA: Sage.

Corsini, R., & Rosenberg, B. (1955). Mechanisms of group psychotherapy: Processes and dynamics. *Journal of Abnormal and Social Psychology, 51,* 406–411.

Forester-Miller, H. (2002). Group counseling: Ethical considerations. In D. Capuzzi and D. R. Gross (Eds.) *Introduction to Group Counseling* (3rd ed.). Denver, CO: Love.

Forester-Miller, H., & Davis, T. E. (1996). *A practitioner's guide to ethical decision making.* Alexandria, VA: American Counseling Association.

Gladding, S. T. (2003). *Group work: A counseling specialty* (4th ed.). Upper Saddle River, NJ: Merrill.

Hayes, R. L. (1991). Group work and the teaching of ethics. *Journal for Specialists in Group Work, 16,* 24–31.

Kitchener, K. S. (1984). Intuition, critical evaluation and ethical principles: The foundation for ethical decisions in counseling psychology. *Counseling Psychologist, 12*(3), 43–55.

Meara, N. M., Schmidt, L. D., & Day, J. D. (1996). Principles and virtues: A foundation for ethical decisions, policies and character. *Counseling Psychologist, 37,* 156–164.

Sileo, F., & Kopala, M. (1993). An A-B-C-D-E worksheet for promoting beneficence when considering ethical issues. *Counseling and Values, 37,* 89–95.

Yalom, I. D. (1970). *The theory and practice of group psychotherapy.* New York: Basic Books.

Yalom, I. D. (1995). *The theory and practice of group psychotherapy* (4th ed.). New York: Basic Books.

Yalom, I. D. with Leszcz, M. (2005). *The theory and practice of group psychotherapy* (5th ed.). New York: Basic Books.

CHAPTER 2
Getting the Group Started

LEARNING OBJECTIVES

After studying this chapter you should be able to

- Explain the different considerations when starting groups in school settings and in community settings.
- Prepare a proposal for a group.
- Write an effective purpose statement.
- Explain how site selection impacts group success.
- Create an effective advertisement for a group.
- Undertake the processes of screening members, making referrals, and selecting the group members.

STARTING GROUPS IN SCHOOL AND COMMUNITY SETTINGS

You might be wondering how helping professionals decide to run groups. While there may be multiple factors in those decisions, in most school and community settings, groups are formed as a response to student or client need, school or agency need, and leader interest. In this chapter we will first look at these general considerations for starting groups. As we discuss these issues, we will refer to two case examples, one in a school counseling setting and one in a community agency setting. Then we will outline the steps a group leader would take to start a group once the need for a group has been established.

Before we proceed with the examples, we would like to talk briefly about the relationship between the school and community agency settings. You may be curious about the relationships between schools and communities and about how the groups in the two settings are similar and how they may differ. First of all, it is important to remember that both schools and community agencies serve children. Schools typically serve most of the children in a community; school counselors provide a range of services to all students, parents, faculty, and staff as well as to the larger community. School counselors often provide group counseling to a small subset of the student body. Often these groups are short term and topic focused.

On the other hand, community agencies often provide group counseling for select groups of school children. These groups are usually led by counselors or social workers with clinical licenses. Although the groups are sponsored by community agencies, the focus of the groups may be on improving students' (members') behaviors related to school and to homework since school is such an integral part of students' lives.

There is no hard and fast line that divides school and community groups for children. While groups in community agencies often address both home and school issues of members, groups in schools may address issues related to the *Diagnostic and Statistical Manual of Mental Disorders* (DSM IV-TR) (2000) diagnoses in the category of Disorders Usually First Diagnosed in Infancy, Childhood, or Adolescence (for example learning disorders, mental retardation, or attention deficit and disruptive behavior disorders). Depression and anxiety disorders may also occur in children and may be addressed through groups in school. In the end, whether children who can benefit from group counseling receive it from the school or the community agency often depends on such factors as school policy, time availability of school counselors, duration of counseling needed, financing, and parent preference.

Starting Groups in School Settings

In our first case example, Sue, Pablo, and Meg are school counselors at a kindergarten through eighth-grade school. As part of their overall counseling plan for the first half of the school year, Sue, Pablo, and Meg are offering a number of small groups. During the first two weeks of the school year, the counselors conduct a needs survey, soliciting requests for group topics from students, parents, faculty, and administrative staff. Table 2-1 outlines the types of groups requested. The first column summarizes the requested group topics organized by grade level, the second column shows the number of requests received per topic, and the third and fourth columns outline the counselors' quarterly plan based on needs and number of requests.

Table 2-1 Quarterly Plan for the First Half of the School Year Based on Needs Survey

Grades and Topics	Requests*	First Quarter Day/Leader	Second Quarter Day/Leader
Grades K and 1			
Bus Safety	36	Mondays/Meg—Tuesdays/Pablo	
Friends	7	Wednesdays/Meg	
Grades 2 and 3			
Friends	8		
Grandparent Loss	14	Thursdays/Meg	Mondays/Meg—Tuesdays/Sue
Depression	3		
Social Phobia	3		
Grades 4 and 5			
ADHD	10	Tuesdays—Meg	
Alcohol Use Prevention	12	Mondays—Pablo	Mondays—Pablo
Depression	1		
Study Skills	10		Wednesdays/Meg—Wednesdays/Sue
Grade 6			
ADHD	3		
Alcohol Use Prevention.	20	Tuesdays/Pablo—Thursdays/Pablo	Tuesdays/Pablo—Wednesdays/Pablo
Career Exploration	4		
Depression	5	Mondays/Sue	
Study Skills	21	Tuesdays/Sue—Tuesdays/Pablo	
Grades 7 and 8			
ADHD	3		
Alcohol Use Prevention	10	Mondays/Sue	
Career Exploration	25	Wednesdays AM and PM/Sue	
		Wednesdays PM/Meg and Pablo	
Depression	6	Thursdays/Sue	
Study skills	20	Thursdays/Pablo	

* Total unique requests from students, parents, faculty, and administration.

      Organizing groups by grade level has a couple of advantages. First, it narrows the age range within any one group so that the students are approximately at the same developmental level. This makes it easier for group leaders to choose discussions and activities that appeal to most of the members. In addition, organizing requested topics by grade level allows group leaders to tailor the group program to address the fact that needs vary by age. In the case example, the majority of topic requests for kindergarten and grade one were related to bus safety and the difficulty very young students may have developing friendships in a new and unfamiliar setting. Note also that since these topics—particularly bus safety—represent immediate needs, the counselors have scheduled all groups for children in kindergarten through first grade in the first quarter of the school year. The counselors

have decided to run two bus safety groups and invite all the students who were referred on this topic to join the group.

If you become a school counselor, you may face similar decisions about prioritizing both timing of groups and extent of groups on a particular topic. Another decision you will have to make is who will lead each group. Counselor interest and expertise as well as desires to balance workload among counselors may be factors influencing your decisions. In the case example, Meg plans to lead the majority of groups for kindergarten through third grade because she prefers to work with the younger children. She is also particularly interested in the topic of loss of grandparents, which corresponds well to the most frequent group topic requested for Grades 2 and 3. Meg has decided to offer one group on grandparent loss in each of the first two quarters so that she will be able to respond to any losses that develop after the school year starts. While there were some requests for a group on depression, the counselors have decided not to offer a group in that area but rather to offer individual counseling or provide referral. Similarly, you may not be able to meet all requests for groups. However, you should attempt to arrange alternate care to address concerns identified by prospective group members.

Alcohol use prevention was the most commonly requested group topic for grades four through eight. Pablo has more expertise and interest in substance abuse prevention groups and was hired by the school because of this expertise. Therefore, he will lead the vast majority of those groups. Sue prefers to work with older children in the school and will lead most of the groups in this age range that are not substance abuse focused.

Groups for the third and fourth quarters of the school year will address sex education for Grade 6, suicide prevention for Grade 7, and high school transition for Grade 8. These topics reflect the priorities of the school board and comprise 90 percent of the groups offered for the second half of the school year. If you plan to work in a school setting, it is wise to respond to appropriate requests from administrators. Such requests are not uncommon. Meg and Pablo will lead the sex education and suicide groups while Sue focuses on high school transition.

Starting Groups in Community Settings

In community agencies, private practices, and residential or other forms of inpatient care, one way that helping professionals decide what groups might be needed is to examine data about the frequency of diagnoses for specific age groups. Table 2-2 was devised by community counselors Jack, Sherry, and Ernie in response to the inpatient data in a diagnosis frequency table created by their counseling center's administrative staff. In Table 2-2 both the names of the diagnoses and the code numbers for the diagnoses are listed according to client age in the first column (diagnosis code numbers ending in XX indicate that all subtypes of the diagnosis were counted together). The second column lists the number of clients diagnosed, and the third column outlines the counselors' plan for January and February based on needs indicated by the data.

This agency has numerous clients. Groups will enable the agency to deliver effective treatment to more clients, and they will also help the agency operate more efficiently by treating clients with the same diagnosis simultaneously. Those clients

Table 2-2 Counseling Center Group Plan Based on
Diagnosis Frequency Table 2005–2006

Diagnosis	Number of Clients	January and February Group Schedule
Ages 40–60*		Monday PM 3 groups/Atypical features—Jack
296.xx Depression	178	Wednesday PM 4 groups/mild depression—Ernie
		Thursday PM 2 groups/moderate depression—Sherry
300.04 Dysthymic Disorder	37	
300.01 Panic Disorder without Agoraphobia	76	
300.21 Panic Disorder with Agoraphobia	4	
296.89 Bipolar II Disorder Ages 10–17	3	
314.xx ADHD	154	Monday 16 and 17/Jack and Ernie
		Monday 14 and15/Jack and Ernie
		Monday 12 and 13/Jack and Ernie
		Tuesday 10 and 11/Sherry and Ernie
296.xx Depression Ages under 10	15	
314.xx ADHD	46	Wednesday 8 and 9/Ernie
313.89 Reactive Attachment Disorder	30	Tuesday Foster mothers of children with attachment disorders/Ernie

*Note that there are no clients between the ages of 17 and 40 and none over 60 in the table. Such a situation occurs here because the referrals and funding at this counseling center come from two different grants, each of which has age boundaries as part of its parameters.

who for some reason or another are not included in groups are seen individually. In the table below, groups were planned for some of the clients with the most frequent diagnosis. Groups might range in size from 8 to 15 members depending on the diagnosis, its severity, the age of members, the experience of the leader, and the availability of coleaders.

Notice that in the older age range, many of the clients are experiencing depression of some type. Depression is more common than many other diagnoses. In reality, depression is too broad a descriptor to accurately and usefully describe a client's combinations of symptoms without more subsets of descriptors. While you will need to read DSM IV-TR (2000) and have some detailed instruction to get a clearer picture of the complexity within the DSM category of depression, we will mention two types of descriptors here to help you better understand Table 2-2. Depression can range in severity from mild (the client has fewer of the symptoms of depression and/or has them less frequently) to severe (the client has many symptoms of depression and

has them frequently). Depression includes multiple possible symptoms, which may occur in varied patterns. Depression with what the DSM refers to as *atypical features* has a symptom pattern that includes mood reactivity (for example, the client's mood seems happier when talking about things that we would expect to make her feel happy) and two or more of the following (DSM IV-TR, 1994, p. 386):

- Significant weight gain or increase in appetite.
- Hypersomnia (sleeping more hours than normal).
- Leaden paralysis (arms and legs feel heavy).
- Long-standing pattern of interpersonal rejection sensitivity (not limited to episodes of mood disturbance) that results in significant social or occupational impairment.

The agency counselors in our case example have decided to focus the groups offered on the clients with depression and to create separate groups for clients with atypical, mild, and moderate depression. The counselors plan to provide different treatment for each group. For example, the group for members with mild depression will be scheduled to last 10 weeks, while the groups for moderate and atypical depression will last approximately 20 weeks. All members of the groups for moderate and atypical depression will meet with the agency's physician or with their family physician to be screened for antidepressant medications. Medication compliance will be included among the goals for these groups. The group for atypical depression will focus in part on hypersomnia and weight gain. In contrast, the group for members with mild depression and the group for members with moderate depression will include discussion about increasing sleep and more regular eating, since lack of sleep and decrease in weight or appetite are typical symptoms of depression.

While a fair number of agency clients in the 40 to 60 age range have panic disorder (a "disorder defined by recurrent and unexpected panic attacks" (First & Tasman, 2004, p. 845) without agoraphobia ("anxiety about being in a place or situation that is not easily escaped or where help is not easily accessible if panic occurs") (First & Tasman, 2004, p. 846), the counselors have not scheduled groups for them because many of these clients skipped some of their appointments for individual counseling. The counselors are concerned that similar no-show rates during group counseling would be constantly working against the effectiveness of the groups.

Thirty-seven clients in the 40 to 60 age range suffer from dysthymic disorder, which "is defined by the presence of chronic depressive symptoms most of the day, more days than not, for at least two years" (First & Tasman, 2004, p. 772). In this case, other counselors within the agency preferred to see the clients individually.

In the 10 to 17 age group, the counselors have decided to use some group work to help deliver services to the large number of children diagnosed with attention deficit/hyperactivity disorder (ADHD). The counselors have grouped the 16- and 17-year-olds into the Monday group and the 10- and 11-year-olds into the Tuesday group. Since they expected these groups to range from 15 to 20 people, Sherry and Ernie will colead each group. The counselors will reexamine the group schedule at the end of each sports season since many of the members' free afternoons will change when the boys move from football to basketball and the girls move from volleyball to basketball. (In a similar way, if you are a counselor working with school-age

clients, adjusting your counseling schedule around the students' after-school activity schedule may facilitate students' participation in and enthusiasm for counseling and therapy groups.) Most of the agency's clientele under the age of 10 are in therapeutic foster care. Ernie has the most expertise working with foster children and foster parents, so he will lead the two groups planned for the foster parents.

You may have noticed that neither the group plan for the school nor the plan for the community agency provides enough groups to accommodate all potential members. Some reasons for that include the following:

- Some of the potential members will be screened out of the groups.
- Some potential members will have schedule conflicts, and others will not be able to get transportation to the group at the time and place specified.
- Appropriate meeting space for groups is limited.

Exercise for Active Learning
Starting Your Own Group

The Active Learning Exercises throughout this chapter will parallel the step-by-step process of starting a group by asking you to work through the process using a sample group of your own creation. To begin the process, decide whether you would like your group to be for children or adults. If you choose children, choose also a school setting or a community setting. Finally, come up with a title for your group based on a topic in which you are interested.

_____

_____

_____

STARTING A GROUP

In this section we will refer to the two case examples just described to illustrate five steps in starting a group:

1. Preparing a proposal for the group in order to gain administrative approval.
2. Refining the group's goals by writing a purpose statement for the group.
3. Selecting a meeting site for the group.
4. Advertising the group to potential group members.
5. Screening members, obtaining referrals, and selecting group members.

Preparing the Proposal

Once you have decided on the need for a group, you should prepare a brief (one- to two-page) group **proposal** that can be presented to agency administrators, clinical supervisors, school boards, and others from whom you might need approval. The proposal should include the following:

- Group information including a brief description of the target population, a statement of the purpose of the group, the meeting site, and a cost estimate.

Title of Group: Getting Organized for School

Members: This group is for students ages 10 and 11 who have been diagnosed with ADHD and who are having difficulty organizing themselves and their school materials in the morning prior to school and staying focused on their schoolwork during the school day.

Purpose Statement: The purpose of this group is to teach self-coaching skills to members to help them organize their school work and maintain focus during the school day. The self-coaching approach is primarily cognitive-behavioral in which students modify their behaviors and thoughts to help them achieve their goals.

Screening Plan: The screening sheet for this group is shown in Figure 2-3.

Meeting Site: The group will meet in Room 8 of John Adams School.

Schedule and Leaders: The group will meet Tuesdays at 3:00 PM for one hour throughout September and October. The leaders will be Sherry D. Page, LPCC, and Ernie E. Grant, LPCC, Supervisor.

Cost Estimate: The group will have eight members, and the cost will be $300 total per member.

Figure 2-1 Proposal for ADHD Group Serving Children Ages 10 and 11

- A proposed advertisement.
- A screening plan.

The sample proposal for an ADHD group in Figure 2-1 originates from the community counseling center chart presented in the previous section. Note that four ADHD groups (each of which focused on a different age group) were listed. Each group would require a separate proposal, not only because each group would be different in terms of member age, but they would also all have different issues related to how ADHD impacts their lives. The group illustrated in Figure 2-1 is for children ages 10 and 11. Its purpose is to help the children learn skills for getting themselves organized for school (completing homework, gathering their books, gym clothes, lunch, etc.) and staying focused on their schoolwork.

Figure 2-2 shows the proposed advertisement for the ADHD group for ages 10 and 11. If they wanted to make their ad a bit more inviting, Sherry and Ernie might have added a few pieces of clip art—dealing with organizing materials and focusing for learning—reflecting the two general goals of the group.

The screening sheet (Figure 2-3) for this group is set up to solicit multiple perspectives (student, parent, and teacher) on members' needs. You should know that in order for a counselor to discuss group members with school personnel, the counselor would need to obtain the informed written consent of the member and his or her parents. The screening sheet also has space for information about medications, since it is likely one or more of the proposed members would be taking medications.

Getting Organized for School Group

This group is for students ages 10 and 11 who have been diagnosed with ADHD. The purpose of this group is to teach self-coaching to help members organize their school work and maintain focus in class and on homework.

Members will learn to

- **Organize school materials at home.**
- **Pack school materials to be ready for school bus.**
- **Organize materials for each class.**
- **Focus during class and maintain working focus.**
- **Organize homework and be ready for bus.**

Parents, please note that parental consent is required for this group.
Please contact group leaders Sherry D. Page, LPCC, (260-555-1234) or Ernie E. Grant, LPCC and Supervisor, (260-555-1254) to sign up, request further information, or discuss questions/concerns.

Starting Tuesday, September 2, the group will meet Tuesdays from 3:00 p.m. to 4:00 p.m. during September and October at the Community Counseling Center, 821 Fourth Street.

Cost: $300

Call Sherry at (330) 000-1111 for more information or to sign up.

Figure 2-2   Proposed Advertisement for ADHD Group for Ages 10 and 11

Sherry and Ernie might wish to talk with the prescribing physician(s). This would also require informed written consent.

Exercise for Active Learning
Writing a Proposal for Your Group

In the previous exercise you created the name for a group you would like to lead and decided if you wanted your group to be in a school setting or in a community setting. Now it is time to set up the outline of the proposal for your group. Be sure to include all of the essential parts of the proposal, using Figure 2-1 as a model. Fill in as much as you can, including a rationale for why the group is needed, a preliminary purpose statement, a profile of potential group members, a preliminary schedule, and **cost estimates.** Keep in mind that this is work in progress. As you read along in this chapter and learn more about each section of a group proposal, you will be asked to come back to your draft and fine-tune it. Thus it would be best to do this as a word-processing document that you can return to again and again.

Writing the Purpose Statement

Perhaps the most critical aspect of the proposal is its **purpose statement**. The purpose statement focuses the group. Like a compass, it provides a consistent direction for the group and leads the group in the direction of specific goals. One way

Student name:_____

Referral source:_____

Parents' names and addresses:_____

Parents' phone number(s):_____

School and homeroom teacher:_____

Student's concerns:_____

_____

Parents' concerns:_____

_____

Teachers' concerns:_____

_____

Medications and prescribing physician:_____

_____

Academic progress:_____

Informed consent of:_____

Student: _____

Mother: _____

Father: _____

Figure 2-3   Screening Sheet for ADHD Group for Ages 10 and 11

to picture the purpose statement is to think of the group as a train going down the track toward its destination. In this analogy the purpose statement is the train's engine, and the weekly group topics are the train cars being pulled along. If the cars (topics) are directly connected to the engine (purpose), the train progresses toward its destination (goal).

In addition to keeping the group focused, consistent, and directed toward its goals, the purpose statement also provides decision-making guidance for the leader. As long as the purpose statement is kept in mind, the leader will have a means with which to decide whether or not focusing on particular members or topics is appropriate for the group. Generally speaking, if a member's issues are not clearly related to the purpose statement, the leader should give lower priority to those issues in terms of spending group time on them.

Tables 2-3 and 2-4 provide the purpose statements from the school and community groups used as examples in this chapter. Later, multiple examples of purpose statements grouped to reflect the ASGW group work specialties will be provided.

Notice in Table 2-3 that when the school counselors run multiple sections of the same group for the same age level, they generally employ the same purpose

Table 2-3 Purpose Statements of School Groups

Grade	Groups	Purpose Statement
K and 1	Q1—M—Bus Safety— Meg; and T—Bus Safety—Pablo	The purpose of this group is to increase members' understanding of safety issues related to traveling on the bus.
	W—Friends—Meg	The purpose of this group is to help members learn skills to make new friends at school.
2 and 3	Q1—Th—Grandparent loss—Meg; and Q2—M— Grandparent loss—Meg	The purpose of this group is to help members process the loss of their grandparent and to talk with their parents about the loss.
	T—Friends—Sue	The purpose of this group is to help members learn skills to make new friends at school.
4 and 5	Q1—M—Alcohol Prevention—Pablo; and Q2—M—Alcohol Prevention—Pablo	The purpose of this group is to teach members basic facts about alcohol consumption and to introduce skills for refusing alcohol.
	T—ADHD—Meg	The purpose of this group is to increase members' ability to organize themselves and their belongings to promote participation in school work. In addition, members will be coached to listen to rather than argue with parents and adults at school.
	W—Study Skills—Meg; and W—Study Skills— Sue	The purpose of this group is to increase study skills needed for social studies and science in grades 4 and 5.
	Q1—M—Depression— Sue;	The purpose of this group is to decrease the symptoms of depression reported by the members.
6	Q1—T—Alcohol Prevention—Pablo; Th— Alcohol Prevention— Pablo; Q2—T—Alcohol Prevention—Pablo; and W—Alcohol Prevention—Pablo	The purpose of this group is to teach a set of 12 refusal skills. These skills will help students refuse when others offer them alcohol or drugs.
	T—Study Skills—Sue; and T—Study Skills—Pablo	The purpose of this group is to teach study skills needed for new material taught in math in grades 6, 7, and 8
7 and 8	Q1—M—Alcohol Prevention—Sue	The purpose of this group is to teach additional refusal and assertiveness skills.
	W—Career Exploration AM—Sue; W—Career Exploration PM—Sue; W—Career Exploration— Meg; and W—Career Exploration—Pablo	The purpose of this group is to explore potential careers and to discuss the lifestyles typical of persons in these careers. Efforts will be made to provide opportunities for students in grade 8 to do a half day of job shadowing in the community.
	Th–Depression—Sue	The purpose of this group is to teach students more positive thinking—particularly self-statements.
	Th—Study Skills—Pablo	The purpose of this group is to reinforce study skills for students in introductory Spanish and Chinese courses.

Table 2-4 Purpose Statements for Counseling Center Groups

Age	Groups	Purpose Statement
0–10	Wednesday 3 PM ADHD 8 and 9—Ernie	The purpose of this group is to teach self-coaching to help members organize their clothes and bedroom and maintain focus when foster parents and teachers are talking to them.
10–17	Tuesday 10 AM Foster mothers of children with attachment disorders—Ernie	The purpose of this group is to support foster mothers of children with attachment disorders and to help the mothers develop strategies for addressing the child's problem behaviors.
	Tuesday 3 PM ADHD 10 and 11—Sherry and Ernie	The purpose of this group is to teach self-coaching to help members organize their school work and maintain focus during class and homework.
	Monday 3 PM ADHD 16 and 17—Jack and Ernie	The purpose of this group is to teach self-coaching to help members organize their clothes and tools for work and maintain focus during after school and weekend jobs.
40–60	Wednesday PM mild depression—Ernie	The purposes of this group are to increase positive thinking, to begin a regular program of walking, and to promote a regular daily schedule.
	Monday PM atypical depression—Jack; and Thursday PM moderate depression–Sherry	The purposes of this group are to increase positive thinking and to promote an appropriate daily schedule of eating, sleeping, exercise, and social engagement. Medication compliance will be encouraged for those members receiving medication.

statement. This is an effort to provide consistency across multiple groups. One goal of groups in elementary school is to help students talk about an issue and to encourage their discussion of the same issue with their parents at home. The purpose statement for the grandparent loss group for Grades 2 and 3 exemplifies this idea.

When the counselors offered a group like the alcohol prevention group at multiple grade levels, the purpose statements for these groups differed so students and their parents could tell that the group was different than the group at the previous grade level and how the groups differed. Notice that while the alcohol prevention groups address increasing levels of knowledge, the study skills groups rotate subject matter from year to year.

Now let's look at Table 2-4. Once again, the same purpose statement was used for multiple groups on the same topic at the same age level. The purpose of the groups for members with ADHD graduated in focus from home, to school, to work in the community. As the severity of the depression diagnoses increased from mild to moderate, a medication compliance purpose was added.

You may be wondering why the agency counselors organized their groups by age range. You might run a group on the same or a similar topic for members of different developmental levels or ages; however, the activities you would use to address the topics could be very different for 8-year-olds versus 40-year-olds. Early identification of the age of intended members allows you to picture the group

mentally and to consider the members you might recruit. When the group is intended for children, identifying possible members and obtaining necessary consent is more complex than with adult members. Early identification gives you time to obtain the required consent. Therefore, you should consider including the age of the intended members in the purpose statement from the inception of the group. Age and developmental level are not necessarily identical. However, in general, developmental level varies with age. Therefore, in this text it will be assumed that age and developmental level are roughly synonymous. If an example is provided where this is not the case, it will be pointed out to you.

Some counselors like to indicate in their purpose statements that a specific counseling theory is to be the basis of the group process. Whether or not you choose to list the theoretical basis of the group in the purpose statement, the purpose of the group, member goals, leader roles, group processes and activities, and methods of outcome evaluation should be guided by theory so that you are intentional in your practice. Furthermore, whether or not the theory is written into the purpose statement, you should discuss the theory and its implications for group goals and processes with the potential member and parents as appropriate in the process of recruiting, screening, and selecting members. Disclosure of the theoretical foundation for the group is part of informed consent, characteristic of ethical practice.

Exercise for Active Learning
Practice Writing Purpose Statements

Given the information below describing the potential group members of three groups, write a clear purpose statement for each of the groups.

a. Five children have been identified by an assistant principal of an elementary school as needing counseling. The children are in the second and third grades and have had multiple referrals to the assistant principal for physical aggression on the playground.

_____

_____

b. This week, three 17-year-olds were arrested and charged with driving under the influence of alcohol. Since this is their first offense, the judge would like to take an educational approach with them. She wants to be sure that they understand the physiological effects of alcohol on the body and on their ability to drive.

_____

_____

c. The nursing home staff has identified six residents, all in their late eighties, who seem upset when staff members do not have time to listen to the stories of their lives. They have asked you to put together a group for these residents.

_____

_____

Purpose Statements for the Four Types of Groups Described by ASGW

Purpose statements are also influenced by the types of groups being held. The Association for Specialist in Group Work (ASGW) recognizes four specialty types of groups: (1) psychoeducational groups, (2) counseling groups, (3) psychotherapy groups, and (4) task work groups (Association for Specialists in Group Work, 2000, p. 330). Let's define what each of these group types are and simultaneously illustrate how group types impact purpose statements. The types are neither mutually exclusive nor exhaustive of the possible types of groups.

Psychoeducational groups focus on teaching and learning. According to the ASGW, they focus on "the application of principles of normal and abnormal human development and functioning" to groups promoting growth and development and prevention of problems (Association for Specialists in Group Work, 2000, p. 331). As seen earlier in this chapter, school counselors often lead psychoeducational groups in order to promote healthy development in children. In addition, both school and community counselors conduct psychoeducational groups to treat group members with diagnosable disorders, for instance to benefit people with alcohol abuse concerns by teaching them about the short- and long-term effects of alcohol on the body. The purpose statement for a psychoeducational group should highlight the fact that the group's primary focus is on teaching and learning; therefore, these words should appear in the purpose statement, along with other relevant information. Consider the following examples:

1. "The purpose of this group is to teach anger management strategies to middle school adolescents who have been sent to the principal for fighting." Notice that this purpose statement focuses on teaching skills and explicitly uses the word *teach*. Not only that, but the purpose statement directly addresses specific skills that will be taught, rather than vaguely stating, for instance, that "the purpose of the group is to teach students how to avoid fighting."

2. "The purposes of this women's group are to help women learn about the history of female oppression and to help women set personally meaningful goals for the next year of their lives." Again, note how the purpose statement explicitly uses an educational term (in this case *learn*).

Counseling groups focus on addressing issues considered to be within the range of normal human problems. As the ASGW phrases it, members "may be experiencing transitory maladjustment . . . may be at risk for the development of interpersonal problems, or . . . may seek enhancement of personal qualities and abilities" (Association for Specialists in Group Work, 2000, p. 331). An example of a counseling group in a school setting would be a group designed for children who have just moved into a new school and need guidance adjusting to the new environment and new interrelationships. An example of a counseling group in a community agency might be a group for women experiencing fear related to reentering the workforce following a divorce. The purpose statement for a counseling group should clearly indicate that the focus is on group process rather than emphasizing teaching, as in the following examples:

1. "The purpose of this group is to help guide women through the difficult task of reassessing their lives following major changes and setting concrete, achievable

goals for the next year and beyond." Note how this purpose statement contrasts with the psychoeducational women's group's purpose statement above. Here words such as *help* and *guide* indicate that the group's focus is primarily on counseling rather than on education.

2. "The purpose of this online group is to decrease the isolation of stay-at-home mothers of infants by helping them meet other mothers in the same situation via the Internet." In this purpose statement, again the word *help* appears prominently, indicting that the focus of the group is on assistance and building support networks, not on direct teaching.

3. "The purpose of this group is to assist members who abuse alcohol to move from thinking intermittently about their need to change to making a commitment and preparing themselves to enter treatment." This purpose statement again emphasizes counseling over direct teaching. The word *assist* indicates that the group leader will be involved to help facilitate the group, but the process of change will emanate from within and between members themselves.

Psychotherapy groups provide treatment interventions for "people who may be experiencing severe and/or chronic maladjustment" (Association for Specialists in Group Work, 2000, p. 331) beyond the range of normal, everyday problems. Counselors in community agencies, day treatment programs, residential facilities, and hospitals conduct psychotherapy groups as part of their professional practice. Psychotherapy groups are less common in school settings. It is important to note here that counseling groups and psychotherapy groups exist on a continuum. Some groups may be clearly distinguishable as counseling groups, and other groups may obviously be psychotherapy groups. However, some groups may move up and down the continuum from session to session.

There are at least two types of purposes for psychotherapy groups that may separately or together be reflected in the group's purpose statement. One purpose is to address one or more of the symptoms of the member's diagnosis. Another purpose, known as *medication compliance*, is to ensure that members who are prescribed medications in fact take their medications and take them as directed. Purpose statements for psychotherapy groups generally name the clinical condition directly. Purpose statements for groups that may fluctuate between counseling and psychotherapy may or may not state the clinical condition. Below are a few examples of psychotherapy group purpose statements and purpose statements for groups that may exist on a continuum between counseling and psychotherapy.

1. "The purpose of this group is to decrease and/or prevent self-injurious behaviors of women with borderline personality disorder." In this case the group is clearly a psychotherapy group. Not only is the diagnosed condition (borderline personality disorder) clearly stated but also the purpose statement clearly indicates that the group will focus on decreasing a single symptom of the disorder.

2. "The purpose of this group for fifth grade students with attention deficit/hyperactivity disorder is to decrease the time the students are out of their seats and to increase the amount of time they are on task during class." Since time on task should promote academic achievement, this group should promote students' academic success.

3. "The purpose of this group is to assist clients who are struggling to manage depressive symptoms and to encourage medication compliance." Here, the purpose statement indicates that the group is a psychotherapy group. Note also that the purpose of this group is not only focused on managing specific symptoms but also on encouraging medication compliance, another clear indicator within the purpose statement that the group is a psychotherapy group.

Task work groups are characterized by a focus on achieving the task for which the group was formed. As stated by the ASGW, the processes of the group should promote "efficient and effective accomplishment of goals" (Association for Specialists in Group Work, 2000, p. 330). Here is an example of a purpose statement for a task work group: "The purpose of this group is to raise the money needed to repaint the community church." In this text, the focus is less on task work groups than on the other types of groups because task work groups are often led by people in the community who are not members of any of the helping professions. This text is intended for use in training helping professionals, so it focuses on groups they typically lead.

Exercise for Active Learning
Fine-Tuning the Purpose Statement for Your Group

Go back now to the proposal you drafted for the previous section's exercise. Now fine-tune the purpose statement, taking into consideration the type of group you will be leading. Is the group for which you created a proposal primarily psychoeducational, counseling, psychotherapy, task work oriented, or a combination? Make sure that your purpose statement is one that focuses the group, provides a consistent direction for the group, and will lead the group in the direction of specific goals. Your purpose statement will become part of your group advertisement later in this chapter, so try to make it as final as you can.

Selecting the Meeting Site

The next step in starting a group is to select the meeting site. Although this step may seem unimportant in the scheme of things, the meeting site can actually contribute a great deal to the success of the group for reasons explored in more detail later in this chapter. That said, sometimes leaders may be in a position to pick a meeting site, and other times choosing the site may not be an option. However, if the leader does have the option to choose the meeting site, he should weigh the following concerns:

Member Access.   A group is more likely to be successful if it is accessible to all possible members. Members should be able to get to and from the meeting site by public transportation at the time of day the group meets. For those driving to and from the group, ample parking at the group site should be available. Finally, the building, the group room, and the rest rooms should all be wheelchair accessible.

Size and Atmosphere.   Leaders should look for rooms that are large enough for the group to be able to break into smaller subgroups, if desired. Depending on the

planned activities, the group may need space for an art area where the cleanup of paints and so forth is easy, as well as a group area where seating arrangements can be easily adjusted to facilitate activities. Adequate lighting is also an important consideration.

Time Availability.   Leaders should check ahead to make sure that the site is available for all planned group sessions. The site should also be free for at least a half hour before the scheduled start of the group to allow for set-up time, and for at least 15 minutes after the end of each session to allow for time to organize materials and clean up.

Privacy.   If the topic of the group is one for which members are likely to desire some privacy, the leader should try to arrange the location and/or timing of the group so that members do not have to linger in the waiting room or parking lot, where they may not wish to be seen, prior to the meeting.

Supervision and safety needs.   The leader should consider the importance of supervision and safety. For example, you may want a group room that facilitates live supervision by the leader's supervisor. This could mean selecting a room with one-way mirrors, and audio or video equipment. Safety needs might arise because your group members have a history of being dangerous or because others, for example abusive spouses, might try to follow members to group. For some groups, leaders may want to schedule daytime meetings and/or hold the group at a site with security guards.

Exercise for Active Learning
Selecting a Meeting Site for Your Group
Identify three rooms in your environment, and evaluate each room as a possible meeting site for the group you have been setting up throughout this chapter. Consider the impact of member access, size and atmosphere, time availability, privacy, and supervision and safety needs on your group. If member access, privacy, and/or supervision and safety needs are major considerations for your group, be sure to keep that in mind as you create your group advertisement in the next section's exercise.

Advertising the Group

Once the group is approved, the purpose statement is clear, and the meeting site has been selected, all of the pertinent information the group leader needs to advertise the group is in place. A good **advertisement** makes potential members aware of the group and provides them with the information they need to determine whether or not they wish to inquire further about the group. First and foremost, you need to be conscious that truth in advertising affects not only your reputation and credibility but also the reputation and credibility of the school or agency. This is particularly important when advertised groups are designed for minors. Not only members but also parents and faculty will rely on the information advertised. You

should include the following information in the advertisement, in whatever form the advertisement takes (poster, print ad, Web ad, e-mail announcement, etc.):

- An accurate and appealing title.
- A clear purpose statement.
- Information about meeting times and sites.
- Name of the leader(s).
- Qualifications of the leader(s).
- Cost of the group, if there is a cost.
- Contact information on how to inquire further about the group.

In addition to the purpose statement, you may choose to include a list of weekly topics, if the group is organized in that manner. When you advertise the purpose statements (and possibly the select weekly topics), keep in mind that once the group is advertised, members, parents, faculty, and anyone else with a vested interest in the group have the right to expect that the content of the group is consistent with what was advertised. Finally, as previously noted, if a group is intended for children, you must provide applicable additional information for parents and faculty that directly addresses informed consent, such as stating that written permission from the children's parents will be required and providing information that allows for parental questions and/or objections.

The advertisements for the groups might be distributed in a number of ways depending on the group. In schools, a list of groups and the advertisements for them might be included with other materials sent home at the start of the academic year or at the start of each quarter. Advertisements might also be distributed to teachers or posted on bulletin boards as appropriate. In agencies, ads that describe the group program for a period of time are often put together in a flier. This material is distributed to counselors in the agency and in the surrounding geographic area. Specific groups might be advertised on the radio or in the newspaper.

For a good example, refer to Figure 2-2, the proposed advertisement for the ADHD group presented earlier in this chapter. Note that in addition to providing all of the above-stated information—including in this case appropriate information for parents—its layout is visually appealing.

Exercise for Active Learning
Practice Designing a Group Advertisement

Advising officers at a local university have had multiple requests for appointments from "undecided" students who want help establishing a major at the start of their sophomore year. The university has colleges of Agriculture, Engineering, Sciences, and Technology. You are charged with organizing a group to help these students. You decide to title your group "Picking Your Major." Design a poster to use in advertising the group. Include appropriate information in an eye-catching poster.

Advertising Your Group

Create an advertisement for your group, using Figure 2-2 as a model. Be sure to include the name of the group at the top of the advertisement, and include all

pertinent information including the purpose statement you created in an earlier exercise (refine it further if you wish), factual information (your name, qualifications, and contact information, the meeting time/site), and group cost (if any).

Screening and Referral

Once potential members respond to the advertisement for the group, it's time for the leader(s) to start the process of selecting the ultimate members of the group. The process of selecting members for the group being formed is called **screening.** In a sense, a specific and carefully worded advertisement is actually the first step in the screening process, because it appeals to a subgroup of people who might be interested in the group and does not appeal to others.

Ethics Pointer

ACA Ethics Code A.8.a requires counselors to screen potential group members (American Counseling Association, 2005, p. 5).

Some people who express a desire to participate in the group may—for a wide range of reasons—not fit well with the intended group. For example, one particular person might be too anxious to benefit from and contribute to the group you are planning. However, the person may definitely need and want counseling. Therefore, you should make a **referral,** which means attempting to connect a person in need of counseling with an appropriate counselor who can provide the needed services the referring counselor cannot provide. That counselor on the receiving end of the referral may be an individual, group, or family counselor and he or she may either be within the same school or agency as the referring counselor or may be external.

Ethics Pointer

Ethics Code A.11.b requires counselors to suggest referral resources if counselors choose not to enter into a counseling relationship because they determine that they are unable to be of professional assistance to clients (American Counseling Association, 2005, p. 6).

Referral can be an uncomfortable process for beginning group leaders. It is a delicate matter to ensure that the person being referred to another source of help does not feel pushed away or does not feel pathologized. One way you can go about offering to make a referral is to express caring and hope and to listen carefully to what services the person desires. You should provide the person being referred with contact information for three or four agencies or counselors who might be appropriate, rather than just one agency or counselor. You should also provide local hotline numbers in addition to the referrals. If the potential client is a child of school age, we typically suggest to parents that they consider the possibility that the school

counselor might be able to help the child. We tell the parents that it is in the public interest that school counselors help children, and we encourage them to contact the school counselor. We mention that parents are already contributing to the school counselors' salaries through paying taxes; therefore, it is OK for the parents to ask if the counselor might be able to see their child for a few sessions or as part of groups at school. Further, the referral process should direct the person toward the most appropriate services. On this point, consider offering to allow the person to call the referral counselors or agencies right from your office so that the person will have a specific appointment scheduled with an appropriate counselor before leaving you. Some people take the referral information home with them and do with it what they will. If they choose not to enter counseling, it is their right to make that choice.

Once a person becomes a member of your group, a counseling relationship is established. If you need to refer a clearly suicidal member, you must follow the mandates of state law, rather than simply provide a referral the member may choose to ignore.

While there may be complex reasons for screening members into or out of specific groups, the guidelines presented in Table 2-5 below are a good place to start. (These guidelines are based partially on Yalom (1995) and partially on the experience of the authors of this book.)

Table 2-5 Group Screening Guidelines

Screen in potential group members who
- are genuinely interested in being in the group,
- have concerns/goals directly related to the purpose of the group and to other potential members' concerns/goals,
- could reasonably expect to benefit from being in the group,
- can commit to attending all sessions of the group,
- are motivated to work on and try new approaches for addressing their issues,
- can commit to confidentiality and other aspects of the group contract,
- provide appropriate signed consent, and
- are of an appropriate developmental level for the group.

Screen out clients who
- do not have concerns directly related to the purpose of the group,
- may have difficulty interacting appropriately in the group—for example, delusional clients or clients with a recent history of assaulting others,
- are likely to impede the progress of the group,
- cannot commit to attending all sessions of the group,
- have a history of quitting groups (not just counseling groups) they join,
- do not genuinely want to make changes related to their concerns,
- cannot commit to confidentiality and other aspects of the group contract,
- do not provide appropriate signed consent, or
- are at a different developmental level than other potential group members.

To further gain an understanding of the screening process, consider the following two case examples in which the approved group has been advertised and the screening process has begun.

Case Example 1

Maya is a school counselor in a kindergarten-to-eighth-grade elementary school. She is forming a group whose purpose is to discuss parental divorce and help students adjust to changes in family life resulting from divorce. Following an advertisement for the potential group, six potential group members have been identified: Mario, Kyle, Yuri, Anna, and Fred—all first or second graders—and Cliff, a fifth grader. Mario, Kyle, Yuri, Anna, and Fred are making satisfactory if slower than usual progress in their academic work since their parents' divorces, and none have been sent to detention since their parents' divorces. During their screening interviews, Maya learns that their concerns center on feeling insecure and unsafe after losing contact with one of their parents. Cliff's school work has suffered considerably since the divorce. He seems unable or unwilling to talk to either his peers or adults regarding his feelings about the divorce. He has assaulted two boys on the school playground, and he has started wetting his bed at night.

The five first and second graders are screened into the group. Cliff, however, is screened out for several reasons. First, as a fifth-grade student, Cliff is at a different developmental level than the second- and third-grade students. Second, his level of distress seems greater, as shown by the decline of his academic performance and by his increasingly assaultive behavior. Maya further believes that at this time, it may not be safe for him to be placed in a group, particularly a group consisting of children significantly younger than Cliff. Finally, Cliff's difficulties talking about the divorce may predict difficulty participating in the group.

Having screened Cliff out of the group, Maya intends to take some action to help him. She may either take Cliff on as an individual client or she may work with one or more of Cliff's parents to refer him to community counseling. Maya's decision may depend on parental preference, her work load, school philosophy and policy, or a combination of these things.

Case Example 2

Darren, a counselor at a community agency, is forming a group for men who suffer from mild depression. The purpose of the group is to help men with mild depression learn how to make more positive statements about themselves and how to have more positive interactions with others. Seven men called and set up appointments for screening after they saw the advertisement for the group. All of the men had mild depressive symptoms, and all of them wanted to feel better. However, in addition to depressive symptoms, Ed appeared to have significant problems with alcohol abuse. After canceling two screening appointments, Ed arrived smelling strongly of alcohol. When Darren indicated that he could tell Ed had been drinking, Ed began talking about having received two traffic tickets this week, including his second citation for driving under the influence. Darren has screened Ed out of the depression group, because Ed's problems with alcohol make it likely that Ed would be frequently absent from the group and would make it difficult for

Ed to participate in and benefit from the group. Instead, Darren has referred Ed for a comprehensive substance abuse evaluation.

As indicated in the two case examples, screening involves weeding inappropriate members out of the group and screening appropriate members into the group. Under certain circumstances, however, an appropriate member may be screened out of a group. That may occur when a potential member is being treated by another mental health professional but is seeking entry into a new group. In a case such as this, the group leader should obtain written consent of the professional for the potential member to be included in the group. The need to get written consent to include in your group a person being treated by another mental health professional applies to both children and adults. Consider the following case example:

Case Example 3
Dibya, the school counselor in a rural elementary school, is starting a counseling group for students in the third and fourth grades who have grief issues. Mario is in the third grade. His father worked as a plumber for a construction company in the city. Last month Mario's father was killed when the trench in which he was fitting a sewer pipe collapsed. The father was badly crushed in the accident, so at the funeral, which Mario did attend, the casket was closed. Mario is currently seeing a counselor in a specialized grief clinic in Central City once a month. When she saw the advertisement for the school-based grief group, Mario's mother called and asked Dibya to include Mario in the group.

Several points support including Mario in the school group. His concern fits with the purpose of the group, both Mario and his mother would like Mario to be in the group, and Mario is in the same grade as the intended participants. However, as a school counselor Dibya should proceed very carefully. After obtaining a release from Mario's mother, Dibya should consult with the counselor at the grief clinic to determine if the grief counselor believes it would be helpful or harmful for Mario to be a member of the school group. If the grief counselor agrees that Mario should be in the group, Dibya should ask the counselor to mail or fax a brief note to her indicating support for Mario's participation in the school group. Dibya should keep this note along with all other consent forms in Mario's counseling record, and Dibya should try to obtain a release from Mario's mother to allow Dibya to keep in regular contact with Mario's other counselor.

Exercise for Active Learning
Referring a Person Who Was Interested In but Not Selected for Your Group

You are screening potential members for a group on anxiety management. The group is offered by a community agency for persons age 20 to 30. In the process of screening, you become aware that one of the members, Marge, is anxious because of recent physical abuse. The other members of your group do not have a similar history and are far less anxious than Marge. Marge also takes medication for depression. You do not believe that Marge is ready to be in your group at this time. You think she would benefit from some individual counseling prior to starting group

counseling. On the lines below, write what you could say to explain to Marge why you think individual counseling would be better for her at this time and how you could help her locate an appropriate counselor.

_____

_____

_____

_____

Your Proposal

Now return to the proposal you began early in this chapter. Check the content of your proposal to be sure it is complete. Polish your wording and if it seems appropriate, add any artwork that would illustrate the purpose of your group and make your advertisement attractive to the eye of the viewer.

STUDY QUESTIONS

1. What considerations should you keep in mind when conducting a group in a school setting? How could you get information about what groups might be needed in a school?
2. What considerations should you keep in mind when conducting a group in a community setting? How could you get information about what groups might be needed by the clients of a counseling center?
3. What are the five steps involved in starting a group, as outlined in this chapter?
4. List the key information that should be included in a proposal for a group. Who is the primary audience for a proposal?
5. Why is the purpose statement for the group important?
6. Describe the four group work types recognized by the Association for Specialists in Group Work (ASGW). How are purpose statements impacted by group type?
7. What are the five considerations to keep in mind when selecting a meeting site?
8. List the key information that should be included in an advertisement for an approved group. How is accurate advertisement of a group related to ethical counseling practice?
9. Explain how to screen out and select members for a group. Whom would you screen out? Whom would you select?

KEY CONCEPTS

advertisement p. 31

cost estimate p. 23.

counseling group p. 28

psychoeducational group p. 28

psychotherapy group p. 29

purpose statement p. 23

proposal p. 21

screening p. 33

referral p. 33

task work group p. 30

REFERENCES

American Counseling Association. (2005). *ACA code of ethics.* Alexandria, VA: Author.

American Psychiatric Association. (1994). *Diagnostic and statistical manual of mental disorders* (4th ed.). Washington, DC: Author.

American Psychiatric Association. (2000). *Diagnostic and statistical manual of mental disorders* (4th ed., text revision). Washington, DC: Author.

Association for Specialists in Group Work. (2000). Association for specialists in group work: Professional training standards for the training of group workers. *Journal for Specialists in Group Work, 25,* 327–342.

First, M. B., & Tasman, A. (Eds.). (2004). *DSM-IV-TR mental disorders: Diagnosis, etiology, and treatment.* West Sussex, England: Wiley.

Yalom, I. D. (1995). *The theory and practice of group psychotherapy* (4th ed.). New York: Basic Books.

CHAPTER 3

Applying Individual Counseling Skills in Groups: Part I

LEARNING OBJECTIVES

After studying this chapter you should be able to describe the following individual counseling skills and their application to group work:

- Genuineness and congruence
- Unconditional positive regard
- Accurate empathic understanding
- Nonverbal skills
- Attending
- Questioning
- Reflecting skills
- Confrontation

INTRODUCTION: WHY INDIVIDUAL COUNSELING SKILLS?

When you read the title of this chapter, you probably wondered what *individual* counseling skills had to do with *group* counseling. How do we use individual counseling skills and still maintain the integrity of the group process? The answer is that being able to run an effective group is based on the leader's ability to connect a series of individual interactions between the leader and each member, as well as between group members. A great deal of what leaders do is to initiate, sustain, and sometimes influence the production of individual interactions and weave them into a series of meaningful group experiences. Therefore, this chapter and the next will focus on individual counseling skills that apply to effective leadership of groups.

Keeping track of the myriad individual interactions that take place within groups probably seems to be a lot for a new leader to juggle. It is. The skills involved in collecting, organizing, and effectively working with a montage of individual interactions constitute the art of leadership. Each individual interaction is meaningful to the member or members involved. Individual interactions achieve collective meaning when the gestalt of the individual interactions is coordinated by an effective leader. In other words, when the leader is able to derive a meaningful whole out of the patterns set by individual interactions within the group, she has successfully uncovered the group's gestalt. Before we address how you can effectively orchestrate individual interactions into the collective experience of a group, in this chapter and the next we will review the foundational individual interaction skills with special attention to those that connect to group leadership. Along the way, we will provide examples to assist you in moving from simply understanding the skills to effectively practicing them in your groups.

STEPS TOWARD APPLYING INDIVIDUAL COUNSELING SKILLS TO GROUPS

How might you most effectively use these chapters on individual counseling skills to develop your group leadership skills? We recommend following the steps outlined below as a way to developmentally extend the individual skills into group leadership:

Step 1. Review the individual counseling skills presented in the Learning Objectives section at the beginning of each chapter.

You are likely to already be familiar with many of these skills if you have taken a basic counseling skills course as a prerequisite for your group course. We have selected for emphasis what we believe are the essential individual counseling skills that make up one foundation of effective group leadership.

Step 2. Practice individual counseling skills using the exercises provided in each chapter.

As with any acquired skill, practice is key to internalizing the skill, regardless of whether you are training to be a violin virtuoso, a golf champion, a computer programmer, or a group leader. (As counselor educators, part of our enjoyment of teaching these skills to new counselor trainees is that we also benefit from a regular refresher

on these skills.) To help you practice the skills, we have provided exercises you can complete on your own or with a partner.

Step 3. Study the integrative example provided near the end of the chapter.

Studying the integrative example will help you to see both the skills and the way the skills are used in the flow of the group.

Step 4. Find opportunities to apply the individual counseling skills in real-world groups with which you are involved.

After working through these individual counseling skills by reviewing and practicing them on your own, practicing them with training partners, and practicing them via the simulated groups presented in these chapters, your next step is to find opportunities to use these skills in groups outside of the classroom. Many of these individual counseling skills apply not only to group counseling but also within groups unrelated to counseling, for instance in participatory classrooms, in extracurricular groups, or in meetings at the workplace. When you find yourself in such groups, identify individual counseling skills employed by others and practice the skills yourself—of course keeping in mind the appropriateness of the situation. For instance, how does a speaker at a workplace meeting use questioning of meeting attendees to get to the heart of the matter at hand? In what ways might your use of congruence and genuineness positively impact the group when you are speaking during your extracurricular group's monthly meeting?

Now let's discuss in turn the individual counseling skills we have been talking about and how each skill applies in groups.

GENUINENESS AND CONGRUENCE

Definition of **genuineness**   The state of being authentic or truthful.

Definition of **congruence**   The state in which there is no conflict between the counselor's feelings and actions.

Counselor **genuineness** and **congruence** were described by Carl Rogers (1957) as core conditions for therapeutic success. These two concepts are often viewed as two sides of the same coin, because the skill of congruence is the counselor's ability to externalize his genuineness into the counseling relationship. When a counselor is being congruent, there is a match between his internal state and external expression of that state. Rogers (1957) did not feel it was necessary for counselors to live all aspects of their lives in genuineness and congruence. He thought it would be unrealistic to expect counselors to always exist in a state of integrated attitude, feeling, and action through their lives. However, he felt it was essential for genuineness and congruence to exist during the counseling session for the benefit of the client. Rogers (1957) emphasized that being genuine and congruent meant being fully transparent during the counseling session, that is, not presenting a facade to the client. Take for example a situation in which, after several sessions, a counselor is feeling frustrated because a client with a substance

abuse problem is not disclosing anything of any relevance to the problem. If the counselor is genuine and congruent, then she should not only be aware of the feeling of frustration but should also externalize the feeling into the counseling process and convey that sense of frustration to the client. However, the degree to which the counselor externalizes this awareness directly to the client may be a question the counselor should discuss with a supervisor and/or with colleagues. Rogers did not advocate for counselors to always communicate their personal feelings directly to clients, stating that this was a matter for careful consideration. The deciding factor in each case should be whether or not expressing her own feelings is in the best interests of the client.

In groups, genuineness and congruence are important because leaders lead their groups by example. Communicating feelings to the group in a genuine and caring manner as these feelings present themselves models healthy group process for the members. The more that both counselors in training and practicing counselors practice opportunities to be fully aware, real, authentic, and integrated, the more likely they are to bring these skills into the group.

Exercise for Active Learning
Skill Development: Genuineness and Congruence

Practice genuineness and congruence in groups outside of the classroom. For instance, if you are currently working with a group or belong to an extracurricular group, speak up at your next meeting in a way that appropriately entails genuineness and congruence. Describe your experience and how you incorporated genuineness and congruence with classmates or in a classroom discussion.

UNCONDITIONAL POSITIVE REGARD

Definition of **unconditional positive regard**   Valuing the client as a person and respecting each aspect of the client's experience as being part of the client.

Unconditional positive regard is an attitude identified as a counseling skill by Rogers (1957), which, when employed in therapy contributes toward successful therapeutic change. The word *unconditional* in this term may make this concept seem too lofty an aspiration to those in the counseling field. We are all human, and even the most likeable people may carry with them personality traits (e.g., aggressiveness, passivity, egocentrism, self-deprecation, timidity, whininess, etc.) that counselors may find difficult to hold in positive regard. Further, many clients may be in therapy for the very reason that they have engaged in actions that most people find problematic, even reprehensible. For instance, it can be difficult for counselors to separate the person from the action when clients have been engaged in criminality, abuse of others, or addictive behaviors, posing a challenge to the counselor's ability to maintain unconditional positive regard. The skill in unconditional positive regard is to maintain your attitude of valuing the client and expressing care and concern for the client as a human being, even as the client reveals undesirable behaviors or aspects he himself considers undesirable.

In groups, unconditional positive regard becomes more complicated than in individual counseling, because the leader must apply this skill to a number of people (members) rather than to one person. There are moments in groups when the leader will feel unconditional positive regard for a member or members, moments in the group when the positive regard will be conditional for a member or members, and moments when the counselor will feel negative regard for a member or members. Rogers believed that negative and conditional regard for clients leads to ineffective therapy. If a leader can accept members in a total rather than conditional way, then progress will occur. From the leader's perspective, unconditional positive regard entails a willingness to accept all members' emotional states for what they are, without condition.

Exercise for Active Learning
Skill Development: Unconditional Positive Regard

1. Reflect on a person in your own life who may have disappointed you in obvious or subtle ways but with whom you maintain an unconditionally positive relationship. What messages do you give yourself to help you maintain unconditional positive regard for this person? Without using names, write down in the spaces below what the person did to disappoint you and the affirming statements you used to maintain unconditional positive regard. When you are done, share and discuss your thoughts with a class partner.

   _____

   _____

   _____

2. Work in small classroom groups and consider the following challenges to maintaining unconditional positive regard as a counselor. Discuss how you might deal with each of these challenges.
   a. A man who has a history of physically abusing his spouse.
   b. A client who frequently makes racist, sexist, and homophobic comments.
   c. A person who continues to engage in a self-destructive chemical addiction.

ACCURATE EMPATHIC UNDERSTANDING

Definition of **accurate empathic understanding**   The ability to deeply sense a client's worldview as if it were your own.

A counselor who has mastered the skill of **accurate empathic understanding** is not only able to understand a client's inner world but also is able to illuminate for the client issues of which the client is both aware and unaware. It is a deep and subjective understanding of the client. Rogers (1957) speaks of the duality of accurate empathic understanding. The counselor must be able to subjectively immerse herself in the client's experiences yet retain the ability to objectively point out issues the client is not aware of—without projecting her own views on the client. In other

words, the counselor must maintain separateness from the client while fully understanding the client's world.

Accurate understanding of another human being is not an easy task, particularly during the early stages of counseling. What are the consequences of a client who feels like the counselor is not *exactly* understanding what he is trying to convey? Most clients are aware that understanding between human beings takes work and do not expect counselors to be superhumanly intuitive; consequently, clients are usually willing to give their counselors latitude as long as the counselors demonstrate a genuine interest in moving toward client understanding. Therefore, another fundamental concept that plays a role in developing accurate empathic understanding is the notion of *interest*. As long as the client feels that the counselor has an interest in appreciating her world and a corresponding willingness to be corrected, then accurate empathic understanding can develop over time during the counseling relationship.

In groups, accurate empathic understanding occurs in various ways. For instance, a member may receive a sense of accurate empathic understanding not only from the leader but also from other members. The power of accurate empathic understanding within a group is that the potential for healing is magnified by however many members are in the group. Importantly, and similar to individual accurate empathic understanding, group accurate empathic understanding requires that the understanding is communicated back to those being counseled, that is, each member of the group. Also similar to individual accurate empathic understanding, complete and immediate accuracy is not always possible and not necessary at the outset, just so long as members feel that the leader and the other members are interested in understanding their worlds and willing to be corrected should they falter in their empathic understanding.

Exercise for Active Learning
Skill Development: Accurate Empathic Understanding

Accurate empathic understanding involves the counselor being able to understand the client's world at a deeper level than the client presents his world. In this reflective exercise, think of a situation in your life (good or bad) that had a lasting emotional impact on you. In the spaces below, write three sentences about the situation, the first sentence describing the situation, the second sentence capturing the emotional content of the experience, and the third sentence demonstrating an accurate empathic understanding of the situation. When you are done, share and discuss your thoughts with a class partner.

> *Example:*
> *(1) In 1992, while returning home late at night from the convenience store, I was mugged at knifepoint by someone who was obviously very agitated and desperate. (2) During and right after the mugging I acted surprisingly calm (perhaps that was adrenaline, which kicks in during crisis situations), but for months afterward, I experienced frequent panic attacks that didn't seem at all related to the mugging. (3) I have since come to an understanding that my panic attacks were the result of my sense of personal safety having been violated for the first time in my life and didn't necessarily need to be triggered by memories of the mugging itself, just by*

experiencing the same sights, sounds, and smells of the neighborhood in which I lived and in which the mugging also occurred.

_____

_____

_____

_____

_____

_____

NONVERBAL SKILLS

Definition of **nonverbal skills**   The set of skills involved with interpreting the meaning behind clients' nonverbal behaviors, such as body position, body orientation, facial expression, gestures, and eye contact, and making sure that your own nonverbal behaviors are congruent with what you intend to communicate to your clients.

Mastering **nonverbal skills** is important in establishing and maintaining a good counseling relationship. When doing individual counseling, the effective counselor begins to notice the nonverbal behaviors of the client in the very first session. Is the client using direct eye contact with the counselor when reporting some feeling or experience, averting her eyes, or looking at the floor? Does the client shift around in his seat or show other signs of discomfort when addressing some difficult or disturbing issue? Does the client's position and body posture indicate anything about how the client might be feeling? Are the client's hand gestures consistent with the topic of conversation, or are they communicating something different? Does the client's facial expression match what the client is communicating verbally?

At the same time, clients notice the nonverbal behaviors of counselors, so it is important that counselors make direct eye contact, use appropriate gestures, and communicating trust and interest through their own body language, facial expressions, and so forth.

Group leaders must not only be able to interpret individual members' nonverbal behaviors but they must also be aware of the nonverbal signals between members. We have found that working with coleaders allows leaders to better track nonverbal behaviors. It is surprising how much a coleader can pick up on the group's nonverbal behaviors when the other leader is otherwise engaged in a particular group interaction.

Exercise for Active Learning
Skill Development: Nonverbal Skills

Videotape or record via TiVo/DVR several minutes of a talk show on television. If you don't have TV video recording capability, locate a clip of a talk show on an online video website, such as YouTube, Google Video, or AOL Video. (If you share this recording with some of your classmates, you will later be able to share and compare your observations.) Watch the show with the sound turned down, and observe

the nonverbal behaviors exhibited by the interviewees/participants. Write down your impressions in the spaces below.

_____

_____

_____

_____

_____

Now watch the clip with the sound turned up, and see how well you were able to understand the group dynamics without any verbal cues. Put check marks next to the correct observations and Xs next to those that were incorrect. (If you shared the recording with classmates, get together to compare your observations.)

ATTENDING

***Definition of* attending**   Paying close attention to what a client is conveying during your communication—both verbally and nonverbally—expresses your open and nonjudgmental interest in the client.

In addition to nonverbal interpretation skills, counselors must also be proficient in establishing and maintaining successful individual counseling relationships via the skill of **attending**. Attending entails listening attentively (rather than appearing removed from the session, talking too much, or only listening selectively) while not making assumptions or jumping to conclusions too quickly. Counselors must demonstrate that they are listening to their clients attentively and are completely focused on the client's revelation of personal (perhaps painful) details. Looking out the window or getting up to pour a glass of water while a client is talking, not speaking when the client has stopped talking, or spending too much time talking and not enough time listening, all convey that the counselor doesn't care about the client or doesn't want to hear what the client has to say.

Attending to multiple members of a group is a difficult challenge for leaders to master. Through experience, leaders learn to listen to the discussion, interpret individual members' nonverbal behaviors, and attend to all members of the group simultaneously. Working with coleaders allows leaders to fully attend to the entire group. Coleadership is particularly useful when leaders must attend to large groups, groups in which members have intense and immediate needs (e.g., recent death of a parent), or groups in which members have mental health diagnoses (e.g., bipolar disorder).

Exercise for Active Learning
Skill Development: Attending
Watch again the recording you made for the nonverbal skills exercise above. Observe how the host/interviewer exhibits attending behaviors. If this were a counseling session rather than a TV talk show, what aspects of the interviewer's attending behaviors would be

appropriate? What aspects would be inappropriate? In the spaces below, write down your thoughts. When you are done, share and discuss them with a class partner.

_____

_____

_____

_____

QUESTIONING

***Definition of* questioning**   A way of eliciting information from clients regarding their thoughts, actions, or feelings by asking open or closed questions.

Questioning is an obvious part of the counseling process. Questioning is a skill rather than simply an action, because it involves knowing what types of questions to ask and when to ask them. Questioning can employ *closed questions* (those that can be answered yes or no or that ask for specific information and don't elicit further probing, e.g., "Did you grow up in Denver?" or "Where did you grow up?") and *open questions* (those that elicit longer responses and that ask clients to provide a narrative response regarding an experience, thought, or feeling, e.g., "Why do you think you had an unhappy childhood?"). Closed questions commonly ask for specific, factual information and often begin with words such as *where* and *when*. In contrast, questions that begin with *how* or *why* tend to be open and elicit broad responses that provide the counselor with a clearer picture of the client and her history, concerns, and previous attempts to address the concerns. A question beginning with *what* can be either closed or open, depending on how the question is phrased (e.g., "What is your mother's name?" is a closed question, while "What do you think of your mother?" is an open question).

Blending closed and open questions forms the overall process of questioning. Be aware, however, that the tone of your question as well as the timing of your questions should communicate interest in and caring for the client. If either the tone of the question or its timing is incorrect, the client may experience questioning as interrogation rather than caring.

Questioning is more frequently used during the early stages of both individual and group counseling. A counselor will use questions to engage new clients, obtain contextual or clarifying information from clients, overcome reticence on the part of new clients, and/or get clients to more fully voice their experiences, thoughts, and feelings. A common goal for a client in individual counseling is to get the client to initiate his own questioning, signaling a willingness on the part of the client to move in a forward, healing direction. This self-questioning is a reflective process. It is also desirable for members in groups to be reflective. Member interactions may involve questioning of other group members, or leaders may encourage members to make statements directly to other members rather than posing questions.

Haney and Leibsohn (1999) argue that questioning is overused by beginning counselors leading groups. Often, inexperienced leaders fall into the trap of filling silences by asking too many questions, which has the effect of making the leader appear to be the "expert," which shuts down member participation. As integrity and trust between members develop over time, questions will more frequently originate from members. Unless the leader facilitates a shift from leader to member-initiated questioning, the leader may be forever burdened with originating all of the questions for the group. Leaders can help groups move toward an increase in member-initiated questions by letting members know that an intrinsic part of group process is for members to ask question of one another; that is, they should not expect the group leader to be the "expert," but to be the facilitator.

Exercise for Active Learning
Skill Development: Questioning

Listen to an interview on a reputable television or radio program (not on a "fluff" celebrity-focused television or radio show, but on a news broadcast or more serious program, such as 60 Minutes, All Things Considered, Investigative Reports, *etc.). Pay attention to the types of questions the interviewer asks (closed versus open-ended) and how these types of questions are mixed together. Do you see a pattern developing during the interview process? Does the interviewer order and pace the questions in a particular way? What have you learned from listening to the interview that you might take with you into a group leadership role? In the spaces below, write down the program you watched and your thoughts as you watched it. When you are done, share and discuss your responses with a class partner.*

_____

_____

_____

_____

_____

REFLECTING

Reflecting is a way of responding that demonstrates that the client has been heard and understood while helping the client to think more deeply about the issues she has brought up. We will discuss three types of reflection: reflection of content, reflection of feeling, and reflection of meaning.

Reflection of Content

Definition of **reflection of content**   The process of repeating to the client key factual information brought out during the discussion. It is a way to demonstrate that the client has been heard and confirm that the client has been heard correctly.

Reflection of content may seem at first to be the simple act of restating the information shared by the client. However, as with questioning, it is in fact a nuanced skill insofar as the counselor must become proficient not merely in repeating information back to the client but more importantly in knowing when and in what format to reiterate the information. There are two primary ways of reflecting content: paraphrasing and summarizing.

Definition of **paraphrasing**   Capturing the content of what a client says, condensing it to a short statement, and saying it back to the client.

In the following section and as we discuss several group facilitation skills in this chapter and in Chapter 4, we will give you some structured approaches to help you learn and practice the skills. As you become more comfortable practicing the skills and as you move to the more complex area of groups, you will need to develop flexibility in wording your interventions and in applying them to leading groups. Ivey and Ivey (2007, p. 161) break the structure of effective **paraphrasing** into four parts:

1. *Using a sentence stem*, or beginning the paraphrase with words that prepare the client for receiving the reflection; for instance, "What I have heard you say is . . ." or "It looks like . . ."
2. *Repeating key words* (using the client's language) that capture the main ideas of the content, such as, "You have used the words *trapped* and *stuck* to describe your situation."
3. *Capturing the essence of what the client has said*, or taking long portions of dialogue presented by the client and compartmentalizing them into a few phrases, for example, "Basically, what I hear you saying is that you are at a financial impasse and would like to find out if there are reasons other than your salary behind it."
4. *Using a check-out*, or a brief question with which the counselor asks the client to confirm or correct the paraphrase, such as, "Did I get it right?"

Using Ivey and Ivey's four-part format, an example of a complete paraphrase would be, "What I have heard you say is *(sentence stem)*, over time you have worked out an agreement with your husband that 'cheating a little' or 'having quiet affairs' is acceptable *(repeating key words)*, but you think that this liberated, seemingly trusting approach isn't really going to save the marriage as you both thought it might *(capturing the essence)*. Is that correct?" *(check-out)*.

Definition of **summarizing**   A more extensive way to reflect content, typically covering a portion of a counseling session or several sessions.

Strategically employed throughout the beginning, middle, and end of a session, **summarizing** illuminates continuity of topics and/or establishes natural breaking points for topics. Summarizing involves the same format as paraphrasing, including a check-out at the end, but it focuses on major themes brought out during the counseling session. For example, a summary might sound like this: "We've covered a lot of ground, so let's take a break for a moment and focus on the main issues we've been discussing. First, you are unhappy with your relationship situation and feel, as you put it 'trapped' or 'stuck.' You use the same language to describe your job situation and your overall emotional state. Am I correct in saying that you

feel you've made choices in your life across the board that you're not happy with and are seeking major changes in your life?"

Group leaders may reflect content from the contributions of individual members or from the group as a whole. Generally, leaders summarize the work of the group as a whole and do so with several purposes: (1) to point out community of concern or experience and thereby promote the therapeutic factors *cohesion* and *universality*, (2) to start the process of changing the focus of the group, (3) to help members process what they have learned, and/or (4) to process the learnings of members as the end of a session approaches.

Exercise for Active Learning
Skill Development: Reflection of Content

In this exercise you will practice reflecting content by paraphrasing and summarizing. First, practice putting together the four components of paraphrasing by writing a verbal response to the following client statement. Label the components of your response. Remember, the four components of paraphrasing: using sentence stems, repeating key words, capturing the essence of what the client has said, and using a check-out.

Client begins the story: *I can't believe I've been in the same old crummy, boring job for 15 years. It pays the rent, but it sure isn't what I dreamed my life would be like when was a kid.*

Counselor responds with a paraphrase: _____

_____

After the counselor's paraphrase, the client continues: *Yes, that's right. I always loved music and desperately wanted to work in the music industry, but there weren't many job openings that didn't require a college degree, and when I graduated from high school, it didn't seem financially practical to go to college, and now I think it's too late to go to college and too late to make a job change. Have I wasted my life?*

Counselor summarizes the whole of the client's story so far: _____

_____

Reflection of Feeling

Definition of **reflection of feeling**   The process of verbalizing the feelings associated with what the client is saying.

Beyond solidifying the factual information in a client's story via reflection of content, locating the human emotion tied with each facet of the story via **reflection of feeling** helps clients connect external events in their lives with internal emotional states.

Ivey and Ivey (2007, p. 194) break the structure of an effective reflection of feeling into five parts:

1. ***Using a sentence stem,*** or beginning the reflection with words that prepare the client for receiving information, such as, "It sounds like you are . . ." or "You seem to be . . ."

2. **Attaching a feeling label** like "angry," "dissatisfied," or "torn" to attach an easily recognizable emotional name to what the client is feeling, for example, "It sounds like you are angry," or "You seem to be experiencing dissatisfaction."

3. **Adding the context** of the feeling, using words like "because" or "when," which broadens the meaningfulness of the client's reflection. For instance, "It sounds as if you are angry because of recent changes to your relationship with your partner."

4. **Stating the temporal aspect** (past or present tense) using phrases like "at this moment" or "in the past," which clarifies feelings by placing them in the past or in the present, for example, "You feel this way now," or "This is something that impacted you strongly in the past."

5. **Using a check-out**, or a brief question to encourage the client to confirm or correct reflected feeling, such as "Am I on the right track?" or "Do you agree with that?"

Using Ivey and Ivey's five-part format, a complete reflection of feeling might proceed as follows: "I see from the way your expression lights up as you talk about your engagement right now *(using a sentence stem; stating the temporal aspect)* that it makes you feel very happy *(attaching a feeling label)* because it begins a new stage in your relationship *(adding context)*. Am I reading you correctly?" *(using a check-out)*.

Group leaders may reflect the feelings of an individual member ("Ed, you seem sad as you speak") or the emotional tone of an interaction between members ("As you two are speaking, both of you look very angry"). Leaders might also reflect the mood of the group ("From the frowning and staring down at the floor and the slumping in your chairs, I am sensing a mood of sadness in the group today. And I'm guessing that the sadness is because Sarah has left the group. Do you think that's what's going on here today?").

In Chapters 6 and 7 we will discuss ways to link members with similar feelings to promote universality. One great advantage of groups is that the leader can check the accuracy of his reflections of both content and feelings with the other members.

Exercise for Active Learning
Skill Development: Reflection of Feeling

Practice putting together the five components of reflection of feeling by writing a verbal response to each of the following client statements, labeling the parts of the response as we did in this section's example. Remember, the five parts of reflection of feeling are using a sentence stem, attaching a feeling label, adding the context, stating the temporal aspect, and using a check-out.

1. You are leading a group of middle school children, and one member says, "Oh man, I told you I studied for that test, but you don't believe me. You're just like my father."

Reflection of feeling: _____

_____

2. You are leading a group on family stress. One member, Ella, makes the following statement: "To my husband and my kids I'm just the cook, the maid, and the chauffeur. When I'm tired or not feeling well, they don't care."

    Reflection of feeling: _____

    _____

3. Write an open question for the group as a whole that could follow your reflection of Ella's feelings, and seek out similarities between Ella's feelings and those of other members.

    _____

    _____

Reflection of Meaning

A dictionary definition of the word *meaning* is "what is intended to be or in fact is, signified, indicated, referred to, or understood" (Webster's New World Dictionary of the American Language: College Edition). Human beings are constantly seeking to uncover the meaning of things—from the meaning of an infant's cries, to the meaning behind a lover's hurtful words, to the meaning of life and death. In counseling, **reflection of meaning** is important because it helps clients understand their experiences and relate what they learn in counseling to their lives outside counseling. To reflect meaning is to cut through the surface of a client's verbally and nonverbally expressed thoughts and feelings and expose their deeply felt significance.

***Definition of* reflection of meaning**   The skill of verbalizing the implicit meanings that lie beneath a client's explicitly expressed thoughts and feelings.

By reflecting the meaning of what a client is saying, the counselor enables the client to understand the "Why?" of the client's feelings, thoughts, and behaviors, helping the client to better interpret her experiences. Take for example the following client story.

Client: Hank wouldn't move in with me unless I agreed to keep it a secret from our families and the companies we work for, so I agreed to it. But I wouldn't have if I had known how much lying and sneaking around we would have to do. I also didn't know that he would keep secrets from me. He told me that he had to go on a business trip, but later I found out that he actually went on a family retreat. I tell him everything—details about my health, my finances, my work—and he is a good listener, but he never says anything at all about himself. What good is a relationship based on deception?

As with reflection of content and reflection of feeling, Ivey and Ivey (2007, p. 344) have broken down effective reflection of meaning into a step-by-step process. These steps parallel those in reflection of content and reflection of feeling except that in this case the counselor rephrases the client's language in a way that suggests the deeper meaning beneath what the client has said. Using Ivey and Ivey's four-part format, a complete reflection of meaning would look something like the following.

Counselor: I am sensing from what you've said [*using a sentence stem*] that you value honesty and intimacy in relationships most of all and that Hank's "deception" and "secrecy" [*repeating key words*] challenge your values and the very reasons why you are in the relationship. [*capturing the deeper meaning of what the client has said*] Does that make sense to you or am I off base here? [*using a check-out*]

Leaders may reflect meaning to individual group members, to a pair of members who are engaged in an interaction, or to the group as a whole. Leaders probably would not follow all reflections with a check-out process but would use such a process if the reflection was not affirmed (perhaps nonverbally by a head nod) by the member or members to whom it was addressed. One time when it might be wise to check out the reflection is when it addresses a deeper level of meaning than the member was expressing verbally.

The process of checking out the accuracy of the reflection may have two parts. One part is to check out the reflection with the member, pair of members, or group to whom it was addressed. When the reflection is addressed to a member or pair of members, the leader can check the accuracy of the reflection with the remaining members who might comment on its accuracy, correct it, or add to it.

Exercise for Active Learning
Skill Development: Reflection of Meaning

Practice putting together the four components of reflection of meaning by writing a verbal response to each of the following client stories and labeling the parts of the response. Remember, the four parts of reflection of meaning are using sentence stems, repeating key words, capturing the essence of what the client has said, and using a check-out.

Client 1: "I feel really bad that I stole that bracelet from my sister. It's not something that I ever thought I would do, because I love my sister and I think stealing is reprehensible. But it was so beautiful. I'm wondering if I have a psychological problem."

Reflection of meaning: _____

_____

_____

_____

Client 2: "There's nothing I hate more than a guy who looks you right in the eyes and lies to you, not even blinking or giving away that he's lying. But I had the facts and that made it even more disgusting when he lied right to my face. So that's basically why I broke up with him."

Reflection of meaning: _____

_____

_____

_____

Client 3: "I used to be really close with my cousin, but he turned into a real hypocrite somewhere along the line. I don't understand how he can be so into his religious beliefs but at the same time make nasty comments about women and gays all the time. Still, I miss hanging out with him because we were really tight and he's family, but I think his opinions will have to change before I reestablish the relationship."

Reflection of meaning: _____

_____

_____

_____

CONFRONTATION

***Definition of* confrontation**   The skill of effectively challenging a client's conflicting or incongruent personal thoughts, feelings, and behaviors (content) or attitudes.

As we use it in everyday life, the word *confrontation* brings with it harsh connotations. We think of arguments that we have gotten into in which both parties walked away angry and without resolution. In counseling settings the term has a somewhat different meaning. In counseling, **confrontation** is a planned action, not an emotional event. When used by counselors, confrontation varies in intensity from a gentle statement calling some incongruence into awareness, to a strong, direct statement. In groups, most of your confrontations should be on the gentle end of the continuum, because keeping your confrontations gentle respects members' rights to determine the pace of their work and provides for member safety.

Confrontation is one of the most difficult skills for counselors to master, but it also offers the greatest potential for healthy client change. Why does confrontation work so well in counseling but not so well in our daily lives? In our daily lives we are not usually prepared to be confronted by a challenge to change our behaviors, or we feel threatened by those who demand or even just suggest that we change. And when we confront others, we may be dealing with people who are not open to change at the moment. The scenario is different in counseling settings. Confrontation in a therapeutic setting is an expected part of the counseling process. In addition, counselors are trained to practice confrontation in an empathic, caring way, which may not be the case outside of counseling, when people tend to confront each other based on strong emotions they feel at the time of confrontation. In the supportive environment of counseling, when clients hear about how others see them differently than they see themselves, this creates a state of internal disequilibrium that opens clients up to the possibility of searching for safe, alternative ways of being.

In groups, not only are members confronted by the leader but they may also be confronted by other members.

Members may initially experience difficulty coping with requests to change their behaviors. Often, however, these requests ultimately lead to more growth

opportunities for them. Members can learn not just how one other person sees them but also how others see them in general [**YTF Reminder:** Interpersonal learning input]. Groups are generally caring environments that provide a context of support for members who try to respond to challenges contained in confrontations. In addition, groups allow members to see that confrontation works to the greater good of the group as a whole, that the process of change is not all about themselves. Finally, the effective modeling of confrontation in groups teaches members how to effectively confront other people in their daily lives outside of the group.

Ethics Pointer

> ACA Ethics Code A.8.b requires group leaders to protect members from being harmed by other members (American Counseling Association, 2005, p. 5). When members confront other members, leaders should monitor the confrontation process to provide for member safety. In groups where members have mental health diagnoses, leaders must be especially alert, allowing one member to confront another only if the timing and intensity of the confrontation is likely to be healing rather than harmful to the member being confronted.

Various authors have outlined their own versions of the steps that make up the confrontation process (Ivey & Ivey, 2007; Chen & Giblin, 2002; Young & Chromy, 2005; Haney & Leibsohn, 1999, Hutchinson, 2007). Following is an amalgam of steps derived from these various authors' versions and applied to the group setting.

Step 1. *Identify the discrepancy*. In order for the discrepancy to be explained to the group or to a member, it must first be clearly identified.

Step 2. *Explain the discrepancy*. Although discrepancies may appear obvious to leaders and/or other members, they may not be obvious to the entire group (in cases where the leader is confronting the entire group) or to the particular member being confronted.

Step 3. *Explain the impact of the discrepancy*. Not only should the discrepancy be explained to the member or group, but the member or group should also understand the impact it has either on an individual member or on the entire group.

Step 4. *Acquire recognition*. Look to the member or group confronted for recognition of why the confrontation occurred. Encourage response from the confronted member or group.

Step 5. *Evaluate the outcome of the confrontation*. Determine if the confrontation was effective by asking questions such as, "Did the confrontation add to the member's self-understanding?" or "Is the group as a whole going to run more effectively as a result of the confrontation?"

The three types of confrontations that may occur in groups are member-to-member confrontations, leader-to-member confrontations, and leader-to-group confrontations. *Member-to-member confrontations* generally result from *content* concerns between members (that is, discrepancies in members' personal thoughts, feeling, and behaviors. For instance, one member has made two incongruent statements, and another member

challenges him on the discrepancy. The role of the leader in member-to-member confrontations is to contain the confrontation process, making sure the confrontation is balanced, making sure it follows the steps outlined above, and stepping in when necessary.

Ethics Pointer

ACA Ethics Code A.8.b requires leaders to protect clients (members) (American Counseling Association, 2005, p. 5). The intensity of member-to-member confrontations can range greatly, from one member appropriately and empathically bringing a discrepancy to another member's awareness, to one member outright attacking another member. The leader should monitor the tone of confrontations and cut off any confrontations that have a tone of attack.

Leader-to-member confrontations are initiated by leaders and often involve confronting members about content discrepancies. Just as often leader-to-member confrontations involve confronting members about breaking group norms, that is, inhibiting the effective running of the group. In such confrontations, the leader's comportment provides a model for future member-to-member confrontations.

Leader-to-group confrontations do not occur as often as the other two types of confrontations and are almost always a result of the whole group breaking group norms. Table 3-1 provides dialogue examples of each of the five steps of confrontation introduced above in the context of member-to-member confrontation, leader-to-member confrontation, and leader-to-group confrontation.

Table 3-1 Steps in Confrontation in Member-to-Member, Leader-to-Member, and Leader-to-Group Confrontations

Steps in Confrontation	Dialogue
	Member-to-Member Confrontation
1. Identify the discrepancy.	*John:* Sam, whenever you speak about your dad, you talk about how wonderful a person he is, but you sound very angry to me.
2. Explain the discrepancy.	*Leader (to John):* Could you explain to Sam what that means to you, John?
	John: Sure. Sam, I feel like you are holding in something about your dad and that your praises for him are not true.
3. Explain the impact of the discrepancy.	*Leader:* How does that affect you John?
	John: Well, it makes it difficult for me to believe Sam, and if I don't believe him, it makes it hard for me to trust him.
4. Acquire recognition.	*Leader:* Sam, what do you think about what John has just said?
	John: Yes, Sam . . .
	Sam: I was always told to respect my parents, so that is why I praise my father, but there were things about our relationship that I wished were different. That is what makes it hard for me to speak convincingly.

(continued)

Table 3-1   *(continued)*

Steps in Confrontation	Dialogue
5. Evaluate the outcome of the confrontation.	*Leader:* Sam, was John's observation about the way you speak of your father true for you?
	Sam: Yes, I can see it.
	Leader: Sam, how are you experiencing John now that he has pointed out this difference in *what* you say about your father and *how* you say it?
	Sam: I think I can trust him more to speak to me honestly and not hold back.

Leader-to-Member Confrontation

1. Identify the discrepancy.	*Leader:* I am really feeling disrespected by you, John, when in the group you start side conversations with Sue while we are trying to establish group goals. One of the norms that we agreed to was that we would avoid having side conversations and stay with the group.
	John: OK . . .
2. Explain the discrepancy.	*Leader:* You agreed to the group norm of no side conversations, but you aren't following that norm.
3. Explain the impact of the discrepancy.	*Leader:* It impacts me as the group leader because I feel as if I have to "parent" you and at the same time try to treat you as an adult in this group. It becomes a conflict for me as to which way to treat you.
4. Acquire recognition.	*Leader:* I hope you understand how this is affecting me.
	John: Yes, I do, and I am sorry for the disruption. I will try to save my side conversations for breaks and before the group starts.
5. Evaluate the outcome of the confrontation.	*Leader:* I am grateful for your involvement in the group, John. I hope pointing this out was OK with you.
	John: Yeah, sure.

Leader-to-Group Confrontation

1. Identify the discrepancy.	*Leader:* Feel free to correct me, but I am sensing as a group that we are stuck in the brainstorming process. Although we want to work to solve our problems, we continue to stay in the safer mode of thinking up possible solutions rather than picking a few of the possibilities and doing the work.
2. Explain the discrepancy.	*Leader:* Truly wanting to make changes means moving forward and selecting new ways of handling old problems. It means that we have to choose and try some new ways.
3. Explain the impact of the discrepancy.	*Leader:* If we continue to stay in the safe place of brainstorming alternatives, we will never have a chance to test them out.
4. Acquire recognition.	*Leader:* Is anyone else experiencing the group as being stuck in this phase?
	John: Yes.
	Sue: It just seems like we have to make the right choice before we move forward. Until we find the right choice, making no choice is safer.
	Sam: I guess we should face reality and make a choice of what to do next.
5. Evaluate the outcome of the confrontation.	*Leader:* Was it OK for me to bring this up? I sensed that we might be all feeling stuck.
	Sam: You were right, we were avoiding.
	John: Glad you finally mentioned it.

Exercise for Active Learning
Skill Development: Confrontation

Divide into groups of four students. In each group, take four slips of paper, write an X on one of them, fold the slips, and put them in a container. Each member will select a slip of paper, and the member who selects the slip with the X on it should remain silent about it. Start a discussion about concerns you all have about becoming a professional counselor. The member with the X should provide a discrepancy in one of his or her statements. Other members will listen for discrepancies in the conversation and conduct a confrontation when it seems appropriate. At the end of the confrontation, everyone in the group should provide feedback on how successful the group was at finding the discrepancy and handling the confrontation. During feedback, members should reflect on the process and steer clear of individual criticism. After feedback, all members should put the slips of paper back in the hat and repeat the process.

INTEGRATIVE EXAMPLE: ELEMENTARY SCHOOL RESPONSIBILITY GROUP

School counselor Betty is leading a classroom group of 25 fifth-grade students. The purpose of the group is to help the students develop responsibility. The students live in a rural area, and many of them have known each other and each other's families for years. During the first session, the group discussed the meaning of responsibility. This is the group's second session, in which they will more fully explore the topic.

Betty: All of you have grown up a lot since last year. Let's start today by going around and sharing one thing that you are responsible for this year that you weren't responsible for last year. Can someone get us started?

Darren: I can.

Betty: OK, what's your new responsibility? *[Closed question]*

Darren: My new responsibility is mowing the lawn on the weekend.

Kyle: I wish my dad would let me use the lawn mower.

Sarah: My new responsibility is feeding Melody.

Anne: Her dad got her a horse.

Sarah: Yup. She's fun to ride, and I liked feeding her until yesterday. It was only 30 degrees in the morning.

Betty: It wasn't so much fun going to the barn in the cold. *[reflection of content]*

Sarah: It was work, and now it's dark in the morning and too cold to ride much.

Betty: So it felt different when it got cold. Riding was fun in the summer. In the winter you don't ride as much. Mostly you do chores and it's cold. It feels like hard work and not fun. *[Reflection of feelings]*

Sarah: That's right. And sometimes I'm grumpy when my dad wakes me up to go to the barn and it's still dark out.

Betty: Mike?

Mike: My new responsibility is the same as my old responsibility. Mike, take the trash out. Mike, take the trash out. Mike, take the trash out! Nag, nag, I wish they would stop nagging me. I want a new set of skis, but all they want to talk about is "take the trash out."

Betty: You sound frustrated. *[Reflection of feelings]*

Mike: Yeah and mad.

Betty: Mike, let's look at what you say and what you do and see if we can figure out how to help you so that you might be able to stop your parents nagging you. *[Unconditional positive regard (Betty doesn't judge Mike, but simply states, "You have a problem, let's see if we can help you solve it.")]*

Mike: OK. I'm tired of hearing the same stuff over and over, and I want the skis.

Betty: You want the skis, but you don't want to take out the trash. Let's go back to the last time your parents nagged you about taking out the trash. What day was that? *[Closed question]*

Mike: Yesterday, Thursday. The trash collector truck comes on Thursday.

Betty: So the trash truck comes on Thursday. What time? *[Closed question]*

Mike: About 8:30, just after I get on the school bus. Sometimes it is there when the bus is still there.

Nick: Yeah, and sometimes his dad is putting out the trash because he didn't do it.

Macey: And yelling at him.

Betty: Mike, is that true? *[Open question and confrontation]*

Mike: Not all the time. Just sometimes.

Babs: Every Thursday this month . . .

Betty: Mike, if I asked your dad . . .

Mike: You wouldn't do that.

Betty: No, but if I did . . . what would he say? *[Open question]*

Mike: *[Looking down]* He'd say what Babs said.

Betty: So you didn't put out the trash this month, and maybe that is why your parents are nagging you. *[Confronting]*

Fred: They are going to keep nagging you till you do it.

Brittany: Probably won't get your skis either.

[Mike gives Betty a questioning look.]

Betty: Probably not, Mike. You see parents reward responsibility. *[Confronting]* [**YTF Reminder:** Existential factors—freedom and responsibility]

Mike: And I didn't do mine.

Nick: Maybe you could start tomorrow. It's Thursday.

Betty has been attending to Mike's facial expression. The look on his face, which had been rather embarrassed, became more hopeful when Nick suggested starting tomorrow. Betty also has been attending to Mike's eye contact. She's noticed that

when she was questioning him, Mike's eye contact was intermittent—sometimes he looked at her and sometimes he looked at the floor. At the suggestion of a new start, Mike begins to give her more eye contact.

Betty: Mike, one of the things the group might be able to help you work on is setting up a routine so you do the trash every week. We could also coach you about some things that you could say to encourage yourself. Would you like us to help you work on that?

Group members are nodding as Betty speaks.

Betty: How about everyone who is willing to help Mike work on this give a thumbs-up sign.

All members give the thumbs-up sign. They understand that the role of the group is to help the members. [**YTF Reminder:** Cohesion]

Mike: Yeah, I really want my skis.

Clasping her hands in front of her to convey her seriousness, Betty leans toward Mike, looking at him steadily. She doesn't begin to speak again until he has made eye contact with her. *[Nonverbal behavior]*

Betty: Well, Mike, we can't promise that your parents will reward you with skis right away. You might have to prove yourself awhile first. *[Confronting, genuineness]*

Betty has confronted Mike with reality here. This is important so that Mike will not have unfulfilled expectations if he does the trash and the skis don't follow. By pointing out this possibility, Betty is being honest *[Genuineness]* with Mike and not promising a change in parental behavior—something that is not under her control. She watches Mike's facial expression *[Attending]* and notices that he still looks hopeful even after he is confronted with the reality that his parents had not linked doing the trash to new skis.

Mike: Well, Dad won't have to do that, but I think he will because we've had deals like that before.

Betty: So you feel pretty hopeful that your dad will reward you. *[Reflection of feelings]*

Mike: Yes, and yes, I'd like the group to help me.

By attending to Mike's body language, facial expression, and voice tone, as well as his verbal communications, Betty concludes that he does want help from the group. She organizes the group so that all members engage in helping Mike.

Betty: One of the things we do in this group is to help each other. This is a group, and we support each other. The way we are going to do that now is to divide into five small groups—five of you to each group. Go ahead and get set up.

While the students are setting up groups, Betty gives some paper and a marker to each group.

Betty: One of the ways to help others is to help them think of several appropriate alternatives. Your task for your small group has two parts. First, come up with at least two ways that Mike might be able to do the trash. Then, come up with two things

Mike can say to encourage himself and feel good about doing the job. I'll check with each group in five minutes to see how you are doing.

The group spends another 10 minutes helping provide some options for Mike and reflecting on their process. Betty then turns the focus to other members.

Betty: Let's see, Ora, it's your turn. What is your new responsibility? *[Closed question]*

Ora: My dad put me in charge of raking all the leaves.

Betty notices that Ora's voice tone is rather factual. *[Nonverbal skill]*

Betty: What do you think about that? *[Open question]*

Ora: It's practical. He doesn't get home from work till almost dark. I tell myself it's one way to contribute to the family.

Pauline: Do you like that job?

Ora: It's better than doing the laundry, and that's what my sister has to do.

Betty: Nathan, how about you? *[Betty is attending to Nathan's facial expression, which she is not able to interpret.]*

Nathan: My new responsibility is looking after Myra.

Betty: *[Betty now thinks Nathan is about to cry.]* You look pretty upset. Am I reading that right? *[Betty reflects the feelings she thinks she sees on Nathan's face. This is somewhat an interpretation on her part, since Nathan has not said this out loud, so Betty follows her reflection with a check-out question.]*

Nathan: Yes. It's a long time and it's scary.

Betty: So there's at least two parts that are hard. It's a long time and it's scary. Let's talk about them one at a time, OK?

Nathan: OK.

Betty: Now, am I right that Myra is your little sister who is in kindergarten? *[Closed question]*

Nathan: Yes, she's five going on six next month.

Betty: OK, and on a school day, tell me what you're supposed to do. *[Open question]*

Nathan: Well, we both go home on the same bus, and I have the key. *[Nathan shows the key that is on a string around his neck.]*

Betty is attending to his voice tone and notices that it is steadier now that Nathan is describing his situation. She provides encouragement through her own nonverbal behavior, nodding occasionally as he speaks.

Nathan: First, I let us in the house. Then, I'm supposed to put our backpacks up on the counter and empty them out. I give Myra and me a snack—cookies or fruit. Then Myra is suppose to change into her play clothes while I put anything that was left from lunch in our backpacks into the fridge so it won't rot. We can play in the house or in the yard until Mom gets home after work.

Mike: So about what time do you get off the bus?

Nathan:	About three-thirty.
Ora:	And about what time does your mom usually get home?
Nathan:	About six.
Paul:	That's about two and a half hours that you are in charge.
Nathan:	Umhmm. It's not too bad until about five. Myra usually does what I ask her to do until then.
Betty:	And what does she do around five?
Nathan:	She wants more snacks that she's not supposed to have, and yesterday she went next door to Mrs. Flupps and asked her for snacks. Mom was upset because I let Myra go out of our yard, like it was my idea. I didn't know she left the yard, and I couldn't find her.
Mike:	What did you think when you couldn't find her? *[Questioning about thoughts]*
Nathan:	I thought she was lost or someone took her. I was worried.
Nick:	That must have been pretty scary. *[Reflection of feelings]* What did you do? *[questioning about actions]*
Nathan:	I called my Aunt Ella in Dover and told her. I'm not supposed to call Mom at work because her boss doesn't like it.
Betty:	So is the backup to call Aunt Ella?
Nathan:	Or Aunt Maddie.
Betty:	So you followed the plan your mom gave you about how to get help *[Summarizing]*, and what did Aunt Ella say or do?
Nathan:	She told me to wait another five minutes, and if Myra was not home to call the police, but Mrs. Flupps brought Myra home just before the five minutes were up.
Ora:	How did you feel then? *[Questioning about feelings]*
Nathan:	Pretty mad at Myra.
Betty:	And anything else?
Nathan:	Really glad she was safe.
Betty:	What did you do when Mom came home? *[Questioning about actions]*
Nathan:	I told her Myra went by herself.
Betty:	How did you feel when Mom scolded you? *[Questioning about feelings]*
Nathan:	I felt like she didn't care about me . . . but I know she does. It's too hard to take care of Myra.
Betty:	It's very hard to take care of little ones. *[Reflection of feelings]* It's a huge new responsibility. I'm wondering if any of the rest of you have that responsibility this year.

Betty searches for others in the group who have similar responsibilities. She hopes to link Nathan with others who have the same experience and promote cohesion and universality. In response to Betty's question, five others raise their hands.

Betty: Sonja?

Sonja: My mom started working this year and I have to watch Heidi, but it's not that long, only about an hour, and Heidi is two years older than Myra. It still scares me sometimes when I can't find her. She went up in the attic and brought down some of Mom's old beads, and Mom was unhappy with me. Last year it would have been Heidi's fault, but this year it's my fault if she does anything wrong.

Betty: So it feels like now she doesn't have to be responsible. *[Summarizing]*

Sonja: And I have to be responsible for both of us.

Donny: Last week when I was watching Danny, he got a knife to cut up the apple that was his after-school snack, and he cut himself by accident.

Sonja: That sounds scary.

Donny: It was. The blood squirted out of him and all over him and me and the kitchen. I wrapped a towel around it and clamped my fist over it. Then I carried him over to the fire station across the street, and the firemen fixed him. After I gave him to the firemen, I realized my heart was beating fast, and I was scared. Mom said I didn't follow the plan to call her, but what I did was good enough and showed good judgment.

Betty: Good, you kept your head and took action to help your brother.

Donny: But what if it happens again?

Jeff: I'd be scared.

Donny: I am.

Betty: Donny, being scared is very understandable. *[Reflection of feelings]* It's a big thing to be responsible for children. Most of you will be caring for younger brothers and sisters soon if you aren't doing so already. *[Universality]* Would you, not just Donny, but all of you like to spend a little time sharing and going over how to deal with safety issues that are likely to come up?

STUDY QUESTIONS

1. Why is it important for the counselor to be genuine during counseling?
2. How can a counselor have unconditional regard for a client who has hurt another person (for example, a client who has physically beaten another person)?
3. Describe what it means for a counselor to have empathic understanding.
4. Give an example of a nonverbal skill and an attending skill.
5. Discuss types of situations in which a counselor would want to use an open question versus a closed question.
6. Discuss similarities and differences between reflection of content, reflection of feelings, and reflection of meaning.
7. Distinguish between situations in which a counselor might use a mild confrontation versus a strong confrontation.

KEY CONCEPTS

accurate empathic
understanding p. 43
attending p. 46
confrontation p. 54
congruence p. 41
genuineness p. 41
nonverbal skills p. 45
paraphrasing p. 49

questioning p. 47
reflection of content p. 49
reflection of feeling p. 50
reflection of meaning p. 52
summarizing p. 49
unconditional positive
regard p. 42

REFERENCES

American Counseling Association (2005). *ACA code of ethics.* Alexandria, VA: Author.

Chen, M., & Giblin, N. J. (2002). *Individual counseling: Skills and techniques.* Denver: Love.

Haney, J. H., & Leibsohn, J. (1999). *Basic counseling responses.* New York: Brooks Cole.

Hutchinson, D. (2007). *The essential counselor: Process, skills, and techniques.* Boston: Lahaska Press.

Ivey, A., & Ivey, M. B. (2007). *Intentional interviewing and counseling: Facilitating client development in a multicultural society* (6th ed.). Pacific Grove, CA: Thompson/Brooks Cole.

Rogers, C. R. (1957). The necessary and sufficient conditions of therapeutic personality change. *Journal of Consulting Psychology, 21,* 95–103.

Webster's new world dictionary of the American language: College edition. (1968). Cleveland, OH: World Publishing.

Young, M. E., & Chromy, S. (2005). *Exercises in the art of helping.* Columbus, OH: Pearson/Merrill Prentice Hall.

CHAPTER 4

Applying Individual Counseling Skills in Groups: Part II

LEARNING OBJECTIVES

After studying this chapter you should be able to describe the following individual counseling skills and their application to group counseling:

- Focusing
- Feedback
- Self-disclosure

INTRODUCTION: CONTINUING THE DISCUSSION OF INDIVIDUAL COUNSELING SKILLS

This is the second chapter in which we look at individual counseling skills as they apply to group process and leadership. As in Chapter 3, each skill will be explored in turn, first via a brief definition, next a description of the individual counseling skill, then an application of the skill as applied to groups, and finally an exercise to help you practice and internalize those skills. At the end of the chapter, an extended group example will be provided as a means of bringing these individual counseling skills into a real-world group setting. By the end of the chapter, you should have a handle on the myriad skills presented in Chapters 3 and 4 and the many ways in which group leaders put them into practice.

FOCUSING

***Definition of* focusing**   The skill of selectively attending to what a client is conveying verbally or nonverbally and directing the conversation so as to maintain its focus on the selected topic or issue.

In individual as well as group counseling, the skill of **focusing** is generally employed as a means of keeping the conversation organized, a matter of sequentially working through clients' issues and maintaining an appropriate amount of engagement around a topic before moving on to the next issue. But counselors also routinely employ the skill of focusing to choose the most productive topical direction for the conversation to take at any particular moment. Take for example a new client who answers the question, "Why have you come to the clinic today?" with "Well, I was arrested for DWI, and the judge made me choose between jail time and therapy time, but I'm not the one who should be here—it's my moron of a husband who needs therapy; he's the one who's doing it with the babysitter, not me." As you can imagine, there are a number of possible directions in which this conversation might go at this particular time. The next thing the counselor says will be based on a conscious choice to focus on one of the topics raised by the client over another.

Hutchinson (2007) goes a step further and suggests that a counselor's choice of focus is often related to the theoretical orientation with which the counselor works. For instance, cognitive behavioral counselors may focus on issues related to the client's thought processes and behaviors, whereas family therapy counselors may focus more on client issues related to family relationships. To prevent a session from losing its client orientation, Hutchinson suggests that counselors occasionally provide reflective topic summaries during the session and give clients the choice of which topic to explore next. Not only does this method assure the session stays client oriented, but it also gives the counselor a clearer understanding of what the client considers important in her counseling session.

Focusing is one of the more challenging tasks for group leaders. The group leader must engage the focus of each member regarding a similar task, sometimes with the competing distraction of side agendas by some members. The challenge of obtaining a compromise on members' individual agendas and agreeing to focus

Ethics Pointer

ACA Ethics Code A.2.b, which addresses informed consent, requires counselors to inform clients about "... the purposes, goals, techniques, procedures, limitations, potential risks, and benefits ..." of counseling (American Counseling Association, 2005, p. 4). If the counselor's choice of focus points or goals in counseling are substantially influenced by a specific theory or theories, this influence should be explained to the client in the process of obtaining informed consent for counseling.

on a combined agenda can be an ambitious, time-consuming process in groups. Leaders need to be able to convey that the group as a whole needs to maintain a focus while at the same time supporting each member's individual issues.

It might be helpful to think of focusing as a means of steering a counseling session in a particular direction. In responding to a client's statement or answer to a question, a counselor has three general choices of direction: a **situational focus, emotional focus,** or **experiential focus** (Chen and Giblin 2002).

Definition of **situational focus**   Focus on the specifics of the situation (or problem) and its context related by the client.

Definition of **emotional focus**   Focus on the client's overt or covert emotions (or feelings) associated with the situation.

Definition of **experiential focus**   Focus on the client's in-the-moment experience of relating to what is happening in the session.

Most of the topics brought to a group can be sorted into these same three categories. At first, both individual counselors and group leaders have a difficult time deciding if a client's statement calls for an emotional focus, a situational focus, an experiential focus, or a combination of two or more focuses. Consider the following statements and the possible different focuses called for by each:

- *"I am feeling pretty upset right now with my kids. They never seem to listen."*

This statement might call for either an emotional focus, since the client has used the word "upset" to indicate emotion, or it may call for a situational focus, since the client seems to be asking for help with the specific problem of disciplining his children. Finally, it may call for an experiential focus to help the client discuss why he brought up the issue of his children at this particular time and how he is coping with having brought up the problem for examination in the here and now of the counseling session.

- *"If I could just learn to face the day with a little more optimism, perhaps people would treat me with more respect."*

This statement might call for an emotional focus, as the client talks about a lack of optimism, which may be another way of saying "sadness" or "despair." It may call for a situational focus, because the client is expressing a particular day-to-day problem of not receiving the respect of her peers. Or it may call for an experiential focus on how the client feels sharing this information at the moment or perhaps on probing

to learn if the client might include the counselor among the "people" who would respect her more if she were more optimistic.

- *"With the pressures of school and work, I do not have much time for a relationship. At least one that I can take seriously."*

This statement may call for an emotional focus, insofar as the client seems to be unhappy with his relationship situation. Or it may call for a situational focus, as the client may be suggesting that he wishes to "fix" the existing situation/problem of too much pressure at school and at work and too little time for relationships. A second situational focus might be found in the client's remark about not having a relationship that he can "take seriously." Finally, it may call for an experiential focus, because the client may want to explore how he feels about sharing this information with the counselor, leader, or group.

Focusing in Two Steps

Chen and Giblin (2002) break focusing down into two steps. The first step is an *empathic statement*, followed by the second step, which is a question or statement that leads the client in the direction of the chosen focus. The following example illustrates the two steps of the process:

Ella (client): I am upset with my progress in school. I thought I would be further along in my studies than I am now. I wanted to graduate in four years, but now that just doesn't seem possible.

Louis (counselor): I can tell from the way you look and what you say that you are disappointed in yourself. . . . *[Step 1—empathic statement]*

Would you talk more about what "upset" feels like for you? *[Step 2—emotional focus]*

Could you talk more about how you have seemed to have gotten behind on your program of study? *[Step 2—situational focus]*

What are you experiencing right now sharing your disappointment in yourself with the group? *[Step 2—experiential focus]*

How Focusing Affects Direction

What happens after the counselor chooses a focus? The following examples illustrate how the direction of a counseling session might vary depending upon the type of focus the counselor chooses in response to a client statement.

Example of Situational Focusing

Meg (Client): I'm just very unhappy with my husband, Dave. He won't help me with the housework at all.

Sarah (Counselor): That sounds really important to you—that he help at least some. There are a lot of things that make up housework. Is there one part of the housework that you most want his help with?

Meg: I really want him to help with the dishes.

Sarah: Is there one day or one time that you most want his help?

Meg: If he would just do them Tuesday nights so I didn't have to do them after I pick Jimmy up from soccer practice. If he'd do that, I'd be satisfied.

Sarah: OK, so how about we brainstorm three different ways that you could tell Dave what you want him to do? Then we can role-play with me being Dave and you telling me what you want.

Example of Emotional Focusing

Meg: I'm just very unhappy with my husband. He won't help me with the housework at all.

Sarah: You're unhappy with him about housework.

Meg: Very unhappy.

Sarah: Besides unhappiness, what are some of the other feelings you have about your husband?

Meg: I'm very proud of him because he spends a lot of time doing things for people in the community. I just wish he would treat me as well as he treats the neighbors.

Sarah: So let me see if I'm getting this right. Overall, the big picture is you feel good that your husband helps other people, but you are a bit resentful that he doesn't treat you as well as he treats others. Do I have it right?

Meg: Yes.

Example of Experiential Focusing

Meg: I'm just very unhappy with my husband. He won't help me with the housework at all.

Sarah: Very unhappy with your husband. What is it like for you to say that to me?

Meg: Frightening, frightening because when I say it out loud I know just how true it is. And I realize it's not just about dishes. Dishes are the tip of the iceberg.

Sarah: *[in a very compassionate tone]* Meg, do you want to talk about what's in the iceberg? *[Meg nods.]*

These examples showed how an individual counseling session might unfold depending on which focus was chosen. Now let's look at a process for focusing in groups. One of the difficulties leaders face when focusing is helping members establish and organize the focus when members bring a multiplicity of issues into the group. One helpful strategy is making rounds within the group, asking each member for input as to what the group's focus should be. For example, the leader can start by positing a general question to the entire group, such as:

Leader: We each have an opportunity to contribute something to the group and also to obtain assistance from the group through each of its members. If there is one thing that you would like to ask your group members to assist you with through the group, what would it be?

After posing this question, the leader can go around the group gathering these issues from members while noting common issues among members. Then the leader can present these issues to the group, indicating any connections made regarding focus preferences, as in the following example:

Leader: We've heard from everyone in the group, and some common themes include difficulty in exploring new relationships after a breakup, dealing with difficult relationships with coworkers, and establishing boundaries with parents. We will eventually get to all of these topics, but which one would you like to work on first?

The use of this group-wide focusing technique and having the group select an initial topic for group discussion helps the group move from the initial phase into the working phase. Once a general topic of discussion is decided by the group, the leader can further focus the discussion toward the emotional, situational, and/or experiential.

Exercises for Active Learning
Skill Development: Focusing

1. *Write an empathic statement and three types of focusing questions in response to the following client statements.*

    a. *I feel like I got a lot out of the group tonight. That dressing down was just what I needed.*

    Empathic statement: _____

    _____

    Situational focus: _____

    _____

    Emotional focus: _____

    _____

    Experiential focus: _____

    _____

    b. *A lot of the kids in my class act up when we have a sub, but I'm always the one who ends up in detention.*

    Empathic statement: _____

    _____

    Situational focus: _____

    _____

    Emotional focus: _____

    _____

Experiential focus: _____

_____

c.   *I told her not to go out with that boy. I knew he was no good. But she went anyway. And now look what happened to her. If I was a decent mother, I would have locked her in her room, right?*

Empathic statement: _____

_____

Situational focus: _____

_____

Emotional focus: _____

_____

Experiential focus: _____

_____

2.   *Listen to a professional interview on the radio or television. Notice how the interviewer selectively focuses on something the interviewee has stated. Is the interviewer focusing on the emotional, situational, or experiential? What alternative focusing questions might you ask the interviewee that the interviewer missed or chose not to ask? Describe the interview, and record your thoughts in the spaces below. Share and discuss your thoughts with a class partner.*

_____

_____

_____

_____

_____

_____

_____

_____

FEEDBACK

***Definition of* feedback**   The provision of factual information to a client about the client's behavior with the goal of helping the client understand how he or she is viewed by others.

Feedback is an essential skill employed by counselors to both acknowledge clients' positive behaviors and help clients recognize their negative behaviors and develop

alternative positive methods of feeling, thinking, and behaving. The effective counselor makes sure that every client receives both positive feedback (acknowledging the strengths of the client) and corrective feedback. Balancing corrective feedback with positive feedback is an expression of respect for the receiver. It also helps the receiver listen to and accept corrective feedback. In our opinion it is best to make sure that the amount of positive feedback in counseling and group work vastly outweighs the amount of corrective feedback.

Feedback in groups "is what permits group members to alter their behavior in light of new information" (Kottler, 1994, p. 79). [**YTF Reminder:** Feedback is one process through which the therapeutic factor *interpersonal learning* is activated.]

Feedback can flow in various directions: from leader to members, from leader to entire group, and between members. Leaders are entrusted with the task of ensuring not only that their own feedback is conducted with care but that the feedback between members is appropriate.

Guidelines for Giving Feedback

The following is a composite of guidelines for giving feedback from three sources: Ivey and Ivey (2007); Johnson (2006); and Kottler (1994).

■ *A feedback giver should allow the feedback recipient to decide when and how the feedback will be given.* In ceding control of the timing and form of the feedback to the recipient, the person providing the feedback ensures that the person receiving it is ready and willing to hear it.

Ethics Pointer

ACA Ethics Code A.2.b, which addresses informed consent, requires counselors to inform clients about ". . . the purposes, goals, techniques, procedures, limitations, potential risks, and benefits . . ." of counseling (American Counseling Association, 2005, p.4). Asking the receiver for permission to give feedback can be viewed as asking for informed consent.

There are several methods for ceding control. First, the person giving the feedback can simply ask the intended recipient for permission for feedback to be given, for instance: "Would you like me to give you feedback on what you've just said about your problem?" or "In what way, if any, would you like to hear from me or other group members about that?" Secondly, the person giving the feedback can imply the concession of control by using questioning phrases such as, "I wonder if . . ." and "Perhaps you should . . ." For example: "I wonder if your method for coping with stress is the best method, because stress management seems to be a persistent problem with you." Or, "Perhaps you should consider an alternate way of confronting your partner, because the previous method seems to have backfired."

■ *Feedback should be sensitively expressed, in tones of empathy, kindness, respect, and acceptance.* This guideline speaks to the intention of the feedback as caring. It helps ensure that feedback is neither intended to be an attack nor received as an attack.

Ethics Pointer

> ACA Ethics Code A.1a. " The primary responsibility of counselors is to respect the dignity and to promote the welfare of clients (American Counseling Association, 2005, p. 4). Feedback should provide members with information and perceptions of others that is likely to promote change. Leaders should be mindful not to give feedback to the group that would obviously be embarrassing to members. If it is necessary to give potentially embarrassing feedback to a member, the leader might consider giving that feedback privately before or after the group.

■ *Feedback should be descriptive, not judgmental.* Feedback that is judgmental may be harmful to members. It is not likely to be effective in promoting reflection and possible change. A receiver who feels judged is likely to reject any elements of truth contained in the feedback. It is up to the leader to control judgmental feedback between group members and teach members how to provide appropriate feedback. For instance, the leader can teach a member to rephrase "Stop being a jerk,"—which is both judgmental and not useful—as, "When you speak to me in that tone, I feel you are disrespecting me."

■ *Feedback should be expressed in terms and language the receiver can relate to and understand.* For example, the feedback "When you slam the door to the group room, it hurts my ears. I'd appreciate it if you closed it more gently next time," is straightforward and understandable. Conversely, "Your slamming of the door in disregard of others in the room is narcissistic behavior that you need to learn to control" may be problematic in several ways. It sounds judgmental, but more importantly, it may be confusing if the receiver of the feedback is not familiar with the psychological term, *narcissistic.*

■ *Each instance of feedback should be about one specific behavior, describing the behavior, supporting the description with examples, and describing the impact of the behavior on others.* A leader might give the following corrective feedback: "Fred, this is the third week you arrived an hour late for group, and the two previous weeks you left half an hour before the group was scheduled to end. The message I am receiving from this behavior is that you are not very committed to attending the group." Positive feedback should also follow this format: "Leslie, last time we met I mentioned that you kept looking down at the floor as we spoke, but during most of our session today you have been looking straight at me. Looking at one another helps people communicate better and I want you to know I appreciate your effort to do that today."

■ *Corrective feedback should focus on behaviors that the receiver can change.* Particularly in groups, some members may have unchangeable traits that irritate other members. A member might have an odd or irritating voice or speech impediment; or it might be difficult to make eye contact with a member who wears thick corrective lenses; or a member might be taking a needed medication with the side effect of an unpleasant body odor. An attentive leader will block any attempt by members to give feedback on such issues.

Ethics Pointer

> ACA Ethics Code A.8.b. "In a group setting, counselors take reasonable precautions to protect clients from physical, emotional, or psychological trauma. (American Counseling Association, 2005, p. 4).

■ *Feedback should focus on the immediate, that is, the "here and now," rather than on the "there and then" (Johnson, 2006, p. 59).* Focusing feedback on the here and now—what is happening in the counseling or the group—encourages the receiver to recognize and address issues raised in individual counseling or in the group. Helping clients/members make behavioral changes and giving them the opportunity to practice the new behaviors within the supportive environment of the counseling session or group will give them the confidence to then go and apply the new behaviors to the world outside.

■ *Feedback should be given at a pace that enables the client to integrate one piece before receiving another.* As a trained counselor you may be aware of multiple changes that would benefit each client. However, what may be most useful to a client is to successfully make and sustain one small change at a time. Being successful making one change increases the client's self-confidence and courage for making more or larger changes. Therefore, the effective counselor is mindful of sequencing and if necessary limiting the many pieces of critical feedback that a client may receive.

■ *Corrective feedback should include advice on methods for effecting change.* Offer potential solutions whenever possible. Simply stating problems doesn't give the feedback receiver enough to work with to effect change. The receiver may be well aware of the problem but does not know how to go about making a change. She may be too close to the problem to be able to see potential solutions objectively. The receiver may not be aware of any solutions or may deem those solutions of which she is aware unacceptable. It is a good practice to provide a range of solutions. In groups, the leader can solicit possible solutions from several members not just the member providing the feedback. For example, consider feedback that doesn't provide change options: "Jill, I think you're good at maintaining personal control in this group, but I worry that your pain pill consumption is going to lead to some serious health or addiction problems." Now compare it to feedback that does provide change options: "Jill, I think you're good at maintaining personal control in this group, but you may not be as aware yourself as it is apparent to me that you are developing a dependence on your pain pills. I think you may want to try attending an addiction meeting, or talking with your parents, or maybe discussing this with your physician."

Ethics Pointer

> ACA Ethics Code A.8.b. "In a group setting, counselors take reasonable precautions to protect clients from physical, emotional, or psychological trauma." (American Counseling Association, 2005, p.4). Leaders should be mindful that some members may give harmful advice. Leaders are responsible for cutting off and correcting such advice.

Recognizing Opportunities for Feedback

In addition to knowing how to provide effective feedback, feedback givers also need to know when to provide the feedback by listening for feedback opportunities. This is especially tricky in groups. Kiesler and Van Denburg (1993) suggest that counselors pay attention to two categories of behaviors when looking for feedback opportunities in group settings: (1) when members are engaged in repetitive behaviors, and (2) when members exhibit behaviors in the group that likely parallel their behaviors outside the group.

■ Feedback in response to repetitive behaviors: *I notice whenever the group begins to speak about losses, be they death or divorce, we get really quiet, then someone changes the topic. I would hope that when we talk about these losses in the future, we can encourage the conversation to continue instead of avoiding it.*

■ Feedback in response to behaviors that parallel behaviors outside of the group: *John, I notice how each time a woman speaks in this group you dismiss what she has to say. I'm wondering if this is a familiar feeling, similar to when you were married. It may be more effective for you as a member of this group to listen to the women's stories and hold off on passing judgment.*

Exercises for Active Learning
Skill Development: Feedback

1. *Watch a TV talk show that deals with therapeutic issues (e.g.,* Dr. Phil *or* Dr. Drew; *try to avoid "trash TV" talk shows that sensationalize and often feature fake paid guests), and watch for points in which the therapist provides feedback to the guest client. Pay attention to the feedback closely. Does the therapist concede control to the feedback recipient, avoid judgments, mention strengths, offer advice on obtaining change, and present feedback in way that is concrete, specific, and economical? Do you notice any occasions in which the therapist responds to the cues of repetitive behaviors as opportunities for feedback? Summarize your impressions in the spaces below.*

_____

_____

_____

_____

_____

_____

_____

_____

_____

2. *Practice giving and receiving feedback with a classmate. Both partners should take turns presenting a problem they have recently experienced. When giving feedback, start by focusing on the recipient's strengths and positive attributes as you know them. Then put into play the feedback guidelines discussed earlier. Record your experiences as the feedback provider in the spaces below. Were you able to provide helpful feedback? Which areas of the feedback process did you have trouble with?*

_____

_____

_____

_____

_____

_____

_____

SELF-DISCLOSURE

***Definition of* self-disclosure**   The act of sharing one's personal history, thoughts, or feelings with the client.

Counselor **self-disclosure** can be a powerful tool to assist in deepening the relationship between counselor and client. According to Hutchinson (2007), self-disclosure connects the client and counselor in the immediacy of the session and creates trust. Because self-disclosure is a powerful skill, it is often overused. Beginning counselors and group leaders tend to rely too heavily on it, focusing the counseling away from the client and toward themselves. This section will provide guidelines for how to appropriately gauge your self-disclosure, but first let's look at the components that constitute an effective self-disclosure.

Ivey and Ivey (2007, p. 370) refer to effective counselor self-disclosure as a *1-2-3 influencing pattern:* (1) attend to the client's story; (2) if you have a story or an observation about one of your own experiences that you believe will be helpful to the client, briefly share it; and (3) return to the client's topic focus.

More specifically, the counselor self-disclosure should begin with a sentence stem containing a personal pronoun to clarify for the client the fact that the counselor is self-disclosing, and include a present-tense verb to indicate that the disclosure is in the moment. So, for example, a counselor self-disclosure would begin with phrases such as "I feel . . . ," "My thoughts are . . . ," "I believe . . . ," and so forth. Then, the sentence stem should be connected to the client's topic; for example, "I feel sad when you speak about your imminent finalized divorce and how unhappy and confused you are right now." This initial statement should be followed directly by another statement, this time from the counselor's own experience; for instance, "Your situation reminds me of the way I felt days prior to my divorce being finalized. I felt sad and disoriented.

How could this be happening?" Finally, the self-disclosure should be connected back to the client's story, so the counseling session doesn't appear to be focused on the counselor. Therefore, counselors should finish the self-disclosure with a check-out—an open-ended question leading back to the client's experience, such as, "Is that how you are feeling now?" or "How is it go through these days feeling this unhappiness?" As an additional means of connecting the self-disclosure back to the client, the counselor may want to add a statement about his reasons for self-disclosing; for example, "I share this with you because these are the kinds of feelings I was having during my divorce, and I thought you might be experiencing similar feelings."

Self-disclosure is a difficult skill to master in individual counseling, and it is even more difficult in groups. Whether the amount of self-disclosure you have chosen to make is too much or too little is often very difficult for group leaders to gauge. In addition, the potential for discomfort is magnified when personal material is disclosed to an entire group as opposed to a single client. When done effectively, self-disclosure can be a powerful demonstration of a leader's openness that results in a strong sense of member trust toward the leader.

As with the skill of focusing discussed earlier in this chapter, a self-disclosure can have an emotional focus, a situational focus, or experiential focus, as illustrated in the following examples:

- *I remember feeling very sad and alone for many months after the loss of my father.* [emotional focus]
- *I was once in the similar situation where I had to decide if I should continue to pursue a relationship (which at the time was emotionally satisfying), knowing that the woman was incapable of ever feeling emotionally secure in a long-term relationship.* [situational focus]
- *When you talk about your interactions with your boss, I feel like there are waves of anger coming at me.* [experiential focus]

Deciding When Self-Disclosure Is Appropriate

Finally we consider the important question of when it is appropriate to employ self-disclosure. Many new counselors and group leaders fail to distinguish between the ways they self-disclose with friends and associates in social situations and the kinds of self-disclosures they would employ in counseling. It may be appropriate, and a counselor or group leader may feel comfortable sharing with her close friends a story about an embarrassing situation; however, in the role of counselor or leader, self-disclosure should be limited in its use and shaped to meet the needs of the group. A good criterion for establishing whether or not self-disclosure is warranted and appropriate in counseling, as suggested by Yalom (1995), is for counselors to ask themselves if the self-disclosure is being done in the best service of the group. Therefore, before you self-disclose in a group session, you might ask yourself the following types of questions: Is the self-disclosure more self-serving than client serving? Am I employing self-disclosure as a way to relieve my own tensions as the group leader? Will this self-disclosure help me to link with the group members on an equal footing?

Exercises for Active Learning
Skill Development: Self-disclosure

After reading each of the following client statements, decide whether or not to mention something from your own experience that might be helpful to the client. If you decide to self-disclose, write down the self-disclosure, then explain briefly how you think it will help the client. (Because it deals with private, personal matters, this is an exercise to complete on your own, without sharing with a partner or with the class.)

Client 1: I stood there paralyzed and did nothing while that awful pit bull attacked my cat. The owner of the dog finally got him under control, and my cat survived, but I can't stop being angry with myself for being such a coward.

Self-disclose? No: _____ Yes: _____

_____

_____

How will this self-disclosure help your client?

_____

_____

Client 2: Since I lost my job, I just don't feel like I fit in with this group anymore. All of you have had the same job for years. You have no idea what it's like to be financially insecure.

Self-disclose? No: _____ Yes: _____

_____

_____

_____

How will this self-disclosure help your client?

_____

_____

Client 3: I don't know about the other women in this group, but it offends me, Donald, when you use words like bimbo *and* bitch *and* whore *when you talk about the women in your life.*

Self-disclose? No: _____ Yes:_____

_____

_____

_____

How will this self-disclosure help your client?

_____

_____

INTEGRATIVE CASE EXAMPLE: CRASH WITNESS GROUP

Eight students at a rural school were on the way home on the school bus, when they witnessed a train crash into a pickup truck that had not stopped at the railroad crossing. Because several other vehicles in front of and behind the bus at the railroad crossing were unable to move, the bus driver was forced to wait until the emergency vehicles arrived, cleared up the accident, and interviewed witnesses. As a result, the children on the bus saw much of the rescue attempt and were traumatized. The school principal called the children's parents immediately and arranged for the children to meet with the school counselor, Bart, the next morning. All eight children attended the counseling group: Mark (age 9), Anne (age 8), Pam (age 5), Pedro (age 6), Juan (age 5), Carol (age 9), Jenny (age 8), and Greg (age 7).

Bart: I'm glad you came to talk with me this morning. I know you were on the bus yesterday and saw the crash. You can help each other talk about what you experienced. **[YTF Reminder:** Universality]

[Bart is working to help the children realize that they were all in the same bus and have a shared experience.]

Your moms and dads said it might be helpful for you to talk together in a group this morning and that you agreed. Is that OK with you?

[Bart is respecting the children and asking for their voluntary participation. Even though school policy allows him to see children in an emergency without parent permission, Bart made every effort to get both parent consent and child consent. Bart is attending to body language and notes that all the children have nodded in agreement.]

Bart: Can one of you tell me what happened? *[Open question]*

Carol: I can.

Bart: OK, you start us off, and the others can help fill in details as we go along. *[Bart is working to get a clear picture of the events that happened. He focuses his questions on what happened—what was done and what was said—because this type of questioning is consistent with the concrete thinking he expects the children might use.]*

Carol: We had dropped off most of the kids, and the bus was going down into that bottom part of the road near the grain elevator.

Juan: And it was thundering and lightning bad.

Bart: It stormed hard for a while. *[Reflection of meaning]*

Juan: The lightning was so close you could hear it sizzle.

Bart: That is close.

Juan: And scary.

Carol: Juan's right. The storm was all around us, and you could barely hear the train whistle. I think that was what caused the accident.

Bart: So you think that the driver didn't hear the train whistle and didn't know to stop. *[Reflection of meaning]*

Carol: Mmhmm.

Bart: Tell me a little more about what happened. *[Bart is working to get the details of the event from the children's perspective.]*

Mark: The train came around the bend and smashed into Mr. Johnson's truck.

Pam: The pig truck. *[looking at Bart questioningly]* You know, the one he uses to drive the pigs around?

Bart: That old green one with the wooden sides? *[Bart asks a closed question for clarification. He is checking to see if he understands Pam correctly.]*

Carol: Yes. The train brakes made that whooshing noise and scraped metal on the tracks.

Mark: And then it smashed into the truck with an awful metal crunching sound.

Greg: And the truck flew up and rolled upside down, and Mr. Johnson was inside.

Pam: And the pigs squealed loud.

Juan: The truck landed on the mommy pig, and the baby pigs ran around.

Carol: The bus driver told us to sit down and don't yell.

Anne: I was scared, so I sat with Carol.

Bart: That was a good choice. *[Positive feedback]* *[Bart reinforces the children's decision to follow the directions of the bus driver in emergencies.]*

Jenny: And she told us not to yell out the window.

Mark: She was talking on the phone to the principal and the fire station.

Bart: So Mrs. Lakes took care of you and then she called for help. *[Reflection of content]*

Carol: Yes. She made sure we weren't hurt. One of the boards from the back of the pig truck flew into the front windshield of the bus, but it missed Mrs. Lakes. She said to stay on the bus because we would be safe there.

Pam: And the baby pigs kept running around.

Bart: *[Gently]* Pam, I can tell you are upset about the pigs. Would it be OK if we talked about what happened and about the people and then after that we can talk about the pigs? *[Focusing the group]* *[Bart acknowledges Pam's concern and the fact that she is upset. He explains how he would like the group to proceed in language that Pam can understand.]*

Pam: OK. Two fire trucks came fast.

Greg: And the ambulance came, and the deputy had to guide them by us.

Mark: We watched them saw the truck open and get Mr. Johnson out, only they covered his face up and put him in the ambulance because . . . *[There are tremors in Mark's voice now]* because he died.

Bart: You didn't expect that.

Anne: Ambulances and firemen are supposed to save people.

Bart:	And you think they should have saved Mr. Johnson. *[Reflection of meaning]* *[Anne nods her head and some tears run down her face. Bart is attending to the other members, and he notices that Mark and Carol are nodding too.]*
Bart:	Mark, do you want to say something to Anne or to the group? *[Bart encourages members to help each other.]*
Mark:	Annie, they save people if they can, but Mr. Johnson got hit too hard in the crash. You could see all the blood on him when they finally got him out of the truck. He was a nice man. *[Mark looks at Bart.]* I saw you play golf with him last weekend.
Bart:	Yes, the Johnsons are friends of my family, and I will miss him. *[Self-disclosure]*
Carol:	Jenny and I cried.
Bart:	It's OK to cry, especially at a time like this. *[Bart gives permission for the children to cry.]* [**YTF Reminder:** Catharsis]
Juan:	That's what my dad said, and he said Pedro and I could go to Mr. Johnson's funeral.
Bart:	Have you ever been to a funeral before? *[Bart is wondering if Juan has any idea what to expect.]*
Juan:	Last year for my uncle. Afterwards there is a big feast. My dad said I could stay next to him like last time.
Bart:	Let's go back to feelings. Some of you cried, and what else did some of you feel? *[Focusing the group]*
Greg:	Scared. My dad drives a truck sometimes, and I asked him if he was going to have an accident like Mr. Johnson did.
Bart:	What did he say? *[Bart recognizes that after experiencing the crash, it is normal for the children to be concerned about their own parents. He helps them explore their concerns.]*
Greg:	He said no, trains don't run into trucks much.
Bart:	And so how do you feel now? *[Open question]*
Greg:	Better, I don't want my daddy to die too.
Bart:	How about the rest of you? *[Bart changes the focus from Greg to the group to see how the other children are feeling.]*
Pedro:	I feel sad and quiet.
Juan:	Me too.
Mark:	My dad told us he works real hard to be safe because he loves us. Dad made all three of us feel better.
Bart:	So all of you talked with your parents last night and that helped you. *[Bart notices heads nodding.]* And now we've talked a little bit here. Are there other feelings you would like to talk about?
Pedro:	I want to be a firefighter like the ones who tried to help Mr. Johnson. They were brave.
Mark:	Yes, they tried to help him even though they had to keep hoses on the truck in case it blew up. I want to be brave like that.
Jenny:	Mrs. Lakes kept cool even though she was almost hurt.
Bart:	Mrs. Lakes did a good job taking care of you. *[Jenny nods.]*

Bart: *[To Pam]* OK, tell me about the pigs now. *[Bart shows unconditional positive regard for Pam by addressing her concern about the baby pigs. He accepts Pam and how she participates in the group at her developmental level.]*

Pam: The three baby pigs don't have any mommy, and that makes me feel sad and happy.

Bart: Sad because they don't have any mommy and happy because . . . ? *[Reflecting and clarifying feelings]*

Pam: Because my mommy told me she would talk to Mrs. Johnson to see if we could adopt two, and Juan and Pedro could adopt one.

Bart: *[Bart knows the Johnsons had hundreds of pigs and is pretty sure that Mrs. Johnson would agree to the children's plan.]* That would be a very kind thing to do. I'm sure you will take good care of them. *[Positive feedback]*

Carol: It's almost time for homeroom.

Bart: Yes, it is. Are all of you feeling well enough to go to homeroom? *[Open question]* *[Bart sees all of them nod.]*

Bart: Thanks for talking with me.

Pam: I feel better.

Bart: Good . . . off you go to homeroom.

STUDY QUESTIONS

1.   Explain the three types of focus the leader might choose.
2.   Discuss the steps listed in the chapter for focusing.
3.   Explain why the receiver should be given control over if and when feedback is provided.
4.   Explain the importance of giving positive feedback.
5.   Discuss appropriate purposes of counselor self-disclosure.
6.   Describe two situations in which you as leader might give a member corrective feedback.
7.   Explain when personal self-disclosure might be helpful versus harmful.

KEY CONCEPTS

emotional focus p. 67
experiential focus p. 67
focusing p. 66
feedback p. 71

situational focus p. 67
self-disclosure p. 76

REFERENCES

American Counseling Association. (2005). *ACA code of ethics.* Alexandria, VA: Author.

Chen, M., & Giblin, N. J. (2002). *Individual counseling: Skills and techniques.* Denver, CO: Love.

Hutchinson, D. (2007). *The essential counselor: Process, skills, and techniques.* Boston: Lahaska Press.

Ivey, A., & Ivey, M. B. (2007). *Intentional interviewing and counseling: Facilitating client development in a multicultural society* (6th ed.). Pacific Grove, CA: Thompson/Brooks Cole.

Johnson, D. W. (2006). *Reaching out: Interpersonal effectiveness and self-actualization* (9th ed.). Boston: Allyn and Bacon.

Kiesler, D. J., & Van Denburg, T. F. (1993). Therapeutic impact disclosure: A last taboo in psychoanalytic theory and practice. *Clinical Psychology and Psychotherapy, 1,* 3–5.

Kottler, J. A. (1994) *Advanced group leadership.* Pacific Grove, CA: Brooks/Cole.

Yalom, I. D. (1995). *The theory and practice of group psychotherapy* (4th ed.). New York: Basic Books.

CHAPTER 5
Planning and Structuring Groups

LEARNING OBJECTIVES

After studying this chapter you should be able to

- Discuss planning a group.
- Discuss structuring a group session.
- Plan and structure a six-session group using the processes described in this chapter.
- Create an evaluation sheet for a six-session group.
- Develop a budget for a six-session group.
- Apply what you've learned about planning and structuring a six-session group to longer- and shorter-term groups.

INTRODUCTION

In this chapter we consider two critical aspects of group leadership: planning a group and structuring group sessions. Groups function with a sense of comfort, confidence, and purpose only when a solid foundation for the group has been laid. Converting the group proposal into a detailed plan of action helps leaders to be clear about what the group intends to accomplish, and it helps them track their progress toward accomplishing the goals set forth during the planning process. If the plan is the foundation of the group, then structure is each session's framework. Our discussion of structure follows the discussion of planning, because a plan must first be in place before a leader can begin to structure the group.

After reading the extended examples from a six-session group and working with the practice exercises that parallel the extended examples, you should be well prepared to plan and structure your own groups. A subsection on the importance of budgeting groups is also included within this portion of the chapter.

PLANNING A GROUP

Definition of **planning a group**   The process of outlining discussions and activities for each session that meet the goals set forth in the group proposal.

In essence, **planning a group** is translating the group's purpose statement into a set of goals or a specific plan of action in which members will be engaged. The planning process, therefore, begins before the group is advertised and before members are screened. As we discussed in Chapter 2, a carefully thought-out proposal forces you to clarify for yourself the intended topics and the processes for addressing those topics. It also forces you to think about ethical matters before the group begins.

Ethics Pointer

> The ACA Code of Ethics (ACA, 2005) requires that counselors obtain informed consent from clients prior to counseling. Section A.2.b describes the information needed from informed consent and includes "the purposes, goals, techniques, procedures, limitations, potential risks, and benefits of services" (p. 4). In order to provide this information to potential members, leaders must develop group plans prior to the group. Section A.1.c requires counselors to "work jointly in devising integrated counseling plans" (p. 4).

By preplanning the group, you are able to discuss the goals of the group with potential members during screening, and if a person appears to be an appropriate member, the member and you, the leader, can work collaboratively to formulate personal goals in addition to the overall goals of the group.

Planning promotes effective counseling in all groups, but it is particularly helpful in brief groups of six to eight sessions, because the time limitations of brief groups call for a particularly efficient use of time. Structuring group sessions is an important part of planning, because it ensures that group activities are directly related to both individual member goals and the goals of the group as a whole.

In other words, it helps the leader maximize time on task rather than allowing the group to spend too much time discussing matters not directly related to goals.

Planning is not just something done prior to the group and forgotten. It also impacts the outcome of the group, because it entails setting the goals to be reached at the group's conclusion. Therefore, outcome evaluation processes are also brought into play during the planning process to measure or record members' progress on the goals. Although pre-group plans do not include the names of members, they can be adapted into evaluation forms for members, identifying both the planned goals for the group and how they apply to the members' goals as identified during the screening process. We will discuss evaluation in more detail later in this chapter. Finally, we will touch on another planning task, preparing a budget for a group, at the end of the chapter.

Ethics Pointer

> Section A.1.c of the ACA Code of Ethics requires counselors to keep "sufficient and timely documentation . . . to facilitate the delivery and continuity of needed services" (ACA, 2005, p. 4).

STRUCTURING GROUP SESSIONS

Definition of **structuring group sessions**   The process of organizing each session of the group into distinct parts that cumulatively lead to fulfilling the session's goals.

Structuring group sessions is the process of giving each session a specific form. Unless the group is a single-session group, leaders should always plan each session so that it leads one step at a time toward achieving the planned group goal or goals. Structuring helps ensure that activities are not only geared toward fulfilling the group's goals but that they are also appropriate in length.

The type of structure a leader chooses depends on the type of group being conducted. Typically leaders will structure a group by dividing each session into three parts: a **beginning,** a **working focus**, and a **processing and closure** part (Hulse-Killacky, Kraus, & Schumacher, 1999). At the beginning of the session, the members get connected and start talking; during the working focus of the session, members make direct progress toward the goals of the session; and during the processing and closing of the session, members reflect on their experiences during the session in order to understand the meaning of these experiences. Our method of illustrating the three-part structure is shown in Figure 5-1, and the sections below will discuss each of the three parts of a session's structure.

The Beginning of a Group Session

In Figure 5-1 the beginning of a group session is represented by an arrow pointing toward the working focus of the session, because what happens during the beginning should lead directly to what happens during the working focus. In the beginning of a session, members will typically make connections with each other and talk among

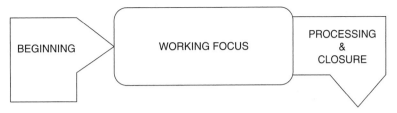

Figure 5-1   Structure of a Group Session

themselves. If it is the very first session of the group, the leader will focus on introducing and linking members, reinforcing the purpose of the group, and encouraging participation of all members. However, at the beginning of all subsequent sessions, the leader's goal is to begin the session by paving the way for the working-focus part of the session. One way to structure the beginning of a session is for the leader to do some direct teaching, thereby more efficiently and purposefully pointing the beginning of the session toward the working focus. For example, during the beginning part of a session on body image, the leader might start by talking about the influence of the media on people's concepts of a desirable body shape. The activities during the working focus of the session might involve responding to images from the media. Thus, the beginning and working focus of the session are directly interconnected. Two other examples of appropriate beginnings that lead directly to the working focus are provided next. Note that one beginning involves a group discussion leading into an activity in the working focus, while the other beginning involves moving almost immediately into the activity in the working focus, with just a brief introduction to the activity. Either beginning approach would be appropriate because it leads directly to the working focus.

Example 1:

Leader: *Let's go around the room. I would like each of you to say which part of the media— movies, TV, or magazines—most influences your sense of what a desirable body shape is. Then we'll do an activity related to the discussion.*

Example 2:

Leader: *On the handout sheet you've each been given, four popular movies with female movies stars are listed. I'd like you to work with the person next to you and compare your own body image with that of the female star listed for each movie.*

In contrast to Examples 1 and 2 above, note how the beginning in Example 3 does *not* lead directly to the working focus because the beginning discussion and the working focus are not directly focused on the same topic (the first is about body image related to a significant other, the second is about body image in relation to the media).

Example 3:

Leader: *Let's start by talking in pairs and discussing the body shape you desire and the body shape your significant other wants you to have. Then we'll discuss how you feel about comparing your own bodies to those of female movie stars.*

The Working Focus of a Group Session

As Figure 5-1 illustrates, the working focus is the main part of a group session and should therefore take up more than half of the session. During the working focus, it is important that the leader keeps the group focused on a specific goal so that progress occurs. The leader might use one or more of the following formats to address a specific goal during the working focus:

- *Discussion Groups.* Breaking the larger group into small groups or pairs to discuss topics. For example: "OK, we're going to break into pairs now and discuss the extent to which you find yourself comparing yourself to images of beauty depicted in the media. After that, we'll open up the discussion to the whole group."
- *Activities.* Conducting group-wide activities to help members better understand particular topics. For instance, "Now let's do this blackboard exercise, which is based on what we just talked about."
- *Direct Teaching.* Providing direct instruction on particular topics for the whole group. For example, "Before we go any further, I want to talk about the history of advertising around body image for a few minutes so that you can see that advertising has a lot to do with the way we feel about our bodies."
- *Rounds.* Facilitating around-the-room discussions on particular topics. For instance, "Let's go around the room and see how we all feel about this. Marcy, you start and then we'll move clockwise."

The total length of the session determines the length of the working focus. In a longer working focus, leaders might incorporate multiple formats, but each format should contribute to overall goal of the session.

The Processing and Closure of a Group Session

In the third and final part of a session, the leader needs to help members make meaning of their experiences during the working focus of the group (processing) and provide a conclusion to the session (closure). Thus, in the body image group it would not be not enough for the leader to begin with an introduction and follow with a related round, discussion, direct instruction, or an activity during the working focus. The working focus would by necessity need to be followed by processing and closure. Yalom wrote that experience (working focus) in and of itself, is not sufficient to be therapeutic. Members "must also *reflect back upon that experience*" (1995, p. 27). This reflecting, or processing, is what allows for the construction of meaning within members' minds.

During this final stage, leaders typically use open-ended questions and/or rounds to help members identify their experiences and internalize what they have learned from their experiences. This is processing. Closure occurs when the leader concludes the session with a brief statement, assigns homework (if appropriate), perhaps briefly states what will be discussed in the next session, and ends the session on time. Note that closure doesn't mean the topic is closed; it means the session is closed. Members may then make use of what they have processed by bringing it into the outside world and into future group sessions.

In Figure 5-1 the processing and closure part of the session is illustrated by an arrow pointing downward to remind you as the leader that as you process and close the session, you must return the emotional level of the group to a normal level so that members are not emotionally upset. They must be ready to leave the session and go out of the group room and on with their lives. An example of this lowering of the emotional level would be a member who responded to the working focus of a grief group by sobbing. The reflective/cognitive processing of the session should help decrease the emotional intensity the member is experiencing and help her be able to safely drive home from the group.

Putting It All Together

To put into practice what we have just discussed above, let's look at a plan for structuring a group session. This particular group consists of eight men, all in their early to mid-twenties, who are relatively new to the workforce and are having difficulty dealing with work stress. The goal of the group is to help the members identify the sources of their stress and to learn strategies for stress reduction. During the screening process, the leader learned that most of the men have long arduous commutes to work, so in his group plan he has included focusing on commuting stress in the fourth session (Table 5-1). In the discussion of the group plan during the first session of the group, the men all agree that coping with commuting stress will be a helpful topic that they look forward to covering.

Note the following five aspects of the sample session plan:

1. The single session topic (commuting stress) mutually agreed upon by the members and leader is appropriate because it is time appropriate and relates directly

Table 5-1 Plan for Session 4: Coping with the Stresses of Commuting to Work

(Length 1.5 hours)

Beginning—7:00 PM

- Briefly introduce the purpose of this session, which is to discuss commuting stress.
- Activity: Pass out paper and pencils. Ask members to write down five adjectives that describe their experience commuting to work this week.

Working focus—7:10 PM

- Lead a round in which each member reads their list of adjectives.
- Initiate group discussion of adjectives—similarities and differences of experience. In what ways are the stresses of commuting similar to the stresses you experience on the job?
- Direct teaching: Summarize the techniques for stress reduction on the job that were discussed and practiced in the first three sessions.
- Open-ended question: How might those techniques for reducing stress on the job be used, or be adapted for use, to reduce stress during your commutes?

Processing and closure—8:10 PM

- Round: Tell the other members what you learned in group today.
- Open-ended question: What small change might you make as you commute to work in the next few days?
- Brief session summary: Thank members, remind them of next meeting, and end at 8:30 PM.

to the overall goals of the group (identifying the sources of work stress and reducing work-related stresses).

2. The session is broken into three distinct parts by the leader. There is a beginning, a working focus, and processing and closure.

3. The beginning of the session is brief and leads directly to the working focus.

4. The working focus takes up at least half of the session and might consist of one or more activities or discussions or a combination of activities and discussions.

5. Processing and closure utilizes a mixture of rounds and open questions to help group members process their experiences in the session and then closes with a brief wrap-up and reminder about the next session, ending on time.

PLANNING AND STRUCTURING A SIX-SESSION GROUP

This section of the chapter presents a brief, six-session group as a means of extending the planning and structuring discussion earlier in this chapter. The basic processes of planning and structuring groups can be applied to groups with fewer than six sessions or more than six sessions. The process of using a six-session group will be demonstrated, because six sessions effectively shows the overall process of planning and structuring multiple-session groups. In conjunction with the six-session demonstration, exercises are provided to help you work through the process in a hands-on manner yourself.

Topic, Purpose, and Developmental Level of the Group

Figure 5-2 shows three aspects leaders must consider as they begin to plan and structure a six-session group: the topic of the group, the purpose of the group, and the **developmental level** of the group's members. In Chapter 2 we discussed the first aspects: topic and purpose. Before we proceed to looking at planning and structuring specific groups, let's pause to consider what we mean by the developmental level of the group and how different developmental levels affect the group.

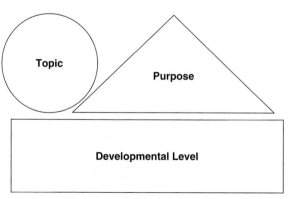

Figure 5-2   Three Aspects of Planning and Structuring

Considering Developmental Level

Definition of **developmental level**   The emotional, intellectual, and behavioral stage of life the person is in considered against the norms of that person's age group.

In general, social, emotional, and intellectual development in human beings roughly corresponds to age. For example, a person in her twenties is typically at a developmental level wherein she is able to handle the challenges associated with sustaining intimate relationships, adapting to various environments, maintaining certain responsibilities, and so forth, that most other people in the same age group are able to handle. This person would be considered to be at a developmentally normal level.

Developmental level can vary greatly among children and teenagers just a few years apart from each other in age. Compare, for example, children you know who are four or five years old with children who are seven or eight. The four- or five-year-old children employ a limited vocabulary, have shorter attention spans than the older children, and respond better to play- or activity-based groups than to discussion-based groups. In contrast, the older children employ a broader vocabulary than the younger children, have longer attention spans, and might prefer discussion-based groups over play- or activity-based groups. When leaders choose a developmental level for a children's group, they should group children within a two-year or a two-grade level (at most, a three- or four-year age span). In this way group members will be roughly similar in vocabulary and attention span, will have had similar life experiences, and will respond positively to the same types of group activities and experiences.

In contrast to children and teenagers, developmental levels for adults vary in wider age ranges, typically in decades. The typical concerns of people in their twenties might include starting a career in a field they love, buying a house or renting an apartment, falling in love, starting a family, and so forth. In contrast, people in their fifties are more likely to be concerned with fulfilling their lifelong dreams, maintaining active lives, helping their children become functioning adults, planning for retirement, and the like. Not only do the topics of practical importance vary between adult age groups, but the perspectives from which they view life also vary. If a group's topic is primarily developmental in focus, for example if the topic is retirement, group leaders may want to select members at or near retirement age. If the topic of the group is not primarily developmental in focus, for example if the topic is cancer support, then leaders might select group members at developmentally different levels, but do so while ensuring that there is not one member developmentally different from all of the other members. For example, a leader should not put five 20-year-olds and an 80-year-old in the same group. The 80-year-old may connect with the other members around experiences related to cancer, but he may be so developmentally different from the other group members regarding life experience and perspective that he will feel isolated from the rest of the group.

Planning the Topic and Purpose

Once topic, purpose, and developmental level are taken into consideration, the planning and structuring of the six-session group can begin. The extended example we will use throughout the next several sections, each section dealing with a different phase of planning and structuring the six-session group, concerns a group

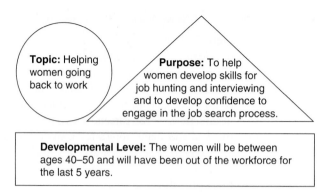

Figure 5-3   Women-to-Work Group: Topic, Purpose, and Developmental Level

focused on women who have been out of the workforce for more than five years and want to return to work. First, the leaders, Beth and Maya, mapped out the group by listing on a chart the topic, the purpose statement, and the developmental level of the members, as demonstrated in Figure 5-3. Knowing that the topic was helping women reentering the workforce, they then fleshed out the topic by writing the following purpose statement: *The purpose of this group is to help women develop skills for job hunting and interviewing and to help them develop confidence to engage in the job-hunting process.* The purpose statement expanded upon the topic by containing three potential focus points: job-hunting skills, interviewing skills, and confidence building. Finally, to further map out the group, Beth and Maya considered the developmental level of their proposed members and decided the developmental level of the women who would most likely benefit from this group would be women who had recently gone through a divorce or who had been married for a number of years, so they reasoned that their members would typically range in age from 40 to 50.

Exercises for Active Learning

Consider a group you would like to run. Write the topic, the purpose statement, and the developmental level of the intended members on the lines below. Be sure to first choose an over-arching topic, then create a more specific but concise purpose statement (one that contains two to three focus points), and finally consider the most appropriate developmental level of potential members as befits the topic.

Topic

_____

Purpose Statement

_____

_____

Developmental Level of Members

_____

Brainstorming, Selecting, and Sequencing Session Topics

Once Beth and Maya had mapped out the topic, purpose, and developmental level of potential group members, they further honed the group's purpose by brainstorming a list of potential session topics. At first the list contained many more topics than the six-session group would allow. They then combined topics that fit together and could be dealt with together in single sessions, indicating next to each topic how it fit directly with the three focus points of their purpose statement. At this point, they still had too many topics for a six-session group, so they further combined topics until they had developed a final sequence of six balanced and time-appropriate sessions. Their movement from brainstorming to sequencing the six sessions is illustrated in Table 5-2.

Having honed the topics down into a sequenced list of six workable sessions, Beth and Maya listed the session topics on a chart in order to visualize how the six sessions would lead into each other in a cumulative manner, as illustrated in Figure 5-4.

The structure of Beth and Maya's six sessions mirrors the structure of an individual session: There is a beginning session (just as there is a beginning part of an individual session), working-focus sessions that take up most of the group's time (just as individual sessions are dominated by the working focus), and there is processing and closure (just as all individual sessions end with processing and closure).

Table 5-2   Brainstorming the Sequencing of the Six-Session Women-to-Work Group

Initial Brainstormed Topic List	More Finely Tuned Topic List (Initial topics combined, overall group purpose indicated for each)	Final Sequence of Topics for Six Balanced and Time-Appropriate Sessions
1. Looking for ads in the newspaper	1. Identifying strengths related to working (confidence building)	1. Identifying strengths related to working (confidence building)
2. Practicing interviewing	2. Thinking about working conditions, salary, and benefits (job-hunting skill)	2. Thinking about working conditions, salary, and benefits (job-hunting skill)
3. Deciding what job or jobs to consider	3. Deciding what job or jobs to consider (job-hunting skill)	3. Deciding what job or jobs to consider, and looking for ads in the newspaper (job-hunting skill)
4. Writing a cover letter	4. Looking for ads in the newspaper (job-hunting skill)	4. Writing a cover letter and a resume (job-hunting skill)
5. Identifying strengths related to working	5. Practicing interviewing (interviewing skill)	5. Feeling good about being a working woman again (confidence building), working on interviewing skills, and wearing appropriate clothes for interview (confidence-building and interviewing skills)
6. Writing a resume	6. Writing a cover letter and a resume (job-hunting skill)	6. Practicing interviewing (interviewing skill)
7. Feeling good about being a working woman again	7. Feeling good about being a working woman again (confidence building)	
8. Working on clothes for interviewing	8. Working on interviewing skills and dressing properly for the interview (confidence building and interviewing skills)	
9. Thinking about working conditions	9. Fitting working and family life together (confidence building)	
10. Thinking about salary and benefits		
11. Fitting working and family life together		

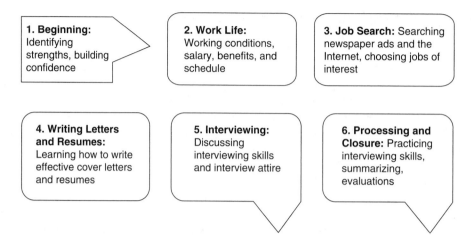

Figure 5-4   Women-to-Work Group Six-Session Diagram

Note that as Beth and Maya have envisioned it, the fifth session combines a working focus and processing and closure. Depending on the group topic, it is not uncommon for leaders to plan more than one beginning session or more than one processing-and-closure session. First—and often second—sessions of multiple-session groups emphasize having the members get to know each other and begin to participate (beginning). The middle sessions emphasize working on goals related to the purpose of the group, including dealing with emotionally intense topics now that trust and cohesion have developed within the group (working focus). The final one or two sessions focus mostly on finishing work already started, processing experiences, and evaluating progress, not introducing new emotionally intense topics (processing and closure).

Exercises for Active Learning

Continue the planning of the group for which you created the topic, the purpose statement, and the developmental level in the previous exercise. Create a three-column table on a blank sheet of paper. In the first column make a list of possible weekly topics; in the second column further refine the list by combining topics and indicating how each topic fits with your purpose statement's focus points; and in the third column, finalize the list of topics into six balanced and time-appropriate sessions. Be sure that your final list includes a beginning session, at least three working-focus sessions, and one or two processing and closure sessions.

Planning Individual Sessions

With the brainstorming, selecting, and sequencing of topics for the full six sessions now complete, Beth and Maya were ready to plan and structure the individual group sessions. The first, or beginning, session had been narrowed down to focus on introducing the group and identifying the women's strengths as workers. Because

every session also needs its own beginning, working focus, and processing and closure, Beth and Maya broke the first session down into these three phases by using the structuring diagram, as illustrated in Figure 5-5.

The beginning of the first session would be focused on introductions and connecting group members [**YTF Reminder:** Cohesion]. The working focus of this first session would be on the positive process of identifying the women's strengths as workers. Beth's emphasis as she closed the session would be encouragement and building a sense of expectation among members that the group would be helpful to them [**YTF Reminder:** Instillation of hope].

Within the structure of the first session, members would work in dyads (DY in Figure 5-5), small groups (SG in Figure 5-5), and as a single large group (LG in Figure 5-5). Using dyads and small groups in the beginning and first part of the working focus phase would help the members get to know each other and help them to build connections among themselves. At the same time, Beth and Maya would incorporate working as one large group into the first session to set a norm

BEGINNING	WORKING FOCUS	PROCESSING & CLOSURE
Maya welcomes the members and restates the purpose of the group. Leader introductions. Put members in dyads. In dyads (DY)—Share name and a little bit about yourself. In large group (LG)—partners from dyads introduce each other. Leaders link members with similarities. Beth reviews purpose of group and norms, stressing supporting each other in efforts to return to work.	In small group (SG)—Share the last two jobs you had and a couple of strengths you had in each job. Simultaneously—Leaders prepare work tables with quilting squares, liquid embroidery, and a grid with squares marked the same size as the quilting squares. (LG) Members use liquid embroidery to write a strength on each of four or five squares. They embroider their names on each of their squares. The group works together to map out the quilt and pin squares in place. Note: Beth will watch time and make the transition at the end of the working focus.	Round: How could one of the strengths you identified help you in a job you're considering now? Round: What was it like for you to be in group today? Beth closes with praise for the courage the members show in going back to work. She reinforces the expectation that the group will be able to help the members with this transition.

Figure 5-5 Women-to-Work Session 1: Identifying Strengths

that the group does work as a whole. Notice that in the first session, the activities the group would do in the large group were the preliminary introductions and an art activity directly related to one of the group's three primary purposes, gaining confidence. These are low-risk activities that were intended to make the members feel comfortable and supported.

Exercises for Active Learning

Following through from the previous exercise, structure the first session of your group, using the three-column format of Figure 5.5. Be sure that the structure of your first session includes a beginning, a working focus, and processing and closure, and be sure that the activities you choose support one or more of your group's purpose focus points.

Beth and Maya wanted the group's second session to focus on work life, including such factors as working conditions, salary, benefits, and schedule. Again, being sure to not only incorporate a beginning, a working focus, and processing and closure, but also making sure that the session remained geared toward their group purpose statement, Beth and Maya devised a second session structure as illustrated in Figure 5-6.

Note how the session as they have planned it begins on a positive note [**YTF Reminder:** Installation of hope] by hanging the strengths quilt created in the first session. Because this is to be the second session and introductions have already been made at the beginning of the first session, the beginning of the second session is to be educational rather than introductory. Beth and Maya plan to do some direct teaching about today's workplace realities as a means of updating members long absent from the workforce [**YTF Reminder:** Imparting of information]. During the working focus, members discuss matters of work life, including working conditions, salary, benefits, and schedule, all of which are geared toward the group's purpose: developing job-hunting skills and confidence building. At the same time, members work in small groups, promoting the therapeutic factors of interpersonal learning and cohesion. During the processing-and-closure phase of the session, Beth and Maya plan to promote the therapeutic factor of universality via a round of discussion intended to show the members that they are all in the same situation. The processing will address what members have learned and how they feel about it. Their reflections will be recorded and saved for the next session in order to carry learning from the first session over into the next session.

For the third session, the focus is to be on searching job advertisements, including those found in newspapers and on the Internet, and choosing jobs of interest. The plan Beth and Maya devised for the third session is illustrated in Figure 5-7.

As with the second session, the third session's beginning focuses on encouragement [**YTF Reminder:** Installation of hope] and on instruction; however, the focus is to be on job searching as opposed to work life. Since the members will have been out of the workplace for some time, Beth and Maya have designed a group with a slower pace, giving priority to skill building and confidence building rather than to finding employment rapidly. During the working focus of the third session, members will focus on both gaining computer skills and processing their questions and feelings. Most importantly, Beth and Maya will emphasize collaboration and

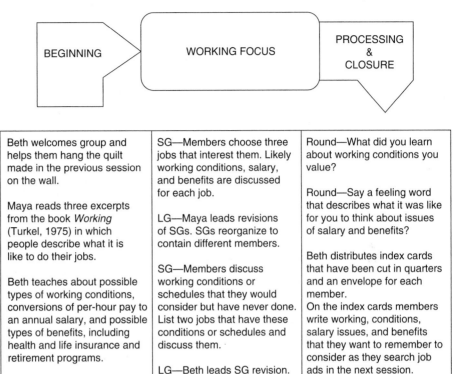

Beth welcomes group and helps them hang the quilt made in the previous session on the wall. Maya reads three excerpts from the book *Working* (Turkel, 1975) in which people describe what it is like to do their jobs. Beth teaches about possible types of working conditions, conversions of per-hour pay to an annual salary, and possible types of benefits, including health and life insurance and retirement programs.	SG—Members choose three jobs that interest them. Likely working conditions, salary, and benefits are discussed for each job. LG—Maya leads revisions of SGs. SGs reorganize to contain different members. SG—Members discuss working conditions or schedules that they would consider but have never done. List two jobs that have these conditions or schedules and discuss them. LG—Beth leads SG revision.	Round—What did you learn about working conditions you value? Round—Say a feeling word that describes what it was like for you to think about issues of salary and benefits? Beth distributes index cards that have been cut in quarters and an envelope for each member. On the index cards members write working, conditions, salary issues, and benefits that they want to remember to consider as they search job ads in the next session. Maya leads a closing round in which each member says something encouraging to another member.

Figure 5-6   Women-to-Work Session 2: Work Life

support during this session. Even if several members choose the same job ad to investigate, they will be coached to support each other with a positive attitude rather than view one another as competitors [**YTF Reminder:** Promoting group cohesion and universality]. During processing and closure, homework will be given to help members prepare for cover-letter and resume writing in the following session.

The structure Beth and Maya have devised for the fourth session is illustrated in Figure 5-8. This session will function primarily as a supportive work session for members to develop cover letters and resumes. The support includes leader encouragement [**YTF Reminder:** Installation of hope] and skill coaching [**YTF Reminder:** Imparting of knowledge] from Beth and Maya, and peer support [**YTF Reminder:** Altruism] and editing of each other's work [**YTF Reminder:** Interpersonal learning] among members. Note that Beth and Maya will close this session with a reminder that only two sessions remain in the group. This reminder is intended to encourage members to address

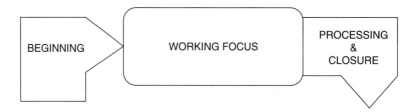

Beth starts group by reminding members to look at their strengths on the quilt. She explains that in this session the group will transition from thinking about work life to looking for jobs. Maya lists Internet sites that have job listings on the local, state, or national level. Maya demonstrates how to find a website and how to copy information to the computer desktop and print it. Beth passes out saved envelopes from last session and has members read their notes from the last session.	DY—Members search state and local newspapers and the Internet, locating, examining, and printing jobs listings of interest. Members who are familiar with computer use are paired with those who are not familiar. During this time, Maya focuses on giving assistance with computers, while Beth focuses on helping members process their thoughts and feelings. SG—Members discuss jobs. Each member selects at least one job each from local, state, and national ads. LG—Beth leads discussion of any member questions about how to look for ads.	LG—Round: What is your first choice job? Give one reason why. Round: What is the most important thing you learned about jobs or about yourself in the group? Homework: Consider the jobs you choose. How are your strengths related to these jobs? Compile a list of your past work experience and educational experience with dates to bring to group next time as a starting point to construct a resume.

Figure 5-7   Women-to-Work Session 3: Searching Job Advertisements

any concerns regarding the working focus of the group in the next session or call upon the leaders individually between sessions rather than wait until the final session so that the group can close smoothly at the end of the last session. This is an important point, because all group interaction must end when the group ends. Both leaders and members will likely have other duties awaiting them at the close of the group.

Exercises for Active Learning

Again following the three-column format of Figure 5.5, write your plans for sessions two, three, and four of your group. Remember that all discussions and activities should be directly related to the topic of the session and to the purpose of the group. Continue to keep in mind the developmental level of your group's members and pick activities and discussions appropriate for their level. Also continue to keep in mind Yalom's therapeutic factors as you structure these sessions, as change—learning and healing—occurs when these factors are activated.

Although many six-session groups will feature only one processing-and-closure session, Beth and Maya chose to combine a working focus with processing and

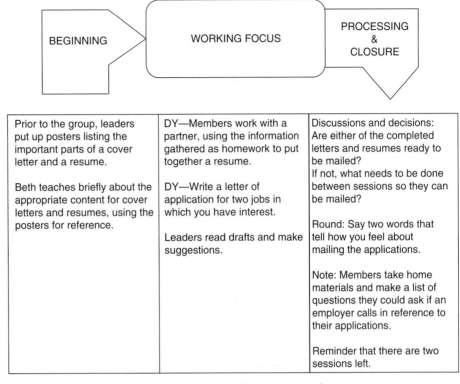

| Prior to the group, leaders put up posters listing the important parts of a cover letter and a resume.

Beth teaches briefly about the appropriate content for cover letters and resumes, using the posters for reference. | DY—Members work with a partner, using the information gathered as homework to put together a resume.

DY—Write a letter of application for two jobs in which you have interest.

Leaders read drafts and make suggestions. | Discussions and decisions: Are either of the completed letters and resumes ready to be mailed?
If not, what needs to be done between sessions so they can be mailed?

Round: Say two words that tell how you feel about mailing the applications.

Note: Members take home materials and make a list of questions they could ask if an employer calls in reference to their applications.

Reminder that there are two sessions left. |

Figure 5-8   Women-to-Work Session 4: Writing Letters and Resumes

closure of the group during the penultimate (second to last) session, as illustrated in Figure 5-9.

During the working focus, Beth and Maya will try to build members' pride in working and confidence in interviewing. The reason the women will be asked to put together two sets of clothes is that many job interview processes have an initial interview followed by a more detailed interview if the applicant is chosen for further consideration. Beth and Maya have designed the processing-and-closure portion of the session—which will take up more than the usual short amount of time at the end of the session—to help calm members' fears of the interview process by promoting the therapeutic factors of catharsis and self-understanding and by confronting existential factors. Their reasoning for starting to process and close the group during the penultimate session was that they felt one session of processing and closure might leave this particular group feeling as if they were not yet quite ready to go out and search for jobs on their own. They want the women to start processing the reality of their own responsibilities a little sooner than other groups might. For this reason, they will start to discuss the reality of the group's end and will invite members to wear their

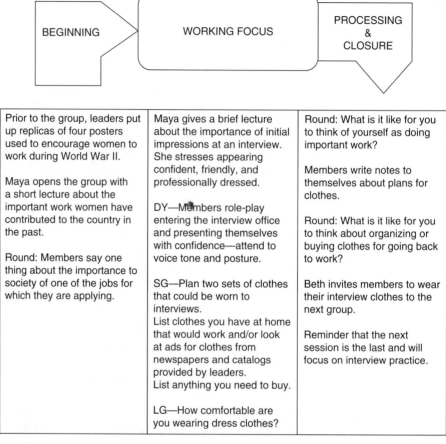

BEGINNING	WORKING FOCUS	PROCESSING & CLOSURE
Prior to the group, leaders put up replicas of four posters used to encourage women to work during World War II. Maya opens the group with a short lecture about the important work women have contributed to the country in the past. Round: Members say one thing about the importance to society of one of the jobs for which they are applying.	Maya gives a brief lecture about the importance of initial impressions at an interview. She stresses appearing confident, friendly, and professionally dressed. DY—Members role-play entering the interview office and presenting themselves with confidence—attend to voice tone and posture. SG—Plan two sets of clothes that could be worn to interviews. List clothes you have at home that would work and/or look at ads for clothes from newspapers and catalogs provided by leaders. List anything you need to buy. LG—How comfortable are you wearing dress clothes?	Round: What is it like for you to think of yourself as doing important work? Members write notes to themselves about plans for clothes. Round: What is it like for you to think about organizing or buying clothes for going back to work? Beth invites members to wear their interview clothes to the next group. Reminder that the next session is the last and will focus on interview practice.

Figure 5-9   Women-to-Work Session 5: Interviewing/Start of Processing and Closure

interview clothes to the final session to make the interviewing process seem more real. Beth and Maya will close this session by reminding members that the next session would be the final session and by clearly stating the focus of the work for that session so that the final session would stay on course and finish on time.

Processing and closure, which will begin in the fifth session, will continue in the sixth and final session, as illustrated in Figure 5-10.

In this last session notice how the beginning has been shortened and more of the time of the session has been given to processing and closure. This is an appropriate adjustment of the structure of the group in the final session, because not only does the final session need to be processed and closed but also so does the entire group. Also, there needs to be time for group evaluation.

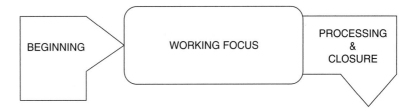

| Beth hands out evaluation forms (see Figure 5.11) and instructs members to try these questions two or three times before adding any other questions. | DY—Members practice interviewing using the initial questions. Interview partner and leaders give feedback and encouragement about performance. Members are asked to practice the same interview two or three times, refining their answers and projecting an increasingly confident presence.

SG—Discussion of multiple ways of answering some questions and pros and cons of each.

SG—Compose additional questions likely to be asked at interview for the job you are interested in.
Each member picks three of these questions to write on her form.

DY—Practice interviewing with a different partner and include new questions. | What was it like for you to practice interviewing?

What did you learn about interviewing that you want to remember when you interview?

Close your eyes for a minute and think back over the entire six sessions. What are some of the important things you learned about finding jobs and the interview process?

What did you learn about yourself?

Round: Say a few words to others in the group about how they have helped you or what you have appreciated about them.

Complete evaluation forms and process.

Leaders close the group on time. |

Figure 5.10   Women-to-Work Session 6: Processing and Closure

Exercises for Active Learning

Continue your preparations with plans for sessions five and six of your group. Depending on the type of group you are conducting, you may want the processing and closure of the group as a whole to begin in session five. Also, remember that in session five you need to let members know that the next session is the last one and that no new topics will be opened in that session. The last session should emphasize processing of the group and allow time for a group evaluation. This means that half to three quarters of the final session should be devoted to processing and closure. The last session should close on time.

Planning for Group Evaluation

Standard practice in any group is to allow time at the end of the last session for group members to evaluate their experience by filling out individual evaluation sheets. The evaluation sheet for Beth and Maya's group is shown in Figure 5-11.

Women-to-Work-Group Evaluation Sheet					
On the scales below, put an X on the number that best describes how you felt at the beginning of the group and circle the number that best describes how you feel now at the end of the group.					
	STRONGLY AGREE	**AGREE**	◄┄┄┄►	**DISAGREE**	**STRONGLY DISAGREE**
I am confident that I can name my strengths related to working.	5	4	3	2	1
I am confident that I understand the working conditions that are important to me.	5	4	3	2	1
I am confident that I can state the salary I need for a job.	5	4	3	2	1
I am confident that I understand the possible benefits that might be part of a compensation package.	5	4	3	2	1
I am confident that I can locate job ads in newspapers and on the Internet.	5	4	3	2	1
I am confident that I can write an effective cover letter applying for a specific job.	5	4	3	2	1
I am confident that I can pick appropriate clothes for interviewing.	5	4	3	2	1
I am confident that I can prepare my resume.	5	4	3	2	1
I am confident that I can present myself confidently in interviews.	5	4	3	2	1
I am confident that I can answer basic interview questions well.	5	4	3	2	1
My overall evaluation of this group is	❏ Excellent ❏ Very Good ❏ Good		❏ Fair ❏ Poor		

Figure 5-11 Sample Evaluation Sheet

Note that the items on the group evaluation sheet directly assess the skills that were taught and practiced in the group. It is important that evaluation sheets be brought into the final session, not only to record the group's experiences but also to promote group discussion at the end of the group and most importantly to evaluate the group's overall effectiveness. Members should leave any group appreciating their progress, understanding where they are in their personal journey, and knowing what their next steps are after the group. In Beth and Maya's group, members will have learned job-hunting and interviewing skills and will have improved their self-confidence. Some may have secured employment before the group ends, while others may not have succeeded in finding jobs. Regardless, all members should leave the group with the skills they need to find employment.

Exercises for Active Learning

Review the purpose statement and session plans for your group, which you created as you worked through this chapter. Then draft an evaluation sheet for your group. Remember to double-check after you finish to ensure that each item on the sheet is directly related to the group's purpose and to what was actually addressed in the sessions. Finish with an overall group evaluation question such as that used in Beth and Maya's evaluation sheet.

Budgeting for a Six-Session Group

One final but very important aspect of planning and structuring groups is budgeting for any items or activities that will cost money. As illustrated in Table 5-3, Beth and Maya used a budgeting table to list needed materials for their group and estimate the costs of those materials. Beth and Maya broke the table down by group session, then by the three phases within each session. Although some sections were blank, Beth and Maya wanted to think through the entire six sessions to ensure that they didn't forget to list anything on the budgeting table. In addition, Beth and Maya listed materials each time they would be needed (for instance, envelopes) to make sure to account for the total costs. In addition to the cost of materials, Beth and Maya might have listed other costs specific to the group beyond general expenses. For example, if they had hired a guest speaker or ordered food or took any field trips, these would have been included in the budget.

Because schools and agencies alike typically function according to an annual budget, creating a budgeting table for any group is critical. Even if the expenses are to be absorbed by members rather than by the school or agency, those expenses need to be accounted for. Notice that Beth and Maya's budget for the group entails about $100 in expenses for materials. If the members are to absorb these expenses, the expenses will need to be divided among the members and included in the cost of the group. In either scenario, thoughtful and responsible planning, open discussions with supervisors regarding expenses, and honest discussions with members about costs is necessary to avoid shortages of funds and associated problems.

Exercises for Active Learning

Create a four-column table such as in Table 5-3 to develop the budget for the six-session group you planned and structured in this chapter.

Table 5-3 Budget for Women-to-Work Group

	Activity	Materials Needed	Cost
Session 1			
▶ Beginning			
■ Working Focus	Strength quilt	Quilting squares	$20.00
		Liquid embroidery	$10.00
▼ Processing and Closure			
After Group		Backing thread	$10.00
Session 2			
▶ Beginning	Book reading	Book	$25.00
■ Working Focus			
▼ Processing and Closure	Recording	Index cards	$2.00
	learnings	envelopes	$2.00
Session 3			
▶ Beginning	Internet	Newspapers	$4.00
	job search	Computers	Agency
		Computer paper	$5.00
■ Working Focus			
■ Processing and Closure			
Session 4			
▶ Beginning	Posters re	4 poster papers markers	$5.00
	letters and		
	resumes		
■ Working Focus	Write letters and		Agency
	resumes	Paper	
		Computers	
			Agency
▼ Processing and Closure		Envelopes	Agency
Session 5			
▶ Beginning	World War II	Posters from WW II	$35.00
	working women		
■ Working Focus	Listing clothes	Pencils and paper	Agency
■ Processing and Closure	Listing clothes	Pencils and paper	Agency
Session 6			
▶ Beginning	Handout on	Paper	Agency
	interview questions		
■ Working Focus			
▼ Processing and Closure			
Estimated Total Materials Cost			$100

SHORTER- AND LONGER-TERM GROUPS

As previously mentioned, we elected to show the planning and structuring processes via a six-session group because six sessions effectively demonstrates how the three phases carry not only through individual sessions but through the entire group. But of course not all groups will be six-session groups. Some groups may be as short as one session, while other groups may last considerably longer than six sessions. In this section we provide two sample group plans designed to demonstrate the planning and structuring process for groups that are shorter and longer than the six-session group.

Planning and Structuring a Single-Session Group

According to Yalom (1983), because of patient turnover, therapists need to develop a "temporal set." In other words, therapists need to train themselves to think in terms of shorter rather than longer groups. In Yalom's words, "The entire life of the group is a single session" (p. 77). While Yalom's comments were written some time ago and with regard to inpatient groups, constant client turnover is common in today's community agency groups, and funds are often limited, so counselors working within community agencies may often find themselves obligated to keep groups short, even as short as a single session. Figure 5-12 provides an example of a plan for a single-session group. The title of the group, "Problems with Taking Medications," identifies the topic to be addressed. The purpose of the group is to help adult outpatients in their 30s and 40s overcome problems with taking their medications.

Note that the single-session group is immediately preceded by the screening of members. Because a single-session group is so time limited, such screening is essential for the group to function efficiently. In addition to pregroup screening, Yalom recommended that structured, active leadership and "explicit orientation and preparation" of members were essential to single-session groups in order for the groups to stay on track during their short durations (Yalom, 1983, p. 108). Therefore, the beginning of a single-session group typically starts with the leader teaching the members what to expect and explaining how the group will work—a less flexible, more directive beginning than would usually be encountered in a longer group. The working focus in single-session groups is typically also more tightly structured than in a longer-term group. As illustrated in Figure 5-12, the group leader might start with a structured round in which the leader calls on members by name rather than awaiting volunteered responses from them. After all members have responded, the leader might be quite directive and explain to the members her plan for how the group will proceed. For example, if four members of the medication group report not taking medications because the medications taste awful and two members report not taking their medications because they ran out of money prior to prescription renewal, the leader might say something like this:

Leader: OK, so I'm hearing two main issues. For some of you, the issue is that your meds run out before your check arrives, and for others the problem is that the meds taste terrible. I want to work on both problems because these are both real problems that are getting in the way of you helping yourself by taking your medications. So this is what we are going to do now: We have about another 45 minutes of the group before wrapping up. We'll take the first 20 minutes until (give specific time) and work together

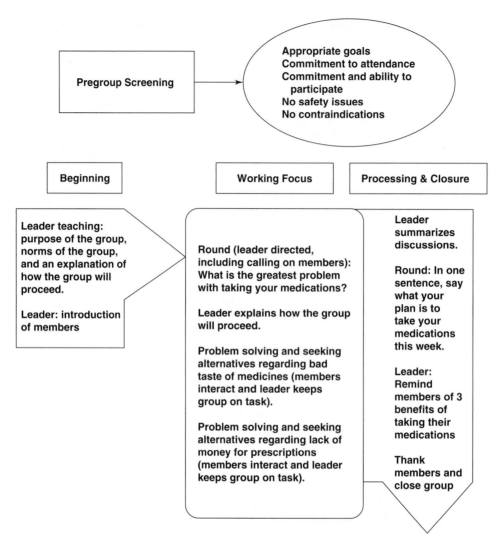

Figure 5-12   Plan for a Single-Session Group: Problems with Taking Medications (Length 1 hour)

on the problem of the meds tasting bad and then from (give time) to (give time) we will talk about what to do if you run out of money to get your prescription refilled.

Note that single-session groups may vary greatly in length, from one hour to an entire morning or afternoon. Therefore, the leader is put in a position wherein he needs to help the group members know specific timeframes for how the group's work be structured. While the leader in our single-session group example divided the time equally between the two topics of concern, that need not be the case. For example, if eight of ten members have one concern and two members have a different concern, the group leader might portion the time according to the number of members interested.

As with the beginning and the working focus of the single-session group, the processing and closure is also quite directed compared to the same parts in a longer

group. While members might participate in a closing round of discussion, the participation requested is usually focused on short responses from members (e.g., in the example above, a one-sentence response). The group leader will then typically conclude with a brief summary, such as in our example a concise three-point reminder to the members about how their medications benefit them. Note how the closing statement is primarily motivational in nature, rather than open-ended. In a longer-term group, the group leader might ask the members a number of open questions about what their group experience was like. In a single-session group, the leader will have to be more selective in using open-ended questions and will have to consciously manage time so that closure occurs as planned.

Planning and Structuring a Longer-Term Group

In contrast to single-session groups, groups that last longer than six sessions may be more open-ended and flexible. You might wonder what types of groups might be longer than six sessions. In schools, the academic quarter often lasts eight weeks, and groups may be timed to match that calendar. Groups in inpatient facilities may be ongoing. In community agencies, groups might be longer because of the program planned or because the treatment required for a diagnosis needed to be applied for a longer time to be effective. For example, if a group member had a diagnosis and if the general functioning of that member was quite low, it might take time for counseling, including group counseling, to help the client make changes in his life and a little more time for the client to learn to maintain those changes with gradually decreasing support from the group and the leader. Oftentimes, longer groups are planned and structured around a book—for instance, a self-help workbook related to the group's topic. Such groups are often structured by focusing on one chapter a week and developing discussion questions or activities related to the topic of the chapter.

Let's consider a wellness group for women in their mid-50s planned around a fictitious book, *Enjoying the Second Half of Life More.* The book has the following chapter titles:

- Chapter 1   In Your Fifties? Now What?
- Chapter 2   Taking Stock of Where You Are Now: How's Your Health?
- Chapter 3   Diet: Eat What You Want to Become
- Chapter 4   Exercise for the Future: Flexibility, Strength, and Confidence
- Chapter 5   Spirituality: Mustering and Using Inner Energy and Purpose
- Chapter 6   Family Legacies and Family Ties
- Chapter 7   Preparing for Your Children's Weddings: How to Let the Weddings Be Theirs, Not Yours
- Chapter 8   Parenting Your Parents: Promoting Their Autonomy and Monitoring Their Needs
- Chapter 9   Planning Finances as Retirement Gets Nearer
- Chapter 10   Contributing to the Human Community and Letting Yourself Feel Satisfied

Table 5-4 illustrates a possible process for planning and structuring a book-based long-term group.

Table 5-4 Planning Table for *Enjoying the Second Half of Life More*

Date	Beginning	Chapter Number and Topic	Processing and Closure
7/1	Leader (L)— introductions. DY—Interview another member. LG—Introduce interview partner. Round: What interests you about this group? L—Review norms of the group.	DY—Say something about your experience of being in your fifties. L—Short teaching about the importance of thinking about your life and life goals. L—Explanation of how the group will use the book. LG—Group reads and discusses the book's introduction.	Processing questions: What did you learn about you or the fifties in the group today? Give a feeling word that describes your experience in group today. L—Assigns homework of reading Chapters 1, "In Your Fifties?" and Chapter 2, "Taking Stock of Where You Are Now" and reminds members to make notes of anything they want to discuss. L—Provides safety information—hotline numbers, etc. L—Expresses hope that members will enjoy book.
7/8	Brief check-in about members' week. Round: After you left group last week, was there any part to the book's introduction you spent time thinking about?	Discussion of Chapters 1 and 2. Processing of feelings and issues related to topics. Processing any need for provision or clarification of any needed medical information. Encouragement for each member to have a personal physician. Chapters' exercises are done in small group and processed. Discussion of any points the members had noted from the reading that had not already been discussed.	SG—Discussion question: What did I learn that I could use in my life outside the group? Are there any questions I want to ask my physician? L—Assigns homework of reading Chapter 3, "Diet," and reminds members to make notes of anything they want to discuss.
7/15	L—Welcome. Round: As you read about diet at home, what were some of the feelings you experienced and how intense were they on a scale of 1 to 5, where 1 is barely aware of the feeling and 5 is overwhelmed by the feeling.	Discussion of Chapter 3, "Diet." Processing of feelings and issues related to topic. Use the chapter exercises to plan desired diet—done in small group and processed. Discussion of any points members had from the reading that had not already been discussed.	SG—Discussion question: Whom do I want to include in my support network as I continue to reflect on my fifties and planning for life ahead? Make a list of five support people. L—Assigns homework of reading Chapter 4, "Exercise for the Future." Reminds members to make notes of anything they want to discuss.

(continued)

Table 5-4 (*continued*)

Date	Beginning	Chapter Number and Topic	Processing and Closure
Middle sessions— 6 weeks or more	Use a variety of rounds or activities that lead to the topic of the chapter.	Continue with a chapter a session, discussing content and processing feelings and concerns; one week may focus on a speaker, a field trip, or an activity related to the purpose of the group instead of discussing a chapter.	Use various rounds or activities that help members process their learning and apply it to life outside the group.
Next-to-last session	L—Give a brief teaching about the life of a group and how this session starts the overall processing of the group.	Finish discussion of final chapter—Chapter 10, "Contributing to the Human Community." SG—Make a map of your community and places that need help. Mark on the map your 1st, 2nd, and 3rd choice of sites where you do or would like to contribute. LG—Combine the maps made by the small groups. Appreciate the impact the group members could make in the local community.	SG—Discussion of overall progress, thinking about the second half of life and what help members might want or need after the group. L—Discuss potluck lunch. L—Assigns homework (could be done in group if desired) looking up resources— books, Internet sites, community groups— related to the topic of the book that the book recommends.
Last session	L—Welcome and brief teaching on the importance of closing well.	Discussion of resources and how they might be used after the group. Card sort—Members write their most important learning on index cards and group them when learning is similar. Evaluation of progress on member goals. Evaluation of group.	Activity in which members express appreciation to each other. Shared potluck lunch. Good-byes. Closure.

Notice that the first session of this longer-term group includes plenty of time for members to get to know each other by splitting into dyads and introducing each other to the large group. The introductions are more member oriented than in the six-session group. Nearly the entire first session is introductory in nature, allowing time to discuss open-ended questions and review the norms of the group. In a book-based group such as this one, the leader sets the most important norms of the group: the importance of doing (and taking notes on) the reading and the importance of calling the hot-line number setup if the topic of the group is an emotionally charged one. Members who seem hesitant to do the reading or seem too emotionally fragile—seem to despair about their future—to benefit from a

book-based group (i.e., they likely need more interpersonal support than a book-based group can provide) should be screened out of the group.

The middle sessions of a longer-term book-based group focus the work on the chapter topics with brief beginning activities that lead to the topic and processing activities centered on identifying cognitive learning, feelings, and applications of book material to life outside the group. Note that in the third week, as members have gotten more into the material of the book, leaders devote time to identifying support networks. The ability to do so is another outgrowth of the extended time available in longer-term groups to process information. In the latter sessions of longer-term book-based groups, the leader has plenty of time to emphasize processing, evaluate progress, evaluate the group experience, and reflect upon personal appreciation of members. Leaders should determine what help members might want after the group, because there is time to provide resources and referrals. For example, if reading the book helped a member identify that a specific area like exercise was of concern, leaders would have time to help the member make a plan or get a referral to someone who could provide help in that area.

RESOURCES FOR GROUP LEADERS

As a novice group leader, you may find it helpful to know that there are resources available in the form of group activity books, preplanned groups, and group planners to help you be more creative and better organized in your group planning. Some examples of useful activity books include: *Creative Counseling Techniques: An Illustrated Guide* (Jacobs, 1992), and *Skills for Living: Group Counseling Activities for Young Adolescents* (Morganett, 1990).

Focal Group Psychotherapy (Mc Kay & Paleg, 1992) is a text that presents preplanned groups on specific topics. This text is particularly useful because the authors provide the conceptual background for each plan. When considering preplanned groups, the burden is on you, the group leader, to evaluate the degree to which concepts and goals in the book match those for your intended group, the degree to which activities in the plan address the goals of your group and do so in a way that matches the developmental level of your members. You should also consider if the activities from the book would be safe for your members. You should select topics and adapt the developmental level of activities to meet the needs of your members.

The Group Therapy Treatment Planner (Paleg & Jongsma, 2000) addresses planning for groups on 28 different topics. Behavioral definitions, long-term goals, short-term objectives, and therapeutic interventions are listed for each topic. In our opinion this planner is most useful to experienced group counselors who have developed a sophisticated understanding of the interrelationships between psychopathology, theory, diagnosis, and treatment. These counselors may find using the carefully worded goals and objectives time saving. Counselors with less experience or training might be wise to use this type of planner in close consultation with their clinical supervisors. Beginning counselors or those inexperienced in group leadership should be mindful that using preplanned groups or planners might lead them to practice beyond the scope of their training and current competency. For example, *The Group Therapy Treatment Planner* provides information to develop plans for a rape survivors group. With the help of this book, a beginning counselor might be able to write an appropriate plan

for such a group. But that counselor will still lack the experience and well-honed leadership skills necessary to run the group in a safe and therapeutic way for members.

Ethics Pointer

ACA Ethics Code C.2.a indicates that counselors practice only within the boundaries of their competence (American Counseling Association, 2005, p. 9).

Beginning counselors who develop plans using treatment planners should discuss with their clinical supervisor their competence to execute the plan.

STUDY QUESTIONS

1. As a leader, what are the advantages of carefully planning a group?
2. What three parts make up a session's structure?
3. How does the work done in each of the session's three parts help the group to do its work and meet its goals?
4. Give some reasons it is important to evaluate the effectiveness of your group.
5. Discuss the importance of budgeting for a group.
6. What goal should the leader keep in mind when setting goals for the work of a single-session group?

KEY CONCEPTS

beginning p. 87

developmental level p. 91

planning a group p. 86

structuring group sessions p. 87

processing and closure p. 87

working focus p. 87

REFERENCES

American Counseling Association. (2005). *ACA code of ethics*. Alexandria, VA: Author.

Jacobs, E. (1992). *Creative counseling techniques*. Odessa, FL: Psychological Assessment Resources.

Hulse-Killacky, D., Kraus, K. L., & Schumacher, R. A. (1999). Visual conceptualizations of meetings: A group work design. *Journal for Specialists in Group Work, 24*(1), 113–124.

McKay, M., & Paleg, K. (Eds.). (1992). *Focal group psychotherapy*. Oakland, CA: New Harbinger Publications.

Morganett, R. S. (1990). *Skills for living: Group counseling activities for young adolescents*. Champaign, IL: Research Press.

Paleg, K., & Jongsma, Jr., A. E. (2000). *The group psychotherapy treatment planner*. New York: Wiley.

Turkel, S. (1975). *Working*. New York: Avon Books.

Yalom, I. D. (1983). *Inpatient group psychotherapy*. New York: Basic Books.

Yalom, I. D. (1995). *The theory and practice of group psychotherapy* (4th ed.). New York: Basic Books.

CHAPTER 6
Mastering Group Leadership Skills: Part I

LEARNING OBJECTIVES

After studying this chapter you should be able to describe the following basic group leadership skills that support setting goals, promoting group cohesion, and balancing group participation:

- Clarifying personal goals
- Direct teaching
- Linking
- Drawing out
- Using rounds
- Cutting off

INTRODUCTION

Group counseling involves a larger set of counseling skills than individual counseling. Not only are individual counseling skills such as questioning, confronting, focusing, self-disclosure, and so forth, brought into the mix in the group, as we saw in Chapters 3 and 4 and carried through the planning and structuring process in Chapter 5, but there are also skills specific to leading groups. This chapter will focus on the leadership skills involved with setting goals and building group cohesion. In the section of the chapter on setting goals, we will discuss the skills of clarifying personal goals and direct teaching. In the section on building group cohesion, we will look at the skill of linking, then discuss balancing group participation, which involves drawing out, using rounds, and cutting off. After reading this chapter and working on its applied exercises, you should be ready to begin to bring both individual and leader skills into your group leadership.

SETTING GOALS

***Definition of* setting goals**   The process of deciding upon the results that the group as a whole and the individual members want to achieve in the group.

As we discussed in Chapter 5, the goals of a group are typically articulated in the group's purpose statement. While the overall goals of the group and the individual members' goals are discussed with members during the screening process, leaders should review the group goals in the first session and may still need to help members solidify their personal goals during the early sessions. The leadership skills of *clarifying personal goals* and *direct teaching* are used to work with group members in **setting goals.**

Clarifying Personal Goals

***Definition of* clarifying personal goals**   The process of helping members develop their individual goals while making sure each member's goals are related to the overall goals of the group.

According to Stockton (1992), leaders should help members clarify their personal goals in ways that are directly related to the purpose of the group, meaningful to the individual members, and achievable in the timeframe of the planned group. Although **clarifying personal goals** may seem on the surface to be a simple, straightforward process, a degree of skill is required of you to make sure that members' goals are both clear and meaningful to them. In addition, you need to be thoughtful about how members' goals fit together. It will be helpful to the group if you can simultaneously address goals of multiple members. During goal setting, you should be thinking of how you will address goals in ways that promote interaction among members rather than interacting with a single member, leaving the other members as spectators.

Ethics Pointer

> ACA Ethics Code A.1.c indicates that counselors and clients should work jointly in planning counseling (American Counseling Association, 2005). The clarification of goals is one manifestation of joint planning.

Consider the following example in which Bart, the leader of a communication skills group, works with Althea, a 24-year-old mother of three young children, to clarify Althea's personal goals:

Bart: Althea, how about you? What goal would you like to work on?

Althea: I want to stick up for myself better.

Bart: Be more assertive?

Althea: Yes.

Bart: Is there somebody specific you want to be more assertive with?

Althea: My mother drives me nuts. She keeps giving me advice about parenting that I don't ask for and, frankly, I don't want.

Bart: She gives you more advice than you want, but you haven't told her that.

Althea: I don't want to drive her away. I just want to be able to let her know what help I want and when I feel I'm doing fine. That's what I'd like to work on.

Bart: That sounds like a goal that you could work on in this group. Maybe we could do some role plays and you could practice how to talk with your mother.

Althea: I think that would help.

Note how Bart has been careful to make sure that Althea's goal is directly related to the overall purpose of the group (this is a communication skills group, and Althea's goal of improving her own communications skills with her mother is directly related to the group's purpose), is meaningful to the group member (Bart has helped Althea clarify her goal, but he has been careful to allow her to articulate her own goal, thereby ensuring the goal is meaningful to her own life situation), and is achievable within the timeframe of the group (Althea's goal appears to be easily achievable, so Bart suggests using role playing as a method for achieving the goal, since other members can be involved in this work).

Exercises for Active Learning
Skill Development: Clarifying Goals

Tia and Franco are leading an anger management group for boys age 13 and 14 who were mandated by the court to participate in the group. All of the boys have appeared before the court for the third time for fighting/assault. The purpose of the group is to decrease the boys' aggressive activities and to teach them more effective ways of managing anger. During the first session, the leaders are helping the members clarify goals.

Paulo:	My goal is to not get in fights on the school ground anymore. My dad said he would make me drop the soccer team if I get suspended again.
Franco:	You're pretty good in soccer, and it would be a shame if you couldn't play.
Paulo:	I really want to play.
Tia:	Matt?
Matt:	I want to know what to do so that I don't fight and I don't run away. And, I don't want to go tell teachers. The other kids won't be friends if I tell on them all the time. *[Tia notices several of the boys nodding.]*
Tia:	So we have to find another choice besides fighting and running away?
Tom:	Yup.
Franco:	How about you Steve, what should be your goal?
Steve:	The other kids make fun of me because I have red hair. When they do that, I want to get even. If I can't hit them, I need to learn some other way to get back at them. That's my goal.

Write a response that Franco or Tia can use to help Steve clarify his goal so that it is consistent with the purpose of the group.

_____

_____

_____

Direct Teaching

***Definition of* direct teaching**   The transmittal of factual information from the leader to members that is related to the purpose of the group.

Direct teaching is a skill that helps set and solidify group goals. Direct teaching helps the group make progress toward reaching their goals by providing members with newer or more accurate information on the group's topic than what they might already possess. Direct teaching is also used to educate members about how the counseling process works. A leader begins direct teaching by informing the group that she is going to give them a short talk on the subject of the group, and they will have a chance to talk afterward. To help members understand how this information is useful to them as they work to reach their goals, the leader's talk is often followed by members discussing the material presented.

You might wonder how to organize direct teaching. Start with a clear statement of what will be taught, how it will be beneficial to the members, and how it is related to the purpose of the group. With the attention span of your members in mind, make a few important points—five or fewer—and relate them to the members' goals. As you teach, you may wish to write on a chalkboard or to refer to an outline posted on the wall of the group room. Handouts may be useful during your talk; however, they may also be a distraction, particularly for members who have a hard time staying focused. One approach might be to write on the

board during your teaching and to provide handouts for the group to take home at the end of the session.

As an illustration of direct teaching, please consider the following example. Millie is the leader of a depression group with the purpose of encouraging medication compliance and positive thinking among members.

Millie: It's good to have you all here tonight. I want to start today by talking about why it is important for all of you to take your medication. I want to go over a couple of points and then we can talk together. First of all, you're all here in the group because you've had episodes when you were seriously depressed, and most of you have thought about or have attempted to hurt yourselves. *[Some members are nodding.]* Most of you found that very scary. Someplace inside, you don't want to hurt yourself, and that's why you are in this group. You have agreed to take your medications and have worked hard to learn to think positively.

Anne: That helps a lot.

Millie: Thinking more positively?

Anne: Yes.

Millie: Good, because I don't want any of you to hurt yourselves. That's why I want to review with you about how your medications help you. For some of you, when you take your medications, you don't feel depressed at all, and for others you don't feel as depressed, and those feelings don't happen as often. Most importantly, when you take your medications, you don't feel like hurting yourselves, because they help you think positively, which goes along with the exercises we do in the group that help you to think more positively, like Anne said. Just learning to think positively is only half of the struggle, so it's very important that you take your medications the way the doctor prescribed them. I want us to talk as a group and go over things that help you to take your medications and problem-solve anything that gets in the way of you taking your medications.

Note how Millie listens to members as she teaches them about the importance of taking medications, but how at the same time, she is doing most of the talking. Also note how Millie not only teaches about the importance of taking medications (which is one of the goals of the group), but she also discusses how taking medication is linked with thinking positively (the other goal of the group), thus reiterating and unifying the group's two central goals.

Exercises for Active Learning
Skill Development: Direct Teaching

Think of leading an anger management group for teens who have been fist fighting at school. List three points that you might include in a direct teaching for this group.

_____

_____

_____

_____

BUILDING GROUP COHESION

Group **cohesion,** one of Yalom's therapeutic factors, means that members have a sense of belonging to the group and feel valued and accepted by the other members of the group (Crouch, Bloch, and Wanlass, 1994). Yalom (1995) describes building group cohesion as the group therapy parallel of building the therapeutic relationship in individual therapy.

Yalom (1995) noted that cohesion is "necessary for other group therapeutic factors to operate" (p. 49). Therefore, a group leader must develop cohesion as early as possible in order for the group to function effectively. The counseling skills of *linking* and *balancing participation* help to promote interaction among members and build cohesion in the group.

Linking

***Definition of* linking**   The skill of connecting group members to one another by pointing out commonalities.

Linking builds cohesion by pointing out to members what they share in common with each other, in essence connecting members to each other. Linking members can be done in two ways. One way is for the leader to make statements pointing out common experiences, feelings, or interests between members or among the entire group. Another and perhaps better way is for the leader to ask members whom the leader has identified as having something in common with one another to speak to each other about those commonalities.

The following example illustrates the skill of linking. In this scenario Lyra leads a group for adult caregivers of elderly parents with Alzheimer's disease and links two of the members, Samantha and Jennifer, who have similar feelings about the caregiving experience.

Samantha: The other day I just yelled at my mother. When I realized what I was doing, tears flowed out. I heard me talking to myself saying, *You are just exhausted, that is what is going on here.* And that is the hardest thing, having to say the same thing to Mom over and over and over again because she doesn't remember. I know she can't help it, but it's exhausting.

Lyra: It is exhausting. *[Lyra sees Jennifer nodding and calls on her.]* Jennifer, are you connecting with what Samantha is saying?

Jennifer: Yes. *[Jennifer looks at Samantha.]* I'm exhausted too, Sam. I finally gave in and got on the list at the county mental health board for some respite care for my mother, and I felt guilty about that. Then I realized that I have to take care of myself, because Mom really doesn't have anyone else.

Samantha: My mom doesn't either. Can you show me how to get on the list?
[Jennifer nods.]

Lyra: Does anyone else feel exhausted like Jennifer and Samantha? We're all here to discuss the same basic issues of dealing with the stresses of helping parents with Alzheimer's. Do any of you have experiences different from Jennifer and Samantha?

In this example, note how Lyra linked two members who used the same feeling word, *exhausted*, and then extended the linking process to the rest of the group in order to build a sense of cohesion among the members. By asking members to compare their experiences with those of Samantha and Jennifer, she opened the discussion for more members to self-disclose in relation to the purpose of the group and promoted cohesion.

Exercises for Active Learning
Skill Development: Linking

Corey and Matt are leading a group for spouses of military personnel who have been deployed to a combat zone. The purpose of the group is to help the members process loss of direct contact with their spouses and learn how to support their families while the military personnel are on deployment. At the start of the second session, Corey invited the members to talk about their feelings during the week between groups.

Golda: I spent most of my time just doing what needs to be done. It's always this way when he is away.

Corey: Could you say a little more about what you mean by "this way," Golda?

Golda: Just managing, getting by, hanging on—just struggling to keep us going as a family for the 60 days he's at sea.

Sarah: Hanging on, me too.

Write a statement or question that Corey or Matt could use to link Golda and Sarah and get them to talk to each other.

_____

_____

Balancing Group Participation

***Definition of* balancing participation**   Leading so that all members participate in and benefit from the group.

One of the benefits of groups as opposed to individual counseling is the "value added" learning that occurs through member interaction. Leaders should work to get all members participating verbally in the first session (Stockton, 1992). Not only should the leader build cohesion in the group via linking and drawing out, but the leader should also set a norm that participation needs to be balanced, emphasizing both group cohesion and member participation during screening and in early sessions.

Balanced participation typically doesn't occur automatically. Once members begin to interact, the leader should monitor relative levels of participation, seeking balance both in terms of the amount of each member's participation and the quality of that participation. We will begin this discussion with the skills used to balance the amount of participation—drawing out, using rounds, and cutting off. Then we will discuss approaches to ensuring that members are participating in productive ways.

Drawing Out

***Definition of* drawing out**   The skill of encouraging members to speak in the group rather than remain silent.

Whereas linking connects members who have made similar statements, **drawing out** encourages members to speak in the first place. Starting with the first session, it is important that you monitor members and draw out anyone who doesn't speak. The lack of participation of even one group member works against group cohesion, because the other members may feel uncomfortable or mistrustful speaking in front of a member they haven't had a chance to get to know. Beginning with the first session and throughout the group, the ideal to aim for is approximately equal member participation. Also, be mindful that even the most talkative members may need encouragement to participate when the group addresses uncomfortable topics or when members experience intense or unpleasant emotions.

There are several ways for leaders to draw out members. You may draw out members by looking directly at them and nonverbally soliciting their participation, by calling on them by name and explicitly asking for participation, or by introducing a round that invites each member to speak in turn (we touched on using rounds in Chapter 5 and will explain using rounds further in the next section of this chapter). As with some of the other skills discussed in this chapter, simply calling on people may not seem like a difficult skill, but because you want to be perceived as a sensitive leader, you may find yourself hesitant to call on members who do not participate. Therefore, you need to practice the skill of drawing out and learn to implement it appropriately. As with any counseling skill, the key to effective drawing out is using the skill tactfully and appropriately, always keeping the overall goals of the group in mind.

Consider how drawing out is used by the leader, Anne, in a group for first-grade students who have been sent to the principal's office for misconduct multiple times during the first month of school. The purpose of the group is to help the children understand appropriate conduct and to begin to participate positively in their classrooms.

Anne: Let's talk about things you have done to help out in your classrooms. Mitchell, I know from the past that you like to talk, so why don't we start with you?

Mitchell: I picked up all the crayons that were on the floor just before lunch.

Anne: That's good. It helped the class be ready to go to lunch on time, and it made the floor safe so no one would slip and fall. *[Anne notices that Jayla is looking attentive as if she wants to talk. Anne looks directly at Jayla and nods.]*

Jayla: I handed out the music books when Mrs. Hassane came in to teach music.

Anne: That helped the class to get started. *[Jayla smiles.]* Now let's go around the room and hear from everybody else. If you're feeling shy or can't think of something, just say your name so that everyone knows who you are. Try to say something if you can, though, because it's fun to participate and get to know other people.

Note how Anne used all three methods of drawing out (direct address, nonverbal address, and rounds) and chose when to use each method based on cues from

the group. To draw out Mitchell, who she already knew was a talker, Anne used direct address. In Jayla's case, Anne responded to Jayla's facial expression of interest and responded with a nonverbal drawing out. In the cases of the other students, Anne used a round and tactfully addressed the fact that some students might be shy, but she also positively encouraged them all to speak by emphasizing the benefits.

Exercises for Active Learning
Skill Development: Drawing Out

Polly Pratt is in an "Adults in College" group. The purpose of this group is to help middle-aged adults who are college sophomores. This is the third session of the group, and Polly has said very little other than her name.

1. Why is it important to get Polly to talk in the group?

    _____

2. Write something a group leader could say to encourage Polly's participation (to draw her out).

    _____

    _____

    _____

Using Rounds

***Definition of* using rounds**   A skill in which the leader poses a question then asks the members to each take a turn replying to the question.

Using rounds may be the most effective way of balancing participation. When the group seems to be headed in an unbalanced direction, a round can get the group warmed up and promote the participation of all members (thus encouraging balanced verbal participation), elicit multiple points of view (thus curtailing dominance and/or submissiveness), elicit group-wide understanding of goals (thus balancing out task and process focus imbalances), and reemphasize the feeling that the group is "in this together" (thus providing positive encouragement for group members whose excessive negativity creates an imbalance in the group).

Rounds are also effective in other ways not necessarily related to balanced participation. Using rounds can help leaders monitor levels of emotions in the group, determine member interest in topics, clarify member understanding of topics, and gauge member progress toward achieving goals. Each of these types of information helps the leader perceive what is happening in the group and helps the leader make decisions about whether or not leader intervention is needed—and if so what the nature and timing of the intervention should be.

Consider how Sofia, the leader of a group for adults who wish to stop smoking, uses a round in the first session. She started the session with direct teaching on the subject of the link between smoking and lung diseases, showed an educational video on the topic, and then noticed that only one member, Vern, spoke

up afterward, and he drifted off of the topic to talk about his past failed attempt at quitting. So Sofia has decided to use a round to encourage and balance participation.

Sofia: I've spent quite a bit of time this morning talking about the link between lung diseases and smoking, and now we've seen the video presentation. I've noticed that only Vern has talked, and some of you look restless, so I'd like to hear from everybody. Let's go around the room and talk about how you are feeling at this point in response to the video. Cloe, let's start with you, since we haven't heard from you in group yet.

Cloe: I think everyone already knows that smoking causes cancer and emphysema, so I'd rather focus on how we're going to actually be able to quit. I've been trying to quit for years, and I doubt it's going to happen.

Sofia: OK, I understand your frustration. But let's try to stay focused on the positive, because you've taken a positive step by joining this group, and it can be a great help to people who want to quit. Because we're in a group focused on the same thing, we can encourage each other, and we stand a much better chance than if we try to go it alone. Vern, we've already heard from you, but you talked about your failed attempts to quit. What specifically did you think about the video, and does thinking about the link between smoking and lung cancer increase your motivation to quit?

Vern: I know there's a link, but it's hard to think of the long-term effects when one cigarette at a time doesn't seem like that big of a deal. I just want to quit now while I'm here and focus on that.

Sofia: OK, we'll spend more time on specific quitting methods from here on in. Alexa, how about you?

Alexa: I'm fine with whatever Cloe and Vern think.

Sofia: Is that what you think, though?

Alexa: Well, I guess I did think the video was helpful because even though I know all that, the photographs of diseased lungs did scare me, so I think that helped me get motivated. Can we talk about how those lung machines work?

Sofia: Sure, let's keep going around the room and talking about the video, though. I'll bring something for you for the next session.

Notice how Sofia used a round to balance participation. First, she made it clear that she wanted to hear from everybody. Secondly, she encouraged participation that stayed on task. In order to keep the group on task, she refocused Vern and volunteered to provide Alexa with the off-topic information she requested (about how the lung machines work) without devoting group time to it. Third, Sofia curtailed negativity by letting Cloe know that she had been heard, but also pointing out that she had taken a positive step by joining the group.

In addition to balancing participation, Sofia's use of round also resulted in other benefits, such as gaining a sense of member interest in and emotional reactions toward the topic. In later sessions, Sofia might use rounds again to help clarify the goals of the group and monitor group progress.

Exercises for Active Learning
Skill Development: Using Rounds

You are leading a group on weight loss. As one member expresses the strong opinion that all members should eliminate desserts from their diets, you notice from the facial expressions of the other members that there may not be total agreement on the subject of dessert. On the lines below, write what you could say to start a round and hear from all members on this issue.

_____

_____

_____

Cutting off

Definition of **cutting off**   A skill in which the leader stops a member from talking.

While drawing out and using rounds are perhaps the most effective ways of balancing participation, sometimes a leader may need to balance participation by **cutting off** members who are speaking. The phrase *cutting off* may seem severe, even rude, but in certain situations it is necessary, and if done in a situationally appropriate manner, it enables leaders to prevent dominance by one or more members. In addition, the skill is essential in ways not related to balancing participation. It facilitates keeping the group in focus; it enables leaders to transition from topic to topic (as well as from beginning to working focus and from working focus to processing and closure); it helps keep the group within its allotted time frame; and, most important, in certain situations it provides for member safety when one member may be attacking or intimidating another member.

Ethics Pointer

ACA Ethics Code A.8.b requires counselors (leaders) to protect clients (members) (American Counseling Association, 2005). In order to implement this ethics code, leaders must be both able and willing to cut off members who are judging or attacking other members.

Beginning leaders may be hesitant to use the skill of cutting off in an effort to avoid hurting or offending members or being perceived as rude or abrupt. However, by practicing the skill, leaders can learn ways to cut off members in a gentle, coaching manner when appropriate and in a strong, authoritative manner in safety situations.

In the following example Georgia is leading a support group for parents of children who have severe asthma. Georgia uses cutting off not only to discourage member dominance but also to protect member safety, keep the group in focus, and move the group from the working focus to processing and closure.

Mary:	*[Has been speaking for over 5 minutes]* . . . Dillon wanted to play baseball, and we worked with the specialist to get some medication that he could take before games. So far he is OK but I wish . . .
Georgia:	It's good to hear that Dillon is OK, Mary, but now let's move on to someone else, because we need to hear from other members, and you've ended on an interesting note that takes us back to our focus on helping keep our kids active.
Ned:	Neddie wanted to play baseball too, and it turned into a mess.
Mary:	What kind of mess?
Ned:	The doctor gave us medication, but he also wrote on the report from Neddie's physical that he had to carry a needle of epinephrine to every game. When the coach read that, he said he refused to be responsible for carrying it or administering it if there was an emergency. He said either Barbara or I would have to bring the needle to every game and stay during the game. If there was a problem, we would have to give Neddie the shot. Barbara has to work during most of the games, and I . . . I couldn't stick that big needle into my son.
Kyle:	You're a big sissy, Ned . . .
Georgia:	Whoa, Kyle . . .
Kyle:	. . . and you're lazy. What's the . . . *[Georgia holds her hand out toward Kyle as if to stop traffic and speaks in a loud and commanding voice.]*
Georgia:	That's enough, Kyle! Stop right there. *[Kyle stops so Georgia proceeds in a gentle voice.]* Kyle, you're attacking Ned, and that's not OK. The rules of the group are to be supportive. If you can get in the right frame of mind and tone of voice to contribute that's fine, but otherwise I want you to rest. If you need to go get a cup of coffee in the waiting room and calm down that's all right too. OK *[to the whole group]*, it looks like the discussion has gotten pretty heated, and we're running low on time. We need to move on to processing and closure. To help Ned with his problem, next week let's move on to the topic of administering medications to our kids, because this seems to be a major one I've heard from several people.

Note how Georgia used cutting off twice in this exchange. She first opted to use cutting off to balance group participation. In this instance she prevented Mary from monopolizing the group's time and at the same time got the group back on focus. After deciding that Mary was dominating the discussion, she looked for an appropriate stopping point and cut her off. She did so in a skilled, gentle manner as befitting the situation in which a member is simply speaking for too long. In the second instance she took a much stronger, authoritative stance to protect Ned from Kyle's attack. Georgia's purpose in the second instance of cutting off was to preserve member safety. Note how it took Georgia two interventions to get Kyle to stop his attack on Ned, employing first a strong verbal cut-off and when that didn't work, using both body language and tone of voice to cut him off. After she cut Kyle off, she restated group norms, reframed Ned's problem as one the group could help him process, and gave Kyle some

parameters for his behavior as the group progressed. She then used the cutting off as an opportunity to turn the group discussion from the working focus to processing and closure.

Exercises for Active Learning
Skill Development: Cutting Off

1. You are leading a parenting group. During the group, Marianna starts to talk about her 4-year-old son, Alfred, stealing $5 from her purse to buy ice cream from the truck that moves through their neighborhood on hot afternoons. Ten minutes later she is still expounding on how terrible Alfred is. You notice one of the other members rolling her eyes and looking at the ceiling. On the lines below, write what you would say to cut Marianna off.

    _____

    _____

2. You are leading a group at the county jail for men who have been arrested after violating a restraining order. Dan, one of the members, begins a tirade against the judge. On the lines below, write what you would say to cut Dan off.

    _____

    _____

Balancing the Quality of Participation

Aside from the amount members speak, there are other types of balances a group leader should seek to maintain. Some members may express themselves in a dominant manner in the group, while other members may tend to express themselves in a less forceful or even submissive manner. Further, some members may be predominantly positive in their comments, while other members are predominantly negative in their comments. Finally, some members may be primarily task focused (focused more on accomplishing the goal of the group) while other members may be predominantly process focused (focused more on the other members and interacting with them) (Bales & Cohen, 1997). The leader should intervene to balance any or all of these dimensions to ensure the efficacy of the group. To balance these various dimensions, the leader should keep in mind the following:

- All members should participate verbally in the group.
- The amount each member participates should be balanced, not necessarily within the same session, but across two or three sessions.
- Not only should members participate equally, but they should also participate in a way that is on task, that is, in a way that is contributing toward the group's purpose. The leader should work to refocus, restrict, or cut off members who continually drift off task and encourage members who are verbal and remain on task to help other members.

In cases where a member takes a dominant tone or stance toward another member or members, a member seems overly passive, a member consistently makes negative comments or has an overall negative attitude, or a member seems either overly task or overly process focused, the leader should step in and reinstall balance via open discussion, refocusing, drawing out, and/or using rounds.

Exercises for Active Learning
Balancing the Quality of Participation

Mitchell and Dean are leading a scout troop whose 12-year-old members are planning for a weekend of winter camping. Pierre, Stan, and Frank have presented a draft plan to the members who responded quite positively overall. However, Jack has made six negative comments. He finally makes the following statement.

Jack: This is just stupid. We're going to freeze camping out in Maine in the winter. You guys are gonna wish you were home playing computer games.

On the lines below, write what you would say to Jack to move his comments to a more positive tone.

_____

_____

INTEGRATIVE CASE EXAMPLE: JOB SEARCH GROUP

As in Chapters 3 and 4, this chapter has presented a number of skills, which you have practiced via the exercises presented in each skills section. We suggest that before reading this chapter's extended group example, you go back and briefly review each of the skills included in this chapter. As a quick reference, these are the skills that have been discussed in this chapter: clarifying goals, direct teaching, linking, drawing out, using rounds, and cutting off. After you have reviewed the skills, read through the group example below, which brings all of the skills discussed together in a group setting (to help guide you as you read, the skills used are indicated in parenthesis and bold). As you read, pay attention not only to what skills are used but also to the situations in which the leaders choose to apply particular skills. What cues might the leaders be responding to when choosing to apply a certain skill over another? What alternate skills could be employed in each situation? Although they are not called out, what are some of the individual counseling skills applied to groups being used in the example?

In our extended example, Angelina and Rose are counselors at a community agency near a large public university in the Southeast. For the past two years the local economy has been in a slump, and cuts in federal and state funding to higher education have had a drastic impact on the university's budget. Last week, 42 university employees, mostly secretaries and clerical staff, were laid off. The director of the community counseling agency in the small city where the university is located has contracted with the university to offer four-session groups to the people who were laid off. The purpose of the groups, each of which will be co-led by Rose and

Angelina, is to help members plan and begin their job searches or, alternatively, retrain for different jobs.

The five members have been grouped together because all of them have expressed a strong desire to be in a group that starts immediately, because all have indicated a preference to meet in the afternoon, and because all of them indicated during the screening process that they have similar goals *[Clarifying goals]*.
[Rose opens the group by giving a clear purpose statement.]

Rose: Angelina and I would like to thank you for coming to the first session of the job search group. We appreciate that this requires an effort at a time that might be discouraging for you.

Angelina: All of you are here because you were laid off by the university in the recent budget cut and because you are taking action to find employment. The purpose of this group is to help you plan and begin your job searches or to help you get connected with some job retraining program.

Rose: Angelina and I sense that all of you have some pretty strong feelings about losing your jobs and having to build new futures. In this group we will talk a little about those feelings, but our central focus will be on taking actions to start on a new future. *[First, Angelina states the common circumstances of the members, which promotes group cohesion. She then clearly states the purpose of the group. Rose further clarifies that the emphasis of the group will be taking action more than processing feelings, thus setting goals for the group.* **YTF Reminder:** *Throughout their introductory remarks, both leaders are working to instill hope.]*

Angelina: Let's go around and have each of you introduce yourselves and say just a bit about what you did at the university. *[Using rounds]*

Sally: I'm Sally, and I was an assistant registrar.

Manny: Manny here. I'm a supervisor in the electrical department. I'd been working here 12 years.

Tom: I'm a groundskeeper . . . mostly I operate the machinery and mow lawns or plow snow. *[He sighs deeply.]* This was a good job.

Angelina: You liked it here.

Tom: I'm going to miss it.

Adrian: Yeah, me too, Tom. I'm still angry, but that's what makes this hard. I will miss it. I was senior administrative assistant in the student health center. I liked the people there, and I will miss them.

Sarah: I was a file clerk in the geology department. I'm scared. I don't think it will be easy for me to get another job with health insurance.

Sally: That's one of my biggest fears. At my age, going on the open market and purchasing health insurance will be very expensive.

Manny: Yeah, and the university insurance covered my family and many companies only cover the employee. I'm concerned about by wife, Ella. She has problems with her eyes and has to take expensive drugs. I don't know how we would pay for them without insurance.

[Now the group is moving to the topic of health insurance that is of interest to the members. The leaders could focus the discussion on health insurance, or they could return the group to the job hunting focus and deal with insurances later. Since the purpose of the group is starting the job search or starting job training, Rose acknowledges the importance of the insurance issue and then uses the purpose to refocus the group.]

Rose: I can see that benefits, particularly health insurance, are important to all of you. Lack of benefits is an additional financial vulnerability for you and your families. The only way I know to get rid of that vulnerability is to help you get reconnected with a good job. Rather than talk more about benefits right now, let's work on finding the jobs or the job training that gives you and your family a chance for income and benefits.

Angelina: We're going to start by thinking about your strengths on the job—the skills or personality characteristics that make you good at what you do and good to work with.

Rose: I put some chalk up on the chalk tray, and I want you to work with a partner or two, since there are five of you, and list five strengths each of you has, then write your name and those five strengths on the chalkboard. *[The group does so over the course of several minutes before Angelina opens up the discussion anew.]*

Angelina: Those are really good lists you made. Could anyone say a little bit about your own strengths and then maybe say how they might be similar or different from what others put? *[No one speaks.]* Sally, how about you, can you tell us more about your strengths? *[Drawing out]*

Sally: I'm pretty good with computers—word processing, financial accounts, and stuff. I seem to learn that type of thing faster than other people do. The programs I've used at work have many different screens that you have to pull up to enter and cross-check data. It feels like a kind of intuition. I seem to know what screen to pull for what I am trying to do. I helped some of the others a lot. I really believed we were a team.

Rose: So you have some skills that would be useful in a number of jobs, and you have some attitudes about how to work together with coworkers that are strengths.

Sally: Mhmm . . .

Angelina: How about what the other folks listed as strengths? *[Drawing out]*

Sally: Well, I'm like Adrian.

Rose: Tell him how. *[Rose links Sally and Adrian. She encourages direct member-to-member interaction to promote cohesion.]*

Sally: Adrian, like you I do the whole job—all of my job—and I get along with the other women. Our office was all women, and that's different than the grounds crew. *[Adrian is nodding.]*

Adrian: For me that is key, getting along with a lot of people. It's one reason I feel optimistic about getting another job. My bosses and coworkers will give me good references. I think most of the folks in this group would be great to work with. How am I different? Well . . . I'm most different from Manny. *[Adrian looks at*

Manny, speaks directly to him, and links with him. Adrian expresses both how he differs from Manny and how he is similar to Manny.] I'm good with people, but I have no idea about electric stuff. All that high voltage stuff scares me to death. I really admire you for working with it.

Manny: Well, you have to pay attention all the time. What scares me is not having a job. *[Manny looks a little hesitant.]* I feel sick. Sometimes I throw up, and men shouldn't do that. The doctor said I am worrying too much and have a stomach ulcer. He said I have to take medicine all the time. *[Manny shakes his head.]* My father is 86, and he told me I have to be strong now. My father worked on the ranch driving stock lots of hours in the heat. He is very strong even at his age.

[Manny is starting to talk more about his medical concerns and the interpretation that he and his father have about what is expected of men. This is a point at which leaders must be aware of what is happening in the group and make a leadership decision. Manny's medical issues may be related to the stress of job loss, and having medical concerns may not fit with Manny's understanding of men's roles. These are serious concerns that leaders might choose to address with the entire group if the group was scheduled to run for more than four sessions and if leaders thought these topics could be addressed in a way that interested multiple group members. The short group time points toward a tight focus on the intended group content. Therefore, leaders may need to address member safety needs, perhaps by referral, and then refocus on the intended goal for the session. In this case Manny has taken the initiative to see a doctor and is receiving care for his medical concerns. Therefore, Angelina redirects him back to the activity at hand.]

Angelina: Manny, your father is right. You do have to be strong now, and you are. *[Angelina looks at Manny and then scans the group returning to Manny.]* When things don't go well, being strong means dealing with reality rather than avoiding it. You went to the doctor and got care for yourself, for your stomach, and now you are coming to this group to get started on finding a job. That is being strong.

Tom: She's right, Manny. Some of the other guys from my section who were laid off have been drunk for the last three days.

Angelina: Drinking isn't going to help them, but we need to make sure the group helps you. *[Cutting off* and *Redirecting]* Manny, let's get back to talking about your strengths.

Manny: OK, I was the man who understood the high voltage lines the best, and the university has quite a few of them because of all the engineering buildings. Maybe I should look for a job with the power company or the phone company. I wish I knew more about fiber optic cable.

[Manny has mentioned an area of interest for him that could be addressed through education. Since helping members start job training is part of the stated purpose of the group, Rose makes a direct inquiry about Manny's willingness to seek training in this area.]

Rose: Would you consider taking a short course in fiber optic cable if an employer wanted you to? *[Drawing out]*

Manny: Yes.

STUDY QUESTIONS

1. Explain how leaders use the purpose group when they help members clarify their goals.
2. Give examples of when you might use teaching to help group members.
3. What are some ways to draw out a quiet member?
4. Why is it important for leaders to link members in the group?
5. Why is it important to promote interaction among members?
6. How does using rounds help to balance participation in the group?
7. What are some reasons that you might cut off a group member?
8. Give an example of what you could say to cut off a member who was off the topic of the group.

KEY CONCEPTS

balancing participation p. 119   drawing out p. 120
cutting off p. 123   linking p. 118
clarifying personal goals p. 114   setting goals p. 114
cohesion p. 118   using rounds p. 121
direct teaching p. 116

REFERENCES

American Counseling Association. (2005). *ACA code of ethics.* Alexandria, VA: Author.

Bales, R. F., & Cohen, S. P. (1997). SYMLOG: A system for the multiple level observation of groups. New York: Free Press.

Crouch, E. C., Bloch, S., & Wanlass, J. (1994). Therapeutic factors: Interpersonal and intrapersonal mechanisms. In A. Fuhriman & G. M. Burlingame (Eds.), *Handbook of group psychotherapy: An empirical and clinical synthesis* (pp. 269–315). New York: Wiley.

Stockton, R. (Presenter). (1992). Association for Specialists in Group Work (Producer). *Developmental aspects of group counseling* [Videotape]. (Available from the American Counseling Association, Alexandria, VA).

Yalom, I. D. (1995). *The theory and practice of group psychotherapy* (4th ed.). New York: Basic Books.

CHAPTER 7
Mastering Group Leadership Skills: Part II

Learning Objectives

After studying this chapter you should be able to

- Explain the benefits and potential drawbacks of coleadership.
- Discuss the reasons why monitoring the group is important.
- Describe monitoring the group with or without a coleader.
- Discuss communicating with a coleader in the group.
- Explain why flexibility is important in group leadership.
- Identify the three types of situations in which flexibility may come into play.
- Explain how people, organizations, and other factors may influence leaders' ability to be flexible.

INTRODUCTION

As you have seen, several chapters in this book have dealt with the mastery of counseling skills, all of which are important in leading groups. Chapters 3 and 4 focused on individual counseling skills, such as questioning, feedback, and focusing, and how those skills apply to group leadership. Chapter 6 took skills mastery a step further by focusing on skills unique to groups such as linking, drawing out, and cutting off. In this chapter we will address coleading and additional group skills: monitoring the group, communicating with a coleader in the group, and developing flexibility. Each skill will be defined, discussed, and demonstrated as we have done in previous chapters, with exercises provided to help you learn to put the skills into practice.

WORKING WITH A COLEADER

This section of the chapter will start by providing information about general aspects of coleadership. We will follow that discussion by considering how coleadership and leader skills interact.

Thinking About Your Role in Relation to Your Coleader

You may have one of several different role relationships with your coleader. You might be a student coleading with another student, a student coleading with your instructor, a student or intern coleading with your supervisor, a student or intern coleading with a more experienced, licensed counselor, an intern or counselor coleading with another intern or counselor, or a counselor coleading with a cultural consultant or expert.

Some of these coleader pairs have either instructional or supervisory purposes resulting in the roles in the pairs being unequal in some way. For example, as a student you may colead with instructors, supervisors, or more experienced clinicians because they have knowledge and skills that allow them to serve as models for you as you learn to lead groups or as you expand the range of clients or topics with whom you work. The inequality in these pairs is centered in inequality of knowledge and experience. The more experienced coleader intentionally serves as a model for you to copy or adapt as you build your own skills and leadership style (Kottler, 1994). Another inequality that you may experience occurs if your coleader is licensed and you are not licensed. In this case, you must follow the in-group lead and the after-group directions of your coleader, because the licensed counselor is legally responsible for clients' welfare while participating in the group.

The inequality you experience in some coleading situations may stem from the fact that one of the coleaders is your course instructor or supervisor. At the end of the group, the coleader in charge is expected to evaluate you—this power differential may affect your experience of leading the group. If you are accepting of your role as a learner and if your skills are reasonably good, you may experience coleading as an excellent learning opportunity.

If you are coleading with a colleague and both of you are of equal and sufficient experience in leading groups, your relationship may be that of providing support for

each other. Your coleader may be a specialist in some area. If, for example, your coleader is a cultural expert, you may learn a great deal about your clients' culture and about the patterns of interpersonal interaction among members of their culture.

Ethical Considerations in Coleading

Perhaps the main point we would to call to your attention is that when you are coleading a group, you remain fully responsible for ethical and professional practice. Coleading does not in any way lessen your responsibility to the members or to the school or agency sponsoring the group. If anything, coleading increases your responsibility since you now share responsibility for the ethical practice of your coleader. This responsibility includes planning the group, screening the members, leading the group, responding to group issues that arise between sessions, keeping accurate records, and submitting accurate and timely bills.

Benefits and Potential Problems Associated with Coleading

One benefit of coleading is having the time and attention of two leaders available to members in the group. Kottler suggests that one leader accept the "responsibility of making certain each person has an opportunity to speak" (Kottler, 1994, p. 188). While this may seem a simple point, we would emphasize that it is primarily the learning resulting from members interacting that is therapeutic for members in groups.

In addition to having benefits for the group members, coleading may have benefits for the coleaders themselves. Carroll and Wiggins (1990) describe one advantage of coleadership as professional sharing. They describe an unequal pair and note that the "novice or counselor in training can try out responses and leads and benefit from an immediate discussion of their value after the session" (Carroll & Wiggins, 1990, p. 75). They further note that both coleaders benefit from mutual support during the session and from post-session debriefing.

Yalom wrote that a coleader can help "beginning therapists maintain objectivity in the face of massive group pressure" (Yalom, 1995, p. 415). When the group unites in wanting to give possibly harmful rather than therapeutic advice or directions to a member, the support of a coleader helps a beginning leader stand up to the group and oppose the counter-therapeutic advice or directions.

Yalom notes that a coleader can help a leader "to weather a group attack upon them and to help the group make constructive use of it" (Yalom, 1995, p. 415). Without the help of a coleader, it may be difficult for a solo leader to clarify attacks or to facilitate exploration of the anger underlying the attack.

Dividing the work may appear to be an advantage of coleading. Certainly, screening five potential members is easier than screening ten potential members. However, Yalom (1995) notes that splitting the screening may lead to a split in the members, with members feeling more connection to the leader who originally interviewed them. Due to the potential for splitting, he recommended all members be interviewed (screened) by both leaders.

Similarly, it is easier to write half the case notes or to alternate weeks of writing them. However, we caution you that when you make such divisions of work, you must take care to remain engaged with all aspects of the work related to the

group. One practice that would help you to do this is for both coleaders to countersign all documents generated in connection with the group. Reviewing and countersigning all documents that your coleader generates will prompt you to stay informed about the members and the group. If, for example, your coleader fields and responds to an emergency call in relation to a group member, countersigning that note as you read it in the record helps you enter the next session knowing what happened and what might possibly come up in group in relation to that event.

Reviewing all documents provides an opportunity for you to make additions to or revisions in the documents that you feel are needed for them to be both complete and accurate. If you and your coleader have disparate views about group process, this should be discussed with your clinical supervisor and documented in the supervision notes.

Coleading has potential problems. Yalom notes that "the disadvantages of the co-therapy (coleadership) format flow from problems in the relationship between the cotherapists" (Yalom, 1995, p. 416). The nature of the problems might include not knowing each other, not liking each other, using different theoretical approaches, or not making or having time to talk with each other about group sessions.

Kottler (1994) suggests that coleaders should complement each other in their personality, style, gender, and points on which they focus during the group. We would note that the complementary nature of coleaders depends on careful selection of coleaders. In addition to choosing someone with whom you work well, you should select a coleader who complements rather than mirrors your strengths and weaknesses. Together you can offer a broader range of expertise on the topic of the group and intervention techniques. In our own introductory classes on group work, we have identified one potential problem when students choose a complementary coleader. This problem occurs when an anxious student pairs up with a confident student. A dynamic is created in which the anxious student looks to the confident student to make him feel safe leading the group. Frequently, neither coleader ends up being satisfied with the relationship. Therefore, we would advise you as a student and a beginning leader to seek a coleader whose confidence level is about the same as yours but who complements you in some of the other dimensions described above.

When you begin to colead groups in your training program, it is important for you to be an equal partner in the coleader team. Being equal partners does not mean that you and your coleader must be alike or that you have to do the same things during the group. It means that you must both make an active contribution to leading the group. For example, it is fine for coleaders to have different roles during group discussion. One may facilitate the discussion while the other makes notes on the board. The coleaders may alternate these roles from discussion to discussion or from session to session. On the other hand, if one coleader always facilitates the discussions and the other coleader always takes notes, the group may come to see one coleader as "the leader" and the other coleader as "a secretary." Worse still is a situation in which one coleader is very active and the other coleader mostly contributes passive head nods. Contributing equally is especially difficult when one coleader is mentoring the other. Carroll and Wiggins (1990) noted that patience is required of the more experienced leader to allow the less experienced leader time to gain skills and confidence.

Finally, in clinical work the financial cost of providing coleaders for groups is a potential problem (Carroll & Wiggins, 1990). However, the advantages of the extra safety provided by coleaders and the extra attention to members may outweigh cost issues in large groups or in groups in which members exhibit a great deal of psychopathology.

Planning Together

In Chapter 5 we outlined a rather detailed process for planning a group. When you colead, you must attend to coleading as part of that planning process, including the following:

- Exploring the quality of the match with your proposed coleader.
- Setting a tone of caring, respect, and collaboration between coleaders.
- Planning your coleading process, including collaboration times, roles in group, acquisition of supervision, and process for paperwork completion.

During between-session meetings with your coleader, you should process the previous session, clarify the goals for the next session, and discuss how you will help individual members work toward their goals during that session. You also should agree which leadership roles each of you will take during the beginning, the working focus, and the processing and closure of the session.

If your group has long sessions with breaks in the middle of sessions, you should spend at least the first few minutes of the break checking in with your coleader. Consider how the beginning of the session went and if you need to make any changes in your plan for the second half of the group. Also review what roles the two of you will take in the next half of the session.

MONITORING THE GROUP

Groups provide a rich, interactive environment for clients' personal growth and development. Interpersonal interaction in groups can be very powerful, but the intensity is a double-edged sword: It can help members immensely, but it can also sometimes hurt them. In their landmark study of encounter groups, Lieberman, Yalom, and Miles (1973) indicated that while some members are "high learners" others can become "group casualties." For this reason, the top priority of group leaders is the safety of members.

Ethics Pointer

> According to the American Counseling Association's ethical guidelines, leaders must "respect the dignity and . . . promote the welfare of clients" (ACA, 2005, p. 4).

The more members in a group, the greater the number of possible interactions and the more challenging it is to keep track of the interactions and the ways in which individual members are reacting to them. Psychotherapy groups may be smaller in size than other groups, but the smaller size may be offset by more complex and

longer-standing member problems. Therefore, **monitoring** is an important skill, no matter the size of the group or the purpose of the group.

Definition of **monitoring**   The skill of observing and keeping track of all members of a group, particularly their participation in and reactions to the group process.

Effective monitoring requires simultaneous activity of the leader's auditory and visual senses. In other words, while you are listening with your ears to the member (or coleader) who is speaking, you are **scanning** the group with your eyes. Scanning enables you to be aware of what is going on in the entire group rather than focusing only on the member who is speaking.

Definition of **scanning**   The skill of looking briefly at each group member to observe facial expressions and body language while listening as a member or your coleader speaks.

Needless to say, monitoring the group tends to be easier when a leader is working with a coleader. One coleader can pay more attention to the member who is speaking while the other coleader scans the group. A group leader working alone must be able to juggle the two tasks simultaneously. Because you have only one set of eyes, you need to learn how to scan the group without making members feel that you are ignoring them when they speak. A leader experienced in monitoring gives eye contact to a member as she begins to speak but then scans the rest of the group to monitor the reactions of other members while continuing to listen carefully to the member who is speaking and giving that member occasional, brief eye contact. The leader attends to the speaking member's voice tones even while scanning the rest of the group and simultaneously attends to the content of the member's comments. At appropriate times, the leader returns to the speaking member and asks questions, summarizes, or in some other way actively leads the group. Good monitoring is a challenge to learn. You will feel awkward doing it at first, but it is a skill you will master with practice.

By being aware of the entire group, leaders can better provide for members' safety and promote interaction among members. For example, if scanning reveals that a member is beginning to show signs of intense emotion, the leader can intervene before the emotion builds. The leader may choose to intervene in a number of ways, such as directing the member showing strong emotion to talk to the speaking member, cutting off the speaking member, checking in with all members to see how they are experiencing the group, or directly addressing any safety issues that seem to be arising. Additionally, scanning the group may also reveal members who are showing signs of agreement, disagreement, or a desire to speak. A leader who monitors the group and notices these things will be better able to lead the group in desired directions. Consider the following examples of effective monitoring.

Example 1

In our first example, Devlin is leading a group for college students who have been referred by student conduct court for substance abuse counseling. In the first session members are doing a round, speaking about the event that got them into trouble.

Ned: It's just my RA. He's so difficult. Anytime I drink, he knocks on my door and tells me to be quiet. I wish he would just go away.

Devlin: He's always there and reprimands you.

Ned: Yeah, me—always me. He has it in for me.

[Devlin scans the group and notices that Jamir looks angry or upset.]

Devlin: Jamir, you look like you're having a reaction to what Ned is saying. *[Drawing out]*

Jamir: *[In an irritated tone]* He knocks on your door because it's 2:00 AM, and we can hear you way down the hall. The other night you puked in the bathroom and didn't clean it up. *[Jamir looks at Devlin.]* I was getting mad that he's not telling the whole story.

In this example Devlin monitored the group via scanning and noticed by Jamir's facial expression that he was having a reaction to the discussion. Jamir might not have spoken had Devlin not called on him, at which point Jamir is able to share his feelings appropriately. The group's process has also been helped, because Jamir has provided information that Devlin and the group need in order to understand Ned.

Example 2

In our second example Heidi is leading a career exploration group for sixth-grade students. The students have worked in dyads and discussed three careers they are interested in. Now the dyads are reporting their discussions to the whole group:

Donna: Well, I talked about working in the shoe shop like my mom or going into the navy, maybe as a secretary. And Clarence talked about being a welder or a nurse. Mostly he talked about being a nurse.

Clarence: I liked welding when we did it in the shop. I also thought about being a doctor like my father, but he works all the time. Sometimes he doesn't come home for a couple of days in a row.

Heidi: You'd like to help people who are sick but not to work all the time?

Clarence: Yup.

[Heidi has been scanning the group and has noticed Bart shaking his head.]

Heidi: Bart? Something wrong? *[Drawing out]*

Bart: Sure is. Nursing is a girl's job. That's what my dad said.

Heidi: That sounds a bit judgmental, Bart. I imagine when your dad was growing up nursing was mostly a job done by women because at that time women weren't allowed to become doctors, so if they wanted to help sick people, they became nurses. Nowadays, all of you can choose the job you want to prepare for.

Clarence: We went to the army hospital to see my uncle Frank when he came back from Iraq. His leg was in bad shape. Some of the nurses who took care of him were men, and they were officers. That's what I might like to do, be a nurse in the army.

In this example Heidi intervened based on her scanning of the group. The intervention protected Clarence and provided important information to Bart and all the members of the group.

Ethics Pointer

> This is an example of a situation in which a leader implemented ACA Ethics Code A.8.b that requires counselors (group leaders) to protect clients (group members).

Monitoring the Three Levels of Group Process

When you monitor groups, you should be mindful of monitoring the three levels of group process: the *intrapersonal* (the way an individual member is responding to the group based on his or her past), the *interpersonal* (interactions of members with each other), and the group as a whole. Leader interventions may address an individual member, interacting members, or the group as a whole.

Rounds, in which all members respond to a question or a direction from the leader, are ideal opportunities for monitoring at all three levels. Sometimes a leader may observe body language that indicates members are reacting to what is being said in the group, but it is not clear how to interpret the meaning of facial reactions or body language. The leader can use a round in such a situation in order to get confirmation or clarification of the meaning of the facial expressions and body language.

Observe how coleaders Michelle and Dawna use rounds to simultaneously hear from and monitor the members of a young mothers' group.

Dawna: Welcome! Let's start by looking at your homework to locate child care that you feel comfortable using. Could anyone get us started?

Dominique: I can. I called six places, but two of them were off the wall for price.

[Dawna, who is looking at Dominique, nods. Michelle, Dawna's coleader, scans the group.]

Dawna: They were just too much.

Dominique: I visited three places that were pretty good. The only thing that might be hard is that they are strict about picking up the kids by 6:00 PM.

[Michelle notices Alexa nodding and looking uncomfortable. She uses drawing out to get Alexa to talk.]

Michelle: Alexa, you're nodding. Did you have a similar experience?

[The coleaders now switch functions. While Michelle's attention is focused on Alexa, Dawna scans the rest of the group.]

Alexa: I found a place that was really good, but they charge a dollar a minute for every minute after six o'clock you are late picking up your child. *[Alexa begins to cry softly.]*

[Michelle sees the tears and tries to clarify what is happening for Alexa.]

Michelle: Alexa, this seems really hard right now.

Alexa: Mmm. Yes. I can't help thinking if my mother were still alive, she would take care of my son. She died last year, and it is so much harder to take care of Joey without her help.

In this example Michelle's monitoring of the group allows her to notice an emotional reaction in another member, Alexa, and make an intervention to clarify

Alexa's apparent reaction to group process. While Michelle then attends to Alexa, her coleader, Dawna, is able to take over monitoring the group. The group's discussion has brought forth Alexa's sense of loss. This loss was related to Alexa's personal past and is an example of the *intrapersonal* level of group process. After acknowledging Alexa's loss, the leaders must make a decision whether to return to the original check in round or to widen the focus and include discussion of possible grandparental involvement in child care. Either decision on the direction of the group would be consistent with the overall purpose of the group. Therefore, leaders have a choice of making the decision themselves or asking the group which way it would prefer to proceed. Michelle decides to let the group decide and sets up a round, using the following language:

Michelle: At this point we could either all talk about the involvement of your parents in caring for your children, or we could go back to the round we were doing. I'd like to hear from each member of the group which you prefer to do now.

In a session two weeks later in the same group, the topic is managing one's budget as a single parent.

Michelle: Dawna and I would like to welcome you to the fifth session of this group for young mothers. The purpose of today's session is to help you manage your budget. *[Michelle states the purpose of the session to help the group focus and begin.]*

Dawna: To get us started, we want to do a short activity. Michelle is passing out a worksheet with a picture of a pie on it, and we would like you to pair up with a partner and divide your pie to show how you spent your money this month. Marta and Dominique, you two sit together. Dorothy and Sue, work together. And, Alexa, work with Michelle.

[The members divide in pairs and begin to work on the budget pie. Dawna has chosen not to pair up and work with a partner. Instead, Dawna scans the group to monitor the dyads. She listens briefly to the discussion in each dyad and then checks in on the next group. After five minutes, Dawna lets the dyads know they have two minutes more. At the end of the two minutes, she calls the group back together.]

Dawna: OK, let's come back together as one group, please. *[The members regroup. Dawna then uses a round to hear from all members about their work on the activity.]*

In situations such as the one just described, it is very important for you to monitor what is going on with each dyad or small group. Sometimes you will need to walk about a room to do this. As you go around you should check to see that the members are on task, respond to member questions, and monitor member safety to be sure that members are not attacking one another within the dyads or small groups.

Exercises for Active Learning
Skill Development: Monitoring

Kyle and Mae are leading a group for high school students who have been placed on probation due to poor grades. According to school policy, while students are on probation, they may neither practice with the team nor play in school-sponsored

games. Members are discussing their efforts to stick to their study schedule. Evan is explaining why he is having problems when some of the members start laughing anxiously.

On the lines below, write what you could say to set up a round to ask the members about their reactions to Evan's disclosures.

_____

_____

_____

COMMUNICATING WITH YOUR COLEADER IN THE GROUP

Definition of **coleader communication**   The process in which coleaders check with each other or talk to each other in order to facilitate group process.

Although **coleader communication** may seem like a simple and obvious skill, it is a vitally important process for coleaders to keep the lines of communication open between them. In order to keep the group moving smoothly, leaders may need to communicate with each other in the group about their roles as leaders, deciding who will take on which role in specific situations. To keep each other on the same page, coleaders may check in with each other about their perceptions of group process, that is, what is happening in the group (Kottler, 1994). Communicating with a coleader might also include checking with each other about

- Readiness to move from one topic or activity to the next.
- Adjusting the timing of group activities.
- Possible changes in the direction of the group.
- When leader roles need to be divided.

Coleader communication involves discussing various types of information vital to keeping the group moving in appropriate and effective directions. The information may be procedural (who is going to do what, when should the group move from topic *x* to topic *y*), cognitive (what are the members thinking about the group process), contextual (what is the surrounding information leading the group to think in such a way), emotional (what are the leaders feeling during the sessions or overall), and so forth. The important thing is that coleaders keep the lines of communication between each other open. Otherwise, you may end up pulling in various directions, impeding group process, and risking member safety.

Ethics Pointer

ACA Ethics Code A.8.b requires counselors (leaders) to protect clients (members) (American Counseling Association, 2005). Good communication between coleaders facilitates member safety.

Here are some examples of the uses of coleader communication.

Example 1

Rusty and Quincy are leading a group to teach stress reduction techniques to boys age 12 and 13 who have problems with anger management. Quincy is leading the group in a meditation exercise.

Quincy: . . . and clench your hands tight. Feel the tension. . . . now slowly let them relax.

[At this point David begins to cry and runs out of the room. Rusty communicates with Quincy about what to do.]

Rusty: Quincy, I'm going to check on David, and you continue with the group.

[Quincy nods in agreement and continues to lead the meditation exercise]

Example 2

In this example Sarah and Nicki are coleading a group for recently (and unexpectedly) divorced women. The members have just discussed their rather grim financial situations. Then, at the suggestion of Sarah, they identify support networks.

Sarah: I believe each of you has identified someone to talk to about your financial situation, right? *[No one responds, but a few members give slight nods. A couple of minutes pass and no one says anything.]*

Sarah: Nicki, I'm wondering what you think is happening in the group right now. *[Sarah communicates with her coleader, Nicki, by asking for her perceptions of what is happening in the group]*

Nicki: *[Looking at the group]* I'm thinking you're all getting tired.

Sarah: *[Also looking at the group]* You've described some pretty tough situations.

Brenda: Tired and discouraged. *[Several members nod.]*

Sarah: I think maybe this is enough for tonight. *[Again, some members nod.]*

Nicki: *[Looking at Sarah]* I think we should end with some encouragement. *[Nicki is communicating with her coleader, making a plan of action]*

[At this suggestion, several members who had been silent and looking down now look up toward Nicki. Sarah also nods to Nicki.]

Nicki: OK, let's go around, and I want each of you to turn to the person on your right and say a few words of encouragement. Who can start?

Helen: I can. Donna, times are tough now, but you are a smart woman and you can find your way through this. Call me if you need to talk. [**YTF Reminder:** Instillation of hope]

In this example, note how coleader communicating facilitated group process. First, the coleaders communicated with each other in the group to break through a lengthy period of silence. Then, the coleaders communicated with each other in the group about how to proceed.

Example 3

In this example, coleaders communicate about the timing of activities within a session. Mac and Jorge are school counselors leading a group of 13- and 14-year-old adolescent boys who are in a group working on anger management. The group has been discussing the last time each member was sent home from school for fighting. Jorge has been leading the discussion while Mac monitors the group as a whole. Jorge communicates with Mac.

Jorge: Mac, is there anything you'd like to add, or do you think we are ready to move on?

Mac: I think this has been a good discussion. Looking at the clock, I'm wondering if we want to do that next activity before or after we take our break.

Jorge: Why don't we take our break now, and after break we'll do the activity.

Mac: *[To the members]* OK, we're going to take our break now and be ready to go again in 15 minutes.

Example 4

In this example we return to the young mothers' group co-led by Michelle and Dawna introduced earlier in the chapter. At this point the group is in its seventh session, which is focused on members' current housing situations and on considering whether or not improved housing should be a goal. Michelle and Dawna started the group by asking the members to draw pictures of their current homes and share their drawings with the group. Then Michelle and Dawna asked the members to work in dyads, first listing the members of their households and then talking about what each household member needs at this time in his or her life. The entire group has now reassembled to process the activity.

Michelle: Before we start talking, I'd like each of you to stand the picture you made of your current home up by the board. Use the chalkboard tray to prop it up.

All of the members do as requested. When all the drawings are displayed together, it appears to Michelle and Dawna that the young mothers and their families are living in adequate housing—all except Dorothy. Her drawing appears to be of a small studio apartment.

Dawna: How about if we do it this way. Go through the members in your household and show us in your picture how that person uses space in your house.

Michelle: *[Looks at Dawna to get nonverbal permission to clarify the point; Dawna nods.]* Show us where they sleep and play and so on. *[Coleader communication]*

Sue: *[Starts pointing to her drawing]* I'll start. Tommy and Tony are twins, so they have bunk beds and share this room. It's not very big, but basically all they do is sleep there. They play on the carpet in the middle of the living room floor. It's big and I find it easy to keep an eye on them there. I sleep in that room and have a desk set up in the corner with my computer so that I can see the boys playing in the living room. Then there's the bathroom and the kitchen, and they are good enough. We don't have a yard, but we are right across the street from the park, and we go there almost every day.

Dominique:	Our place is a little bigger but maybe not set up as well because it's upstairs and downstairs, and my kids are a little older. Mary is five and Anne is nine. Both girls have their own rooms. Mary likes to paint and draw, so I made a corner of her room into her "studio." Anne reads a lot in her room. I decided that I would rather sleep on the couch and let each of them have their own room. It's not great for me, but it's better for them. I don't like sleeping downstairs and having them upstairs. I'd like to move to a one-level apartment, but I'd only move if the girls didn't have to change schools.
Alexa:	Good schools are very important.
Dominique:	You can say that again.
Dawna:	*[Looks at Michelle]* I'd like to hear from Dorothy next. What do you think, Michelle? *[Coleader communication]*
Michelle:	Yes, absolutely. Dorothy? *[Michelle uses drawing out to invite Dorothy to participate.]*
Dorothy:	Our apartment complex has a center area for the kids to play away from the road. You can't see them from the road.
	[Michelle sees puzzled looks on some of the members' faces, and she too is puzzled. She follows with a closed question to get specific information.]
Michelle:	So you like the play area because it's protected?
	[Dorothy puts her head down a little and talks in a soft voice.]
Dorothy:	Yes, I have to protect us from Martin. *[The group knows that Martin is the father of Dorothy's son.]*
	[While Dawna scans the group, Michelle addresses the safety issue directly.]
Michelle:	You told us he threatened you once before. Dorothy, is he threatening you now? *[Closed question]*
Dorothy:	He doesn't know where we are, but he keeps calling my mother and leaving threats on her answering machine. He keeps saying he's going to find us.
Marta:	You're smart to stay out of his way.
Sue:	I know that area. Maybe I could help you look for a little bigger place that is still protected.
Dorothy:	OK. I'd like us to have a better home as long as it's safe.
Dawna:	Dorothy, I'd like to give Martin's probation officer a call and fill her in. Would I have your permission to do that? I think the probation officer might keep closer track of Martin if she was aware that he was still threatening you.
Dorothy:	His probation officer is pretty good. I think she would help. You can call her.

In the preceding example the coleaders communicated with each other multiple times so that they were working together as they addressed a safety issue that emerged during the group. They checked with each other when one member's drawing took the discussion outside the range they expected. When it became obvious that they were dealing with a safety issue, they used eye contact and head nods to

maintain communication as they compassionately but directly addressed the safety issue. At the end of the group, the leaders will have Dorothy sign a release form allowing them to call the probation officer.

Exercises for Active Learning
Skill Development: Communicating with a Coleader

You and Fritz are leading a group to teach parenting skills to parents in their twenties. The group is talking about how difficult it is to be consistent in dealing with toddlers. One of the mothers, Cara, begins to look frustrated or perhaps angry as her husband, Steve, speaks. At the same time Matt, who is a friend of Steve's, begins drumming his fingers on the table. On the lines below, write what you might say to check with Fritz, your coleader, about his perception of what is happening in the group.

_____

_____

Later in the same group you are monitoring the group while Fritz works with a pair of members. You notice that the time is getting close to transition the group to processing and closure. You wonder if Fritz plans to make the transition soon or if he has lost track of the time. On the lines below, write what you could say to Fritz to check out the timing of the group from this point forward.

_____

_____

FLEXIBILITY

***Definition of* flexibility**   The ability of leaders to be open and responsive to new information about the needs of the members and appropriately adjust the direction of the discussion as the group progresses.

We chose to conclude the discussion of group leadership skills with **flexibility,** because it is the skill that enhances the value of all the other skills. Groups are a living organism with fluid processes that can often be unpredictable and move in directions that are unanticipated but potentially more therapeutic than the original planned direction. Effective leaders must be goal directed, but at the same time, they cannot be rigid. They need to be able to move with the flow of the members' needs and interests to the degree that such movement is appropriate in the given group.

In Chapter 5 we emphasized the importance of planning as the foundation of professional and ethical practice. Flexibility enables the leader to respond to the living nature, the live action of the group. Planning and flexibility complement each other. Leaders must both be responsible in planning the group and develop the ability to adjust to the group. Flexibility meets member needs, follows member interest, and uses the energy of the group. Flexibility allows leaders to be creative and spontaneous.

Because flexibility is a complex topic, the discussion will be divided into three subsections. The first subsection clarifies the definition of flexibility by illustrating three typical situations in which leaders are faced with decisions regarding the direction of the group and may need to exercise flexibility. In the second subsection we discuss factors that influence a leader's ability to be flexible. In the third subsection we provide advice on how leaders can improve their flexibility.

Situations in Which Flexibility May Come into Play

Essentially, flexibility comes into play in three situations in groups: (1) when a member or members indicate an urgent need to discuss a particular topic, (2) when an obviously relevant but not originally planned topic presents itself, and (3) when a necessary interruption to discuss content over process (or vice versa) presents itself. As you will see, all of these situations are external to a leader's planning (the first situation arises from the group, the second and third situations develop independent from the planned topic), but all of these situations require leader attention.

Emergence of an Urgent Topic

Sometimes members either open or interrupt the group by requesting the discussion of an urgent topic. Leaders must choose whether to follow the plan for the group or to address the urgent topic. For example, we, the authors, led a skills training group for graduate students in counseling several days after the terrorist attacks on the United States on September 11, 2001. Several members opened the group that evening by saying that they needed to use the group to process what had been going on at their work sites, many of which had been overwhelmed by multiple self-referrals for mental health care in the wake of 9/11. Responding to the members' request to address this urgent topic meant changing the entire plan for the session. Because we had experience coleading so many groups together, we only needed to look at one another to communicate our agreement to make the change. We knew, however, that when leaders decide to change the focus of the group, they should provide an explanation of why and how focus is changing. This is what we said:

Betsy: Tonight we were supposed to focus on developing agendas for task work groups; but as I listen to you, it seems you need to process what it has been like for you at work in a time of crisis. Marty?

Marty: Yes, many of you have had to handle a flood of clients who arrived in crisis mode needing help, and in some cases these clients may have needed hospitalization. You did what was needed for the clients, and now you need to do some reflection and self-care. So that is what we will focus on for the next hour or so.

Betsy: Let's go around and hear briefly what your week has been like and how you are feeling about it now that you have had a chance to catch your breath.

Notice that in this transition we made it clear to the members that the group was going to move in an unexpected direction, we provided a time frame, and some indication of what was expected of members was also clarified. Not all urgent topic

situations will be as all-encompassing as the one above. Sometimes a single member is in crisis and needs to discuss an urgent topic. Whether or not to change the focus of the group is a tougher call for the leader to make in such situations. With practice, however, leaders can become more adept at determining which situations call for transition of group focus and which might be better handled one-on-one outside of the group with that particular member.

Change of Focus

Sometimes the activity or discussion at the beginning of a session may lead to an obvious, relevant focus that was not intended for the working focus of the session. The leader must decide whether to stick with the planned working focus of the session or address the focus that evolved during the beginning of the session. For example, a round in which members are asked about positive aspects of their week may instead result in multiple expressions of deep loss or deep anger from members. In the next example from a natural disaster recovery group, the leader needs to decide whether to pursue a focus on these negative emotions associated with a loss (in this case, a hurricane) or to redirect the group toward the planned focus on positive emotions. In Response 1 the leader decides to pursue the original plan and redirect the members' focus toward the positive. In Response 2 the leader opts to change the focus of the group based on the members' expressed negative emotions.

Response 1

Leader: I'm hearing a really deep sense of loss, a heavy burden. That sense of loss is real and is going to be with you for a long time. You lost so much in the hurricane. Reconstructing your life is going to take a long time. What we have to do in group is to help you process the loss by doing things like we did last week. But we also have to see and appreciate the positives. It's the positives that give hope. We will revisit processing loss over the next few weeks, but right now I am going to ask you to think about the positives and say just a bit about one of them. Clyde, could you start?

Response 2

Leader: What I'm hearing is the losses are too heavy right now. You are still just realizing what they mean to you. What I'd like you to do is to make some groups of three or four and talk for a few minutes about one of those losses you're just beginning to understand.

Notice that in the first response (redirecting the group back to the plan) the leader is careful to acknowledge the validity of the members' concerns while explaining why the group should maintain the planned focus on positive emotions. The leader is working to activate the therapeutic factor *instillation of hope*. In the second response, the leader decides to be flexible and move with the relevant new direction of the group. Neither response is right or wrong. The leader may decide to be flexible or not be flexible, but either way, the leader must clarify his reasons for maintaining or changing focus.

Content Versus Process

Sometimes the leader may notice a point in a session where it becomes clear that the focus of the group should be on content rather than process, or vice versa. For instance, if in a support group for cancer patients, the group is processing fears about treatments and it becomes obvious that some members do not have a clear understanding of the medical treatments under consideration, the leader might redirect the group from processing fears to focusing on the specifics of medical procedures (direct teaching of content). In contrast, if during direct teaching about types of treatments a member starts to cry, the leader probably should shift to a processing focus.

Sometimes it's wise for the leader to not only shift group focus in such situations but to also be flexible regarding the closing time of the group. If the group's work proves emotionally exhausting and members are spent, the leader may end the group early. When doing so, it is important for the leader to help members process and consolidate gains they have made during the session and end the session on a positive note, such as the following:

"You've just done a lot of intense work, and you made a lot of progress. My sense is that thinking about these things has been useful, but you've done about all the work you can for one session. I can see it's about half an hour early, but this is a good place to consolidate gains and end for the evening, so I'm going to explain how we will do that. What I want you to do now is to sit with a partner for just a couple of minutes and talk about the most important thing you learned tonight. After we do that, I'll read the short inspiration piece just as we usually do at the end."

Leader Readiness for Group Flexibility

Leaders have a number of questions to ask themselves when they consider the appropriateness of bringing flexibility into the group.

How well does the leader know the members?   Knowing the members of the group increases the leader's ability to understand member needs and interests and to predict how members might respond to unplanned topics and processes brought into the session. The better the leader knows the members, the better the leader can provide for member safety when discussing unplanned topics and/or responding to unplanned directions in the group brought to light by members or unearthed during discussion.

What are the leader's skills and experience levels?   Beginning leaders with less experience and less finely honed leadership skills are likely to feel more confident leading groups that have a clear structure and don't deviate from the group's plan. As leaders gain experience, they are likely to become more confident being flexible in the group and are likely to make better decisions about when and when not to change plans mid-group.

Is the leader sufficiently knowledgeable on the topic to pursue members' suggested changes in content focus?   A member may ask for a change of focus to an area about which the leader has little expertise and/or has had little time to prepare to discuss. In such cases the leader should be cautious about moving the work

of the group in the new direction. The leader may wish to consider if a coleader possesses sufficient expertise to help shift the direction of focus. If the change in focus is important, the leader should let the group know that the topic is important and will be addressed, but postpone the topic for another session, if possible.

Does the leader have any preplanned materials available that may be used to help pursue an unplanned topic?   If the leader has pre-prepared materials available within easy access on a variety of topics related to the group's focus, these might prove useful when the leader needs to respond flexibly to the needs or interests of members. Leaders should train themselves to develop a set of resources they may consult in such situations. For example, if a leader leads a similar group on a regular basis, she should not simply rely on a set of handwritten notes to follow when leading the group, but spend the time to develop resources (such as overheads, charts, or PowerPoint presentations) based on topics raised in previous groups, resources that can be reused. In short, planning ahead allows for increased flexibility.

What is the leader's comfort level with the proposed topic, and can the leader anticipate the group's comfort level on the topic?   If a leader is significantly uncomfortable with a topic or perceives that other members might not be comfortable with the topic, he may not want to make an unplanned venture into that topic area. For instance, if a group consists of a variety of people dealing with sexual abuse trauma and one member hints that she may be repeating the cycle of abuse on her own children, the leader may not be prepared to confront that issue or ask other members to confront it either. Leaders should, however, discuss their discomfort with their clinical supervisors since that discomfort may represent a limitation of clinical skills. When considering emotions that might be raised in members when dealing with a potentially uncomfortable or explosive unplanned topic, it may be wise for the leader to keep the group within a range of moderate emotional stimulation and avoid promoting extremely intense emotions in the group (Lieberman, Yalom, & Miles, 1973).

Will the group leader be able to maintain overall group goals after venturing into an unplanned topic? Will the leader be able to return to the main plan of the group?   Even if a leader is convinced that the unplanned work of the group has been more valuable and accomplished more than the original plan would have, the leader still needs to ensure that the group remains focused on overall group goals. If an unplanned topic ventures significantly off course, the leader may want to reconsider taking that direction, as the original session plan may need to be eliminated both in the current and future sessions. If the leader does opt to move in that entirely different direction, he will need to adjust the group's processing and closure to reflect the work the group actually did and make sure that the processing and closure is linked back to the group's goals.

Group Member Readiness for Flexibility

As leaders need to ask themselves the previous questions related to their ability to be flexible, they also need to ask themselves a number of questions from the perspective of members.

How central is the topic to the needs of all members?   Sometimes members ask about or begin discussions about topics that are not central to either their own needs or to the needs of the group as a whole. While such topics may be interesting, the resulting discussions are unlikely to help members squarely address issues that brought them to counseling in the first place. Leaders must keep the group focused on productive work directly related to overall group goals.

How interested are all members in an unplanned topic?   One of the leader's goals is to keep the entire group consistently engaged. For that reason, leaders should focus the group's energies on issues of interest to the entire group, not on issues of interest to only one or two group members. If a member brings up an issue important to her progress but of little interest or relevance to other members, the leader should consider working on the issue minimally in the group and provide options for the member to discuss her issue outside of the group, via referral or individual session.

How well do the members understand group process? How cohesive is the group?
To new members, changing the focus to an unplanned topic mid-session might be confusing. After members participate in a group for a while, they will better equipped to deal with the ways in which group process can change. Additionally, members may resent the requests of other members to change focus mid-session when the group is still in its early sessions. As group cohesiveness develops, members may become more open to moving with the group. Leaders may want to gradually introduce the concept of flexibility into the group as group cohesiveness develops and members grow to understand group process.

Is the topic potentially threatening to member safety?   The leader is charged with providing for the safety of all members. Members who seem confident, stable, and open to the unexpected will be able to handle a more flexible format. On the other hand, members who seem anxious, whose stability is questionable, and who respond to the unexpected with anxiety or defensiveness may do better with a more planned group. Therefore, in the interest of safety, if a leader thinks that pursuing an unplanned topic is likely to be unsafe for even one member of the group, the leader should stick to the original plan.

Are appropriate and effective support systems, such as hotlines or additional individual counseling services, available outside of the group if a member needs them?   Safety issues are paramount, and leaders need to be consistently aware of them, not only within the group but outside of the group. Considering member support systems is part of the leader's safety assessment along with being careful about member readiness to address requested topics within the group. Members might ask to address a topic that could be profitably discussed but would require increasing support systems prior to focusing on the topic. Therefore, the leader should be aware of support systems available outside of the group and remind members of what these systems are by reiterating hotline phone numbers and information on obtaining individual counseling.

Factors Influencing Flexibility: Group Purpose, Timing, and Informed Consent

Not only do leaders and members influence group flexibility, but the realities of the group process also come into play. Three factors influence flexibility within a group: (1) maintaining the group's purpose, (2) staying within the group's allotted timeframe, and (3) staying within the informed consent guidelines of the group. The first two factors of purpose and timing should be considered in tandem, because purpose and timing directly influence one another. Even if the leader decides that a new topic is appropriate, he must consider the timing involved as well. Note how purpose and timing are interrelated in the following questions leaders should ask themselves.

Where does the proposed topic fit in a logical sequence of issues related to the purpose of the group?   If the proposed topic does in fact fit appropriately within group goals, the leader should make an attempt to discuss the topic during an appropriate session—not necessarily right away—in order to maximize time considerations. If the topic that is raised or that presents itself is important but would more appropriately fit and flow smoothly within a later session, the leader should let the members know that the topic will be discussed, however, not right away. In this way members will know their request is being responded to and taken seriously.

What is the relative priority of this unplanned topic versus the topics already planned for the remaining sessions of the group?   Leaders should also ask themselves about the relative priority of an unplanned topic. If the topic is appropriate for the group but discussion of the topic would take away from more important topics to be discussed within the group's allotted timeframe, the leader should think twice about changing the group's focus. In cases like this the leader should be honest with the group about why the topic cannot be discussed in depth. If one or more members emphatically want to discuss the unplanned topic, the leader can either deal with the topic quickly, volunteer to discuss the topic with the interested parties outside of group, or recommend alternate resources for the interested parties to consult.

In addition to purpose and timing, leaders must also keep in mind that they need to stay consistent with the consent forms signed by members prior to entering the group. If a member requests a topic that is clearly outside of the informed consent form signed by all members, the leader needs to carefully consider moving into that unexpected topic before proceeding and possibly seek advice from a clinical supervisor. An example of a situation in which a leader might be confronted with an informed consent issue would be a request by an adolescent to discuss birth control methods in a group that was advertised as dealing with a different topic, such as stress. When there is an issue about informed consent, the leader has two possible choices: either tell the members that the group needs to stay within the consent area given, or obtain a supplementary signed consent form from everyone who signed the original consent form. In the above case a new signed consent form would need to be obtained from both members and parents. If even one member cannot or does not want to consent to the new topic, the leader should not pursue the new topic.

Ethics Pointer

ACA Ethics Code A.2.a describes informed consent as an ongoing part of the counseling process (American Counseling Association, 2005, p. 4). This means that major changes in the intended content or process of the group for which informed consent was originally given may require a re-explanation of the group and a revised signed consent form.

Other Factors Influencing Flexibility: The Agency and the Funding Source

Flexibility may also be influenced by matters beyond the control of the leader, such as organizational requirements dictated by the agency within which the group operates and the funding source.

Does the proposed topic fit within the general framework of the group approved by the agency? When the leader creates the original plan for the group, she is likely to have to provide the plan to the agency within which the group operates and gain approval from the agency. The agency may be a nonprofit agency, a school, a federal organization, or other type of agency. Regardless, if the leader wants to change the group's plan based on issues that arise from members or from the discussion, she should get any needed approval from the agency.

How does the group meeting space affect flexibility? Sometimes a leader may lead a group in an office or group room that allows for spontaneous access to materials ranging from art supplies to teaching materials. In such cases flexibility may be easier. In other cases limited access to preplanned materials may result in less flexibility.

Can the proposed topic be related to the requirements of external payers? If a leader or the agency within which he holds the group accepts payments from insurance plans or state or federal agencies, the leader may be limited in the degree of flexibility he can bring to the group. This is true both in terms of the number of group sessions and also the content of the sessions. In general, leaders will have to document that the content of the sessions is related to the group guidelines approved in advance by the payer, or payment may be denied. Further, if a post-group quality assurance review reveals that the leader delivered services not approved by the payer, the leader or agency may be required to return money to the payer. Therefore, leaders need to keep such considerations firmly in mind when deciding whether or not to move in unplanned group directions.

Exercises for Active Learning
Skill Development: Flexibility

Pauline and Anita are leading a group for adults in their 50s who want to examine their career satisfaction and possibly do a midlife career change. Pauline has 6 years' experience since she graduated with her counseling degree. That experience is almost totally in career counseling. Anita is a master's level intern who has very little

experience leading groups. Anita's graduate school provided a strong and wide base of coursework as well as an opportunity to take three electives. For her electives, Anita picked two courses on substance abuse and one on Gestalt counseling.

The group is in the second session when Brad makes the following request:

Brad: What I want is to know how to balance my career versus my marriage. I'd like a more satisfying job, one focused on helping people and not just making money but . . . my wife, she likes money. I think she'd leave me.

Fred: Olag and I had a similar discussion during break. Could you talk about that and maybe have an aggressive divorce lawyer come and talk to the group?

On the lines below, make some notes about the factors that might influence a group's ability to be flexible in this situation.

_____

_____

_____

_____

_____

INTEGRATIVE CASE EXAMPLE: ICE-FISHING-ACCIDENT GRIEF GROUP

In this chapter's extended example, Ed and Jack are counselors working in a popular ice-fishing region in the upper Midwest. Traditionally, every other Saturday from early January through late March a group of eight to ten members of the local volunteer fire department go out fishing together. At the end of the season, the fire department throws a party and holds a mock award ceremony for the biggest fish that got away. They have been doing this for 14 years, but this year things are very different. Starting in early March temperatures were unseasonably warm. Lows did not go below freezing for several nights. But because the wind blew powder snow over the lake, the thinning condition of the ice was not readily apparent, even to the local authorities. Two days ago a group of eight fishers drove their trucks over the ice out to their ice-fishing huts, as they had all winter long. In the evening all of the groups packed up their vehicles just before sunset and began the trip to shore. The first of the three trucks hit a soft spot in the ice and sank into the frigid water. Two of the four passengers in the truck escaped from the windows. However, the other two passengers went under the ice with the truck. Fishers from two other vehicles saw what happened and made a rescue attempt, which resulted in the rescue of one of the two fishers who had gone under but had managed to extract himself from the truck. Alan, the other person who had gone underwater, drowned. His body was later retrieved by special divers from the state police.

For 36 hours following the accident, the seven fishing friends sat around the firehouse, not saying much, but somehow finding comfort in each other's company. Dale, the fire chief, stayed with them all night and the next day. That evening he said, "Hey, go home all of you and get some rest." But when he came back in

the morning, they were all still there. So he phoned the community's counseling center and asked Ed and Jack to run a grief group for the survivors of the tragedy: Janice, Vladimir, Nicholas, Philip, Otto, Mary, and Eric.

Planning the Grief Group

The purpose of this group has been defined by the circumstances under which it is being formed, that is, to help the firefighters involved in the ice-fishing accident talk about the experience they had and the feelings and fears they are experiencing. Because the need for the group is immediate, there isn't much time for planning. Fortunately, Ed and Jack have had experience in the past with crisis intervention groups. They quickly plan for three two-hour sessions to be held the next three nights.

Screening for the Grief Group

It is now two full days since the accident, and Ed and Jack are screening candidates for the group. Ed starts with Vladimir.

Ed: So you're Vladimir, and you were thinking about being in the grief group.

Vladimir: Yes. It was very upsetting. *[Vladimir speaks very softly, and his face looks like he might cry.]*

Ed: It would be upsetting for anybody. You saw the whole thing didn't you? *[Drawing out]*

Vladimir: Our jeep was a ways behind the truck when it went through the ice. We weren't very far from the shore. I was driving, and the others told me, "Get to shore before we go under too." Once we got on shore, Janice went back to pull up the ones that had gone under.

Ed: What did you do?

Vladimir: I stayed in the jeep and called the police and the emergency vehicles. But . . . but I keep wondering if I should have gone back into the water and helped . . . if I might have been able to save them. Last night I had a nightmare about being under the ice.

Ed: So you're having doubts and you're having nightmares. I think this group could help you. The purpose of the group we are planning is to help you talk about the experience you had and these feelings and fears that you are experiencing. It's going to be three sessions—the next three nights—and if you join the group, we expect you to make a commitment to come to all of them. We also ask you to make a commitment to talk about these things with the other members so they can help you, and you can help them.

Vladimir: I will do that. I need to talk it out here because my wife and friends outside the fire department don't understand how upset I am.

Ed: Three sessions isn't very long, but it's long enough to make progress if you set a specific goal to work on in the group. Can you say something specific you would like to work on? *[Here Ed is providing encouragement and helping Vladimir clarify goals.]*

Vladimir: I'd like to talk with the others and feel like we did our best to save Alan and that what I did was worthwhile.

Ed: That sounds like a good goal.

In this screening, Ed has seen that Vladimir is able to talk about his experiences both at the time of the accident and since that time. Ed clarified the purpose of the group and helped Vladimir set a personal goal that was related to the purpose of the group. Further, Vladimir made a commitment to attend and participate in the group. Vladimir appears to be an appropriate member for the group.

Ed's coleader, Jack, is screening Janice. Jack has reviewed the purpose of the group with Janice, who indicates she would like to be part of the group.

Jack: Janice, you were one of the people who went into the water to rescue people. Is that correct?

Janice: Mmhm. *[She sighs deeply.]* Those men in the truck, they've been my friends since high school. *[Janice is in her 40s or 50s.]* I know their families. *[Tears flow down her face.]*

At this point, Jack is wondering if being in the group might be too much for Janice at this time.

Janice: I keep seeing Alan's face; he was the one who drowned. I keep seeing his face in my mind. I keep telling myself this couldn't happen. *[She looks squarely at Jack.]* His wife, Laura, is one of my closest friends. His boys are five and six, and they're not going to have their dad. How will I face them?

Jack: So when you go to the funeral, you're going to see Laura and the boys . . .

Janice: And they're going to ask me why I didn't save their dad.

Jack: Janice, you risked your life, and one person was saved.

[Janice nods. Jack notices that Janice is shaking.]

Jack: You're still shaking when you talk about it.

Janice: I'm still shaking most of the time. I feel chilled to the bone.

Jack: How long were you in the water?

Janice: In and out about an hour. I was shivering pretty badly.

Jack: Janice, have you been checked by the doctor since you came back from the lake?

Janice: No.

Jack: I'd like you to go and be checked out now, for your own safety.

Janice: I want to be in the group. I want to work out what to say at the wake. There won't be anyone to help me then. And . . . and I want to talk with all the others.

Jack: As long as the doctor says you're OK, you can be in the group, but I want to give you permission to take care of yourself now. Can you drive yourself to the hospital, or do you want me to drive you?

Janice: You can drive, and I'd like Mary to come.

Jack: OK. Let's go.

Jack is satisfied that Janice is able to articulate a goal appropriate for the group. She is intensely affected by the tragedy she experienced but is able to talk about it, her condition, and her fears of facing others at the wake. It is likely that

she will both benefit from and contribute to the group. If the doctors clear Janice, Jack will talk with her more about committing to attendance. During this screening interview, Jack has acted to protect the physical health and safety of a prospective member. During screening, you should not hesitate to ask members about health issues that may be related to their participation in the planned group. If the effects of a member's health issues on her participation or the interrelationship between health issues and concerns or symptoms that bring the member to the group are unclear, you should refer the potential member for an appropriate medical evaluation. Your leader intervention protects the safety of the members.

While Jack is at the hospital, Ed is screening Philip.

Ed: Philip, the reason we screen members is to make sure that you are a good fit for the group and that you understand what to expect and it sounds right for you.

Philip: Well, I'm curious, but I don't really understand why you are running a group for the people that let Alan drown.

[While Ed hears the accusation in Philip's reply, he chooses not to focus on it at this point.]

Ed: Philip, tell me a little bit about what happened out there and how it's affected you. *[Drawing out]*

Philip: He drowned, and my truck went through the ice. And I'm going to have to pay a lot of money because it wasn't insured. Makes me so mad . . .

Ed: What did you feel when you were out there?

Philip: I just want to know who is responsible. I'm so angry. When I find out how this happened, someone is going to pay. *[Philip sounds vengeful here. He is clenching his jaws.]*

Ed: Philip, it sounds like you're pretty angry.

Philip: Yes.

Ed: And you're having a hard time thinking beyond that. You need to replace your truck. That is your main goal.

Philip: It was nearly new.

Ed: A new truck is a lot to lose. You might need to focus on that now and maybe later I can help you find some individual counseling or another group. *[Referral]*

Ed quickly noted Philip's angry affect and vengeful goals. He did not lecture Philip but rather screened him out of the group. Note that Ed reworded Philip's goals into positive actions. Ed also indicated that counseling would be beneficial but not in this group, and he offered to help make a referral. Also by screening Philip out of the group, Ed is acting for the safety of the other members—a primary leader responsibility. In all, eight of the nine people involved in the ice-fishing accident were screened into the group.

Leading the First Session

Ed and Jack's goal for the first session is to clarify what happened from the perspective of the different members and identify the feelings the members experienced during the event.

Ed: Jack and I would like to welcome you to the group.

[Ed proceeds to review the purpose of the group. The group agrees to norms Ed suggests for attendance and confidentiality. The group begins to talk about their goals.]

Otto: My goal is to feel more, to feel better. I think I'm still in shock at what happened.

Jack: You feel a little overwhelmed?

Otto: Yes, like numb most of the time and then I woke up last night very sad.

Jack: The feelings are there, but sometimes it is hard to get in touch with them?

Otto: Exactly!

Ed: Janice?

Janice: I have to figure out what to say at the wake when people ask me what happened. I'd like to practice what I'll say to Alan's wife and his two boys.

Otto: That's going to be hard to do.

Janice: Very hard.

Jack: Eric?

Eric: I always felt very safe on the ice before all this. I was careful but I felt safe. I'd like to work on getting my sense of safety back.

Ed: It's going to be harder for you to trust the ice now and to trust your own judgment. *[Several members nod in agreement.]*

Eric: I really love to fish, and I don't want this to ruin it forever.

Ed: Nick? *[Drawing out]*

Nick looks at the floor and says nothing. This is the second time that Nick has acted like he won't participate. He is on his way to becoming a silent member—someone who does not speak in the group. Jack now makes an effort to draw out Nick and help him participate. Note that he does not attack Nick for his silence. Rather than forcing the issue of Nick talking about his goals (a content focus), Jack focuses on Nick's difficulty participating (a process focus).

Jack: This is the second time we've come to you, and you haven't said anything. What is hard Nick? *[Drawing out]*

Nick: It's hard to know that I'm alive and Alan isn't.

[Ed has been monitoring the group, scanning the group with his eyes. He noticed Vladimir nodding, so he now links these two members.]

Ed: You're nodding, Vladimir. You've been thinking about this too? *[Vladimir nods.]* Can you say something to Nick about how you are connecting with him?

Vladimir: *[Vladimir looks directly at Nick.]* I keep thinking I'm alive and Alan's not. It could have been me that died.

Nick: It could have been me, and I don't have any life insurance. What would happen to Alice and my son if I'd died out there?

Ed: The accident brought the issue of your own mortality into center focus. I'm sure you're not the only one more aware of that now.

Jack: Let's finish up doing the goals and then we can come back and talk about mortality as a group and take our time about it.

STUDY QUESTIONS

1. Give two reasons it is important for the leader to monitor the group.
2. What skills could you use to monitor the group if you are leading alone? How do coleaders work together to monitor the group?
3. Give examples of three situations in which you would want to communicate with your coleader in the group.
4. Why is it important to be flexible when you are leading a group?
5. What are some situations in which you might want to move away from the original plan for the group?
6. Discuss ways people and organizations might influence your ability to be flexible in the group.

KEY CONCEPTS

coleader Communication p. 140   monitoring p. 136
flexibility p. 144   scanning p. 136

REFERENCES

American Counseling Association (2005). *ACA code of ethics.* Alexandria, VA: Author.

Carroll, M. R., & Wiggins, J. (1990). *Elements of group counseling: Back to the basics.* Denver, CO: Love.

Kottler, J. A. (1994). *Advanced group leadership.* Pacific Grove, CA: Brooks/Cole.

Lieberman, M. A., Yalom, I. D., & Miles, M. B. (1973). *Encounter groups: First facts.* New York: Basic Books.

Yalom, I. D. (1995). *The theory and practice of group psychotherapy* (4th ed.). New York: Basic Books.

CHAPTER 8
Working with Cultural Complexities and Differences

Learning Objectives

After reading this chapter you should be able to
- Describe ASGW principles for diversity-competent group workers.
- Explain the rationale for addressing cultural complexities and differences in groups.
- Describe the Personal Dimensions of Identity model of cultural assessment.
- Perform a member assessment using the Personal Dimensions of Identity model.
- Discuss concepts of the Stylistic model of cultural assessment.
- Perform a Stylistic model assessment of a group member.
- Integrate multiple cultural assessments into a group process.
- Explain relevant issues for homogeneous cultural groups.

INTRODUCTION

Some groups are expressly designed to have **culturally homogeneous** membership; that is to say, members are chosen because of a particular similarity in their ethnic/cultural backgrounds. However, most groups are **culturally heterogeneous,** that is, members (and leaders) are of mixed ethnic/cultural background. Therefore, to become a skilled group leader, you need to learn how to navigate cultural differences and accept the challenge presented by the multiple cultural realities in a group. You also need to be influential in setting a tone for the members' appreciation of differences within the group.

At the end of this chapter, we will briefly consider some of the factors involved with leading homogeneous groups. The main focus of the chapter, however, is the ways in which you as the leader of culturally heterogeneous groups can gain understanding of cultural differences in your groups and expand group members' understanding of one another's diverse worldviews. Addressing complexities and differences of members may seem counterintuitive to the idea of forming a cohesive working group. It might seem logical that spending time speaking of differences could result in separating members rather then getting them to work together. Three arguments dispel this reasoning. First, avoiding addressing cultural differences sends an incorrect message to members that culture doesn't matter when their cultural difference could be a central factor in how they define themselves. A "colorblind" or "culture indifferent" leadership stance silences members from speaking about a core influence on their identity. Second, by not addressing differences in the group, a group leader may inadvertently miss the opportunity to encourage diverse solutions to group members' problems. The group becomes a monochromatic, culturally stagnant, singular-thinking body without utilizing the strength in alternative solutions that acknowledged diversity can provide. Finally, by not introducing cultural differences into the discussion, a leader can unknowingly perpetuate the oppression that some members will feel living in the dominant culture. Not acknowledging members' differences and the impact those differences have on them replicates in the group what they are experiencing in the world outside the group. By spending time addressing and appreciating differences in a member's culture, you are modeling for the group a norm of healthy exploration and openness.

The task of keeping members' cultural information together and maintaining cohesion in the group is a complicated job for a leader. After reviewing some of the professional mandates for diversity-competent group leadership, we will discuss methods for collecting, organizing, and analyzing group members' cultural information.

PROFESSIONAL MANDATES FOR DIVERSITY: COMPETENT GROUP WORKERS

The Association for Specialists in Group Work (ASGW) has established a set of criteria that leaders should follow in respect to developing and demonstrating cultural competence. The Principles for Diversity-Competent Group Workers by the Association for Specialists in Group Work (ASGW, 1998) follows the same

framework of the Association for Multicultural Counseling and Development's (AMCD, 1996) *Multicultural Counseling Competencies*. The AMCD competencies were conceptualized in 1992 (Sue, Arredondo, and McDavis, 1992), developed into working standards in 1996 (AMCD, 1996), and later established as competencies for the whole counseling profession when endorsed by the American Counseling Association's Governing Council (Paterson, 2007). The ASGW framework involves three major guiding principles: (1) group leaders' awareness of their own worldview, (2) group leaders' awareness of group members' worldview, and (3) group leaders' use of diversity-appropriate intervention strategies. Under each guiding principle are subsections that complete a 3 × 3 matrix of principles. The subsections include attitudes and beliefs, knowledge, and skills.

Exercises for Active Learning
Developing Diversity-Competent Group Leadership

With a small group of your classmates, explore the Principles for Diversity-Competent Group Workers at the ASGW website (ASGW, 1998), http://www.asgw.org/diversity .htm, and discuss potential professional development activities that trainees could do to enhance their diversity competence with groups.

You might be wondering how you can move from reading written standards to applying the standards in your leadership of groups. To begin with, all of the work in your development of cultural competence as an individual counselor applies to you as a leader. You need to fully explore and understand your attitudes and beliefs about your own culture, race, gender, political-economic status, sexual orientation, ability, and religion and spirituality. In addition, leaders need to explore their own negative emotional reactions and stereotypes to diverse members. Developing increased personal awareness is often too quickly overlooked by beginning leaders who might resist exploring their own privilege and oppression of disenfranchised groups. Becoming aware of and admitting our active and tacit oppression of others is difficult. This resistance to self-awareness about one's own culture and negative emotional reactions to different cultures often leads to a rush to learn culture-specific techniques, which is seen in leader training responses like, "Yes, but what do we do with someone who is *different?*" The question is a good one, but in some cases may represent the leader's inability to look at his own cultural history and involvement in privilege.

In addition to exploring attitudes and beliefs that we have about our own and other's cultures, as diversity-competent group leaders, we need to develop a better understanding of members' diverse worldviews. This requires a lifetime of openness and study on the part of the group leader. Most of what you will get from your training in multicultural counseling will only scratch the surface of culture-specific knowledge you will need to learn to work effectively with diverse populations. As a practicing group leader, you have an ethical and professional obligation to continue being open to learning more about diverse populations (D'Andrea, 2000) and incorporate this new knowledge of differing worldviews into who you are as a leader (D'Andrea, 2004). Acquiring knowledge about others' worldview comes from studying other cultures through reading and other media but most

importantly through direct exposure and interaction. In your search for developing an understanding of members' worldviews, placing yourself whenever possible into situations where you have direct exposure to diverse populations will give you learning opportunities that you can apply toward leading groups.

Finally, there are diversity-appropriate intervention strategies. These strategies are not well defined in the group literature, and those that are explained are dependant on the level of the client's acculturation to the dominant culture. The more acculturated the member is to the dominant culture, the less connected she feels to culturally linked interventions. We can take some cues from what some cultures do as interventions and open up members to new possibilities to solving problems. For example, Garrett (1998) describes a technique for groups that involves a Cherokee custom of using a "talking stick" (a beaded stick) that is passed to members when they ask for it and gives them the place to speak in the group. Another Native American custom is the "giveaway ceremony," where meaningful items of persons who have "gone to their ancestors" are given away to remaining friends and relatives. What is given away has personal and spiritual meaning. A modified giveaway ceremony could be used to close the final session of a group. Members could pass onto other members some emotional component that they hope they will carry with them in the group's absence. Whether or not you have a traditional Native American as a member of your group, the talking stick technique or the modified giveaway ceremony could be used appropriately to lead the group communication norms or closure. In these cases the use of this diversity-appropriate technique also helps expand other members' worldviews and ways of seeing problems through another lens.

Given the limited space that we can apply in this book's overview of leadership skills, our goal would be for you to have a few tools for encouraging the understanding of cultural differences in your group. One strategy for organizing our understanding of culture is to employ a *typology of universality* (Carter & Qureshi, 1995), a set of constructs that supposedly cuts across all cultural types. Preparing you as a culturally effective leader would involve educating you in these universal constructs so you could apply them as a means for member assessment, engagement, problem identification, and resolution. Two methods of universal cultural assessment will be described in this chapter: Arredondo and Glauner's Personal Dimensions of Identity (PDI) model (Arrendondo & Glauner, 1992) and McFadden's (2003) Stylistic model. Arrendondo & Glauner's PDI model provides a list of important considerations that make up a member's *personal identity*. The McFadden (2003) Stylistic model provides a framework for structurally exploring a member's cultural narrative. Both methods have application for group leadership in understanding cultural complexities and differences. As we look more closely at the two models, we will begin by studying a brief description of each model, next we will use the model to reflect on our own identity, and then we will look at how the model might be used in selecting members and in leading groups.

PERSONAL DIMENSIONS OF IDENTITY

Personal identity is a term that is commonly confused with racial identity. Cross (1991) attempted to create a distinction between the two terms. *Personal identity* is related to factors that influence personal esteem and interpersonal competence.

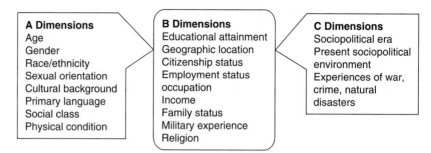

Figure 8-1   The Personal Dimensions of Identity Model.

Racial identity is the group that the individual identifies with racially and involves the racial self-esteem of the individual.

Arredondo and Glauner's (1992) **Personal Dimensions of Identity Model** organizes the different aspects of personal identity into three groups, which they call the *A, B, and C dimensions* (Figure 8-1). **"A" dimensions** are characteristics/attributes that are innate and, by and large, observable to others. They include such things as age, gender, sexual orientation, race, and physical attributes. **"B" dimensions** include such things as educational experience, religion, work experience, and hobbies. These dimensions are not immediately observable to others and are the results of individual experience and achievement. The **"C" dimensions** represent the social and political forces that have impacted upon the individual's life experiences. These "C" dimensions include broad contextual factors, such as the historical era in which one has lived and one's experience of political oppression or privilege, war or peace, a natural environment that is subject to disasters (hurricanes, floods, drought, etc.) or is stable, and an economic environment of poverty or affluence. As shown in Figure 8-1, one's "B" dimensions are influenced both by one's innate "A" dimensions and one's contextual "C" dimensions.

Table 8-1 provides a questionnaire that a group leader might administer at the screening stage to gain important insight into potential group members.

Table 8-1   Questionnaire Based on the PDI Model

"A" Dimensions:

- What is your gender?
- How is your body form expressed phenotypically? (Are you tall, short, small, large?) Are there any other unique genetic phenotypic expressions?
- Do you generally feel mentally healthy? Are you comfortable with your mental state?
- What is your sexual orientation?
- What primary language do you speak? Are there any other languages that you speak?
- What is your social class?

(continued)

Table 8-1   *(continued)*

"B" Dimensions:

- What races, ethnicities, and cultures do you claim as part of your identity?
- What are the ways in which you identify yourself? How do you experience your own identity in relationship to others?
- How long have you lived in this country? To what degree do you associate yourself with the dominant U.S. culture?
- In what country(s) do you hold citizenship status?
- Where do you live geographically? What is the region like? To what degree do you associate yourself with the dominant culture of this region?
- What kind of educational background do you have?
- What kind of work experience do you have?
- What is your socioeconomic status? How does that compare with others where you reside?
- How do you take care of yourself physically, emotionally, and spiritually?
- Do you ascribe to any particular religion, belief, or spiritual practice?

"C" Dimensions:

- Have you had any significant personal or familial experiences during your life or in your family's history that has shaped your identity?
- What kinds of historic or ongoing experiences have shaped your race, ethnic group, or culture?
- Are there political or sociocultural experiences that have shaped your identity?

Now that you have looked at the dimensions of the PDI model and scanned the contents of the three dimensions, you might use the model in the following exercise to help you reflect on these dimensions in your own life.

Exercises for Active Learning
Assessing Your Own PDI

1. Answer the questionnaire in Table 8-1 to complete your own PDI. Keep in mind as you write your answers that in the second part of this exercise, you will be sharing your answers with a class partner, reading one another's answers, and discussing them.

2. Pair up with a classmate and exchange your answers to the questionnaire. Compare your experiences in answering the questionnaire by addressing the following questions:

   a. Which dimensional components were easier for you to answer?
   b. Which dimensional components were more of a challenge for you to consider?
   c. What did you learn about yourself and your own cultural identity by completing this exercise?
   d. What have you learned about one another by completing this exercise?

It will be easier for you to understand possible and likely interactions among group members if you gather information about members' PDI as part of your screening process. This information will help you in several ways: You will be better able to hypothesize about members' *intrapersonal processes* during the group, that is, the personal feelings, cognitions, and experiences that the members bring to the group from their own history and their life outside the group. (An example of intrapersonal process

might be an initial lack of trust in a group member who has been a frequent recipient of discrimination.) You will have a better chance of effectively linking members with similarities and of identifying differences among members that must be talked out (i.e., made overt in the interpersonal process) of the group. You will have a better chance of drawing out members' attitudes, beliefs, and emotions that will help the group progress with its task or purpose. Your group will be more effective. You will be more aware of and more able to block or deal with any differences in attitudes or beliefs that might be the foundation of intense negative interactions among members. Finally, your group will be safer for members.

Incorporating the PDI Model in Group Leadership Strategies

In order to consider how group leaders might incorporate the PDI model into their work with a group, let's look at the following group setting: In a coastal county in southeast Texas that recently experienced a great deal of flooding following a tropical storm, personal, business, and farm property have incurred a great deal of damage from water, soil carried by and in the water, and the growth of mold that has been accelerated by warm summer weather. County leaders have decided to appoint a group of residents to form a county cleanup committee tasked with coordinating cleanup efforts and allocating the meager county funds available for that purpose. Steve and Maria, counselors in a local mental health agency, have volunteered to screen potential group members and colead the committee to help them function efficiently as a team and cope with the frustrations and demands of the group's tasks. To ward off potential accusations of bias, the county leaders have been careful to nominate representatives of the various socioeconomic communities residing in the county. Steve and Maria's screening of the nominees includes collecting PDI information. They have selected the eight individuals listed in Table 8-2 for the committee.

Table 8-2   County Cleanup Committee: Member PDIs

Ramon

A Dimensions—innate and observable characteristics/attributes
Ramon is a 68-year-old Latino heterosexual male. He is a second-generation Cuban exile, who speaks Spanish with English as a second language. Ramon considers himself a member of the middle class. At this point in his life, he is wheelchair bound due to severe arthritis.

B Dimensions—results of individual experience and achievement
Ramon graduated from a two-year college and worked all his life in the petroleum industry. He is currently retired. His current income is $30,000 per year, including social security. He is married, and his children are grown. He lives in Galveston, Texas, in a subdivision of modest, single-family homes. Ramon is a U.S. citizen, who served in the army during the war in Vietnam. He is a practicing Catholic.

C Dimensions—social and political forces that impacted the individual's life experiences
Ramon was born in Cuba and as a small child came to the United States with his parents to escape the Castro regime. His parents were wealthy landowners in Cuba, who came to the United States with three children and only a few thousand dollars in cash and jewelry. They settled in the Cuban exile community of Miami, where his father worked as a bartender. Ramon's mother didn't work. Ramon grew up in a very insular Miami Cuban community during the height of the cold war. He was very frightened by the community's reactions to the Bay of Pigs and

(continued)

Table 8-2   *(continued)*

Cuban Missile crisis. Ramon is proud to be a Vietnam veteran. He hates liberals and "antiwar nuts." Currently he is active in the Republican party and considers himself a true American patriot who does not question the decisions of the American government.

Kyle

A Dimensions—innate and observable characteristics/attributes

Kyle is a 33-year-old African American heterosexual man. Kyle speaks English, and he can read labels of electrical diagrams in several languages. Kyle describes his social class as blue collar. He has a medium but muscular build and has the strength needed to carry construction materials.

B Dimensions—results of individual experience and achievement

Kyle passed the state exam and became a master electrician two months ago. His training was conducted through the electricians' union. He worked his way through classes and extensive on-the-job training at the apprentice, journeyman, and master electrician levels. Kyle lives in an apartment complex in a remodeled warehouse near the construction company for which he works. Last year Kyle made $75,000. Kyle is a U. S. citizen. Kyle is divorced. His wife and child live in Montana. While he has visitation rights, he does not visit. Kyle does not identify with any religion, nor does he have any military experience.

C Dimensions—social and political forces that impacted the individual's life experiences

The men on Kyle's father's side of the family have been enlisted men in the navy for four generations. Kyle's father was an electrician's mate. From his father, Kyle learned to value hands-on work. He learned teamwork was important and not to be afraid to get dirty to get a job done. Kyle also learned to expect to work his way up in the world. During his childhood, Kyle's family lived on four different navy bases. The family suffered the periodic emotional ups and downs when his father was deployed at sea for months at a time. He chose not to go in the navy because he wanted a steadier, more settled life.

Miguel

A Dimensions—innate and observable characteristics/attributes

Miguel is a 37-year-old heterosexual Latino man. He describes his cultural heritage as Mexican. He speaks Spanish and a little English. He is healthy and strong. His social class is lower class.

B Dimensions—results of individual experience and achievement

Miguel has a grade school education. He is an illegal immigrant who travels from Mexico to the United States annually. Each year he works in a different location, generally doing some type of agricultural or ranch work. He can operate a wide range of machinery including tractors, spreaders, combines, trucks, backhoes and automated crop watering systems. Most years he works in the United States from April to December at which time he returns to his family in Mexico. Miguel makes about $10,000 cash a season. Miguel has a wife and three children who live on a ranch they do not own in Mexico. Miguel is Catholic. He has no military experience.

C Dimensions—social and political forces that impacted the individual's life experiences

Miguel grew up on the ranch where his family continues to live. Then as now, the money the family received for working on the ranch was meager. His father and uncles traveled to the United States to make money to support the family. When Miguel was a teenager, Miguel's favorite uncle died crossing the border into New Mexico. Miguel's family viewed the uncle as a hero who died trying to support the family. Miguel has and does experience a great deal of discrimination. His anger about discrimination simmers within him but is not often expressed.

(continued)

Table 8-2   (*continued*)

Anna

A Dimensions—innate and observable characteristics/attributes

Anna is a 69-year-old heterosexual Caucasian woman. Anna describes her cultural background as a mix of English and Native American. She speaks English well and some Navajo. Anna is part of the upper middle class. Her health is good except for some occasional mild pain from arthritis.

B Dimensions—results of individual experience and achievement

Anna graduated from a two-year business school at the age of 20. At this time she works two after-noons a week as a law clerk. She views her occupation primarily as a grandmother. Anna lives in a small but elegant home surrounded by a lot of land in a small town on the outskirts of the city. Anna is a widow. Last year she made $40,000 from wages and $20,000 from stock dividends. Anna is a U. S. citizen. She describes her religion as Native American, and she does not trust the military.

C Dimensions—social and political forces that impacted the individual's life experiences

Anna grew up going back and forth between Texas and the reservation. From her extended family on the reservation, she learned to be peaceful and to be attuned to the natural world. In town in Arizona and in Texas, she experienced prejudice and at times discrimination. As she grew older, Anna studied to become a paralegal so she could help prevent and counter discrimi-nation. In the course of her professional work, she met and married her husband with whom she lived happily for many years. Anna values giving back to the community.

Tyler

A Dimensions—innate and observable characteristics/attributes

Tyler is a 57-year-old Caucasian heterosexual man. He describes his cultural background as western. Tyler speaks English as well as a bit of Spanish and a bit of Louisiana French. He is part of the upper middle class. Tyler hurt his back loading trucks several years ago. He still has some minor pain, and he tries not to do any lifting at this age.

B Dimensions—results of individual experience and achievement

Tyler graduated from a local mechanic school with a certificate in diesel mechanics. He began as a truck driver. Over the years he eventually bought a semi and then a trucking franchise. Tyler lives is a gated community in the suburbs. Last year Tyler made $200,000. Tyler does not identify with any religion. He was in Junior ROTC in high school.

C Dimensions—social and political forces that impacted the individual's life experiences

Tyler grew up in the rural part of the county. His father traveled from ranch to ranch shoeing horses. His father was very gentle and patient with the horses and with Tyler. If people refused to pay for the work he had done, Tyler's father became very confrontational. If a horse kicked Tyler's father and injured him, most often his father washed the blood off and kept on shoeing. Tyler came to value standing up for himself and being tough. He learned that as an adult no one would take care of you but yourself.

Shana

A Dimensions—innate and observable characteristics/attributes

Shana is a 42-year-old African American heterosexual woman. Shana speaks English. Shana considers herself a member of the working class. She is physically healthy, attractive, and in good physical condition (bodybuilder).

B Dimensions—results of individual experience and achievement

Shana is a high school graduate who owns her own hairdressing shop but is struggling to keep it going. Her yearly income, including husband's salary, was $40,000 in good years but lately is closer to $20,000. She is married with four children. Her husband, who lives in San Francisco, has

(*continued*)

Table 8-2   *(continued)*

a full-time but low-paying job in the petroleum service industry. Shana and her children live in a duplex on the edge of Galveston, Texas. Shana is a U.S. citizen. She identifies her religion as Baptist.

C Dimensions—social and political forces that impacted the individual's life experiences
Shana was raised in San Francisco. As a young child Shana was exposed to the civil rights movement by her parents who were very active. They took their children on marches and taught them American history from the perspective of blacks growing up in the racist society of the early twentieth-century South. Shana went to beauty school instead of college. Married with two children, in 1994 Shana was nearly killed when the salon she was working in collapsed during the Northridge earthquake. Shana took her two young children to start a new life in Galveston, a place where she had relatives and "the earth didn't move." Although she is relatively safe from earthquakes in Texas, she is learning firsthand what her parents taught her about living with racism.

Nancy

A Dimensions—innate and observable characteristics/attributes
Nancy is a 45-year-old heterosexual Caucasian woman. She speaks English and French well and enough Spanish to communicate with the store employees who unload the freight trucks. She describes her cultural background as American. She is part of the middle class. Nancy is physically healthy except for being nearsighted, for which condition she wears contacts.

B Dimensions—results of individual experience and achievement
Nancy graduated from the state university with a bachelor's degree in business. She works as a merchandise buyer for a national department store chain that sells expensive clothes for women. Nancy lives in an apartment on the eighteenth floor downtown in the city. Nancy is single. She makes $50,000 a year. She is a U.S. citizen. She does not identify with any religion. She has no military experience.

C Dimensions—social and political forces that impacted the individual's life experiences
Nancy was raised by her mother in the city where Nancy now lives. Nancy's father left when Nancy was five. Her mother worked, sewing clothes for wealthy people in the city and earning enough so that the two of them always had a clean apartment with enough to eat. From her mother, Nancy learned the necessity of constant effort. She also learned that a woman could take care of herself and survive on her own. Autonomy and self-sufficiency are important values for Nancy.

Red

A Dimensions—innate and observable characteristics/attributes
Red is a 27-year-old homosexual Caucasian man. Red describes his cultural background as a New Englander. He speaks English. Red is tall, lean, and athletic. He plays golf regularly.

B Dimensions—results of individual experience and achievement
Red graduated from a small, liberal college in Massachusetts with a degree in recreation management. He is Second Assistant Park Commissioner for the county. Red is single. He lives in a small condo overlooking a golf course. Red holds joint U.S. and Canadian citizenship. Last year he made $30,000 from the county and $30,000 from giving golf lessons at a local country club. Red is Catholic and has no military experience.

C Dimensions—social and political forces that impacted the individual's life experiences
Red's father was American and his mother was Canadian. Most of his childhood Red's father worked as a chef at a resort in New Hampshire. The resort was a pleasant place frequented by the wealthy. Red's family lived in a small home on the grounds of the resort. Red had access to the facilities of the resort. He fell in love with golf and spent most of his childhood on the golf course. His golf game became good enough that colleges recruited him though there were no scholarship offers. Red learned to value diverse lifestyles. He also believes that the outdoors—green space—is essential to the human spirit.

Exercises for Active Learning

Read the PDI profiles of the members of the county cleanup committee, and respond to the questions below.

1. What similarities might you draw on to link Ramon and Kyle?
2. On what issues/values might Roman and Miguel differ?
3. Which members might be more likely to be accepting of Miguel as an illegal immigrant?
4. Red is the only member of the committee who is gay. What strategies might the leaders of this group use to create a welcoming group for people of diverse sexual orientation?
5. Consider the profiles of the three women in the group. What similarities do you see? What are some important differences?

In their first group session coleaders Steve and Maria work with the members of the County Cleanup Committee to get to know one another a little better and hopefully begin to form a cohesive group.

Steve: Maria and I would like you to start this first session by asking each of you to share something of your cultural background with the other group members. On the wall you can see the chart to the dimensions of identity that we talked about when you met with Maria and me for the screening process.

Maria: We realize that in one group you can't talk about all aspects of your identity, so we are asking you to pick one or two of them to share and to talk about how those parts of your identity might influence how you would relate to other group members or how you think about the task that you are charged with—planning for the county cleanup. I'll start. Well, as Steve said, my name's Maria, and I'm half Mexican and half Puerto Rican, so I probably will want to make sure the plans we develop reach out to people of Mexican and Puerto Rican cultures. *[A Dimension – cultural background]*

Shana: My name's Shana, and I own my own hairdressing shop. *[B Dimensions – employment]* I want to make sure that small business people don't get driven out of business due to large losses. Maybe there's some way to at least help businesses get some low-interest loans. And another thing—I was in the earthquake in California and watched my whole world crumble to dust *[C Dimensions – experience of natural disaster]*, and now it seems the same—only like my world is being washed away—and I'm scared of how it might change my life.

Steve: Does anyone else feel like your "world is being washed away"? *[Drawing out]*

[Several members are nodding.]

Maria: Can one of you say something about your feelings? *[Universality]*

Nancy: Yes, that's what's happening to me too. The basement of the store that I buy merchandise for has five feet of water in it, and we received a call saying not to come to work indefinitely—until they call us. I had some emergency food in my apartment, but now only half of it is left. I'm scared too, Shana.

Maria: And that fear about how this situation is going to play out is probably real for most people in the county. We have to make the best plan we can, and get it started.

Miguel: I'm Miguel and work on the farms. *[B Dimensions – employment]*

Ramon: [*Glaring at Miguel*] And you're illegal. [*B Dimensions – citizenship status*]

Steve: Ramon, let Miguel speak for himself. [*Cutting off*]

Miguel: It's true, and now with the flood I'm out of work and I have no place to live—same for the other farm workers. We don't have the money to go home, and we can't get help here. [*Ramon continues to glare at Miguel.*] They really hassle us at the shelter. I speak English OK, but the other workers don't. They told me that at the shelter they said that they had to ask for everything in English only. [*C Dimension – experience of discrimination*]

Ramon: Yeah, well, that's not right. My parents have green cards, but they don't speak English, and they get that baloney all the time in this town. [*C Dimension – experience of discrimination*]

Maria: So, Ramon, you connect with Miguel in that you have both experienced discrimination. [*Linking*]

Ramon: Yes, well I don't have much sympathy for guys who come here illegally, but maybe we could work together to seek out people in the Spanish-speaking community who need help talking with aid workers and making out the applications in English.

Miguel: We could help a lot of people.

Maria: Yes, you could.

In the exchange between Miguel and Ramon, their strong feelings about differences in citizenship status are evident; however, their similarity—being the recipient of discrimination—links them with a common experience and feelings. Their discovery of common ground provides a basis for common action related to the purpose of the group. Note also that Maria immediately reinforces their desire to work together.

Using PDI Profiles to Plan Group Composition

Thoughtful composition of groups may increase the likelihood that members will meet their individual goals. PDI profiles can assist the leader in composing groups that balance the diversity of members' backgrounds and experiences. Groups with greater diversity in members present a wider variety of alternative solutions to problems brought to the group. However, greater diversity also means greater challenges in building trust among members. Members who are less alike need to invest some time and effort in becoming familiar with those different from them. Groups with lesser diversity can have a built-in familiarity but may be challenged to find alternative solutions to those familiar to them. In composing members for a group, a leader needs to find a working balance between member sameness and member difference that safely pushes each member a bit further along in individual growth.

THE STYLISTIC MODEL OF TRANSCULTURAL COUNSELING

Another method for incorporating and understanding culture in work with group members is the **Stylistic Model of Transcultural Counseling** as described by John McFadden (McFadden, 2003). The Stylistic model has developed over the last three decades as a model that counselors can use in exploring the cultural influences, values, and experiences of their clients.

Unlike the PDI model, which is organized around observable and distinct aspects of identity, the Stylistic model includes aspects of individual identity that are intrapsychic. Furthermore, whereas the PDI model does not address client or counselor action, the Stylistic model addresses the current issues that the individual is coping with as a member of a larger society and provides direction to culturally appropriate interventions. After reviewing the Stylistic model, we will consider how the PDI and Stylistic models can be integrated into a diversity-competent group leader's practices.

Like the PDI model, the Stylistic model looks at three dimensions. However, in the Stylistic model, these dimensions are like stories on a building. The foundational story is the cultural-historical dimension. The second story is the psychosocial dimension. The top story is what McFadden calls the scientific-ideological dimension (Figure 8-2).

The **cultural-historical dimension** is the foundational level consisting of the components of a person's history related to his culture(s) of origin. Included in this level are the person's own history and that which is passed on from previous generations: the history of oppression and discrimination or power and privilege experienced by the person and his family, the person's family values and cultural traditions, historic movements in which the person's culture of origin was involved, patterns of communication in that culture, and heroes and heroines identified from personal cultural history. The adaptive strengths and challenges that an individual has derived from the cultural-historical dimension directly influence the composition of the next level, the psychosocial dimension.

The **psychosocial dimension** is the level that addresses an individual's intrapersonal psychological functioning (including cognition and emotion) and interpersonal social functioning. Included in this level are personality development, ethnic and racial identity development, psychological security, and the individual's ways of forming and maintaining relationships with others. The psychosocial makeup of an individual (based on the foundation of the person's unique cultural-historical experience) directly influences the composition of the next level, the scientific-ideological dimension.

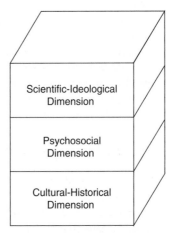

Figure 8-2   The Stylistic Model of Transcultural Counseling

The third level, the so-called **scientific-ideological dimension,** is defined by McFadden as the current nature of an individual's presenting problem(s)—factors in the person's external world that have impacted upon the development of the problem and factors in the external world that impact upon the development of solutions to the problem. Included in the factors that have contributed to the problem formation are the person's place in the larger society—the societal macrosystem that is composed of the individual's economic potency in the world, the goals of the institutions in which she is engaged, media influences, and the current political climate. Factors contributing to the problem solution are the individual's microsystems of problem resolution: the individual's goals, the forming of logical behavioral chains, and ability to conceive of meaningful alternatives to the problem. Because it is the external expression of all that is cultural, historical, and psychosocial in the individual, the scientific-ideological dimension is the focus of most counseling, both individual and group.

McFadden, Jencius, and Bowen (2005) have constructed questions for each dimension that would help group leaders understand their own stylistic dimensions and in turn apply similar questions to their groups. These questions could be used as a screening tool before the group begins or could be serially asked of members in the first session to enhance discussion about members' cultural influence and cultural commonalities and differences of members. See Table 8-3 for some sample questions for each of the Stylistic dimensions. It is not an exhaustive list of reflective questions but will give group leaders a conceptual framework of inquiry by which to explore their own and group members' cultural realm.

Using the Stylistic Model

Whereas gathering PDI data on group members is relatively straightforward, assessing members' stylistic dimensions can be a formidable task. As you read through the following Stylistic profile of a group member we will call Carlos, you may sense that the stylistic dimensions address some of the indicators in the PDI but with greater context. In addition, the scientific-ideological dimension addresses problems that the group member brings to the group and the immediacy of his situation.

Most clients who seek counseling describe their presenting problems from the perspective of the scientific-ideological dimension. In this case example, Carlos might frame his problem to the group as arguments that he and his wife are having over household chores. Other members might indicate that they too have this problem and that they view it as a common fact of modern life. However, doing a Stylistic analysis of Carlos opens up his life in a much deeper and more meaningful way. Often leaders will work with members on problem resolution engaging only from the scientific-ideological dimension, ignoring the cultural-historical and psychosocial dimensional influences. McFadden (1999) would argue that employing all three dimensions of the Stylistic model, not just the scientific-ideological dimension, would enable the leader of Carlos's group to help Carlos and the other members explore the problem in a more meaningful way.

Table 8-3 Questions for Stylistic Dimension Understanding

Cultural-Historical Dimension

- What are key traditions within your culture?
- Are there cultural traditions you have that are not supported in your own environment?
- Are there any cultural traditions that conflict with the majority culture?
- How has ethnic or racial discrimination affected you?
- Could you name one or more persons from your culture that have inspired or motivated you?
- How has your culture's history of oppression affected your daily life?

Psychosocial Dimension

- What types of social forces have impacted your identity?
- How have societal perceptions of your culture either enabled or disabled your success or failure?
- How has your self-development been impacted by your culture?
- What aspects of your personality define who you are?
- From what elements in your life do you derive security?
- What, if any, coping strategies has your culture taught you?
- How does your perception of others affect your interaction with persons from other cultures?
- How do you align yourself with your ethnic identity?
- How do you maintain your human dignity?

Scientific-Ideological Dimension

- How do you identify and set goals for yourself?
- What meaningful alternatives are available that meet your cultural needs?
- What impacts your decision making when faced with life choices?
- What impact has the government had on your family or as an individual in society?
- What images do the popular media use to portray your culture/ethnicity?
- How has the media affected the way your culture is viewed?
- What are some ways the media can promote your culture's success?
- What are the economic barriers affecting you?
- How do the institutions in your environment correspond with your cultural identity?

Adapted from McFadden, Jencius, and Bowen (2005).

Through questioning Carlos using the Stylistic model, the leader would learn about significant cultural-historical influences on Carlos concerning men's role in the family. The leader would also learn about Carlos's family history of economic oppression and reduction to migrant farm work. Carlos's cultural-historical dimension in turn has influenced the way he thinks about himself, how he relates to others, and how he wants to be seen by others (the psychosocial dimension). This dynamic also influenced Carlos's drive to get into college and succeed in a profession that would enable him to help others with his parents' immigrant experience. At the psychosocial dimension, Carlos has enhanced his own psychological security and human dignity through self-inspection of his family's experience. He has also enhanced his psychosocial dimension by working to challenge oppressive perceptions of others regarding the immigrant experience. His strong value of support through the family has helped him develop psychological security and formed a resilient personality to address continued oppression of his people. On the scientific-ideological level he faces a current conflict in his marriage that likely derives from two cultural-historical factors in

Stylistic Profile: Carlos

Cultural-Historical Dimension

Carlos is a 28-year-old male of second-generation Mexican origin. Carlos's father, Roberto, first came to the United States with occasional illegal employment through border crossing to work in the growing fields of Southern California. Roberto faced much of the hard work for long hours and minimal pay that illegals and immigrant farm workers face. Carlos's father met his mother, Edwina, whose family had legally immigrated to the country prior to Edwina being born. Roberto continued to return for work and to see Edwina. They were eventually married, with Carlos being the first of four children. Growing up, Carlos was marginalized by many of his school-aged peers who regarded him and his immigrant family as burdens on the system. Carlos grew up in a traditional patriarchal family where he saw Edwina respond to Roberto's needs and caretaking at home. As the oldest male, Carlos had a certain amount of freedom from household responsibilities and was encouraged to excel with all the opportunities he could get as an American citizen. He performed well in school, which led to an advanced education in social work and community organization. Carlos currently manages a social service agency that addresses the needs of immigrant and illegal aliens in the community.

Psychosocial Dimension

Carlos's experience of growing up was challenging through the ethnic isolation that he faced but that helped him develop a strong Mexican cultural identity. He was able to see his family as a source of strength and internalize this into a sense of autonomy and personal identity. His success in school also improved his self-esteem and enhanced his sense of self-efficacy when it came to education. Having seen his father and mother establish a new life in new country (in a sometimes hostile environment) helped him appreciate the human dignity found at all socioeconomic levels. Carlos still had regular challenges from the dominant culture based on his ethnic origin and the responses of those in the dominant culture who stereotyped Mexican immigrants. Carlos learned from his family and from experiences early on in school to face his critics and to speak out when he was being marginalized.

Scientific-Ideological Dimension

Carlos has been married to Maria for four years. She is a second-generation Mexican immigrant. Maria is working part time and is going to school to study counseling, hoping to be of assistance to the Mexican community. Together, their income is sufficient to allow them to have a comfortable existence and for Maria to continue with her studies to complete her degree. Both she and Carlos were able to obtain educational grant opportunities available for them to extend their education, and in the case of Carlos's employment, work to assist Mexican immigrants. Where they live, the news media does not portray these efforts in a positive light, and their opportunities to better themselves are still viewed as being done at the expense of nonimmigrant families in the community.

Carlos has joined a men's group at the suggestion of Maria, who felt that he was not contributing enough to the chores at home because of his passion for his work and his claim that he is exhausted at the end of the day. She sees his work as important but also would like to see him more involved in support at home.

his life: the oppression his culture has faced by being subjugated into service industry positions, and the roles men play in the Mexican family. On the other hand, Carlos wants to support his wife's career, help raise her social status, and contribute to the partnership. A group leader just skimming the surface by working only in the scientific-ideological dimension would have missed the rich cultural context of this member's problem.

Comparing the Stylistic and PDI Models

The Stylistic model has many similarities to the Personal Dimensions of Identity model previously presented. They both attempt to focus the leader in exploring and understanding the biological, historic, and contextual aspects of the members. They both attempt to capture the individual's experience of oppression in society and cultural influences from their families. The Stylistic cultural-historical dimension and the PDI "B" dimensions similarly look at family influence, values, and cultural history. Both models also capture the cultural identity (in the Stylistic psychosocial dimension and the PDI "B" dimensions). Historic oppression, which captures more of the sociopolitical movements impacting a client, is represented in the Stylistic cultural-historical dimension and in the PDI "C" dimensions.

In what ways, you might ask, are these models different, and where do they overlap? As shown in Figure 8-3, the "A" dimensions of the PDI (the observable and distinct demographics about the individual) are not specifically addressed as a level in the Stylistic model. The "B" dimensions of the PDI are similar to many of the cultural-historical descriptors of the Stylistic model and represent those aspects of the individual that are about personal experience (PDI) or intrapsychic/interpsychic (Stylistic) state of identity. The scientific-ideological dimension is unique to the Stylistic model because it addresses the current issues that the individual is coping with as a member of the larger society. The scientific-ideological dimension also provides direction to culturally appropriate interventions, being the action-oriented dimension in the Stylistic model, whereas the PDI model does not address client or counselor action.

Fundamentally, although there are many similarities of content across both models, the PDI model emphasizes *data* and the Stylistic model emphasizes *dynamics*. Therefore, the approach we recommend to our own group counseling students is to employ an amalgam of both models that helps give a group leader a well-rounded view of each member of a diverse group. In order to get comprehensive information about the members to serve as a foundation for leading the group, you may be well served to devise a member questionnaire based on the exercise you completed earlier (Assessing Your Own PDI on page 164) and some of the Stylistic

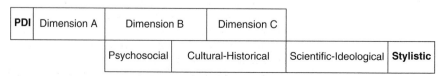

Figure 8-3   Differences and Similarities of the PDI and Stylistic Models

questions provided by McFadden, Jencius, and Bowen (2005) in Table 8-3 and administer it during screening. You can also incorporate exploration of additional questions to ferret out further similarities and differences among members in the first and second sessions of the group.

ASSESSING MEMBERS' PDI AND STYLISTIC DIMENSIONS

In order to demonstrate using the Stylistic model supplemented by the PDI model to conceptualize and lead groups, we will use as an example the men's group of which Carlos is a member. The member profiles in Table 8-4 give you brief information about each member's PDI followed by a more extensive analysis of the member's cultural-historical, psychosocial, and scientific-ideological dimensions. After you read these member profiles, we think you will see the value of using a screening protocol of questions designed to elicit information about the Stylistic and PDI dimensions. By collecting this information at the screening stage, you will start the first session of the group as an informed leader.

Table 8-4   Combined PDI and Stylistic Profiles of Men's Group Members

Key To Abbreviations:

A = PDI "A" Dimensions	*CH = Cultural-Historical Stylistic Model*
B = PDI "B" Dimensions	*PS = Psychosocial Stylistic Model*
C = PDI "C" Dimensions	*SI = Scientific-Ideological Stylistic Model*

Carlos

- Carlos is a 28-year-old heterosexual male, medium build, of Mexican heritage. (A, CH)
- He and his wife of four years, Maria, belong to a growing Mexican middle class. (B, SI)
- Carlos speaks both Spanish and English. (A)
- Carlos claims his Mexican heritage living as an American citizen. (B)
- Carlos and Maria were able to obtain educational grant opportunities available for them to extend their education, and in the case of Carlos's employment, work to assist Mexican immigrants. (SI)
- Where they live the news media does not portray these efforts in a positive light, and their opportunities to better themselves are still viewed as being at the expense of nonimmigrant families in the community. (SI)
- Carlos holds a master's degree in social work. (B)
- He ascribes to the Catholic religion; however, he does not regularly practice his faith. (B, CH)
- Carlos enjoys hiking and backpacking and finds reading and outdoor activity relaxing. (B)
- Carlos's father, Roberto, first came to the United States with occasional illegal employment through border crossing to work in the growing fields of Southern California. (CH)
- Carlos's father met his mother, Edwina, whose family had legally immigrated to the country prior to Edwina being born. (CH)
- Carlos's father immigrated after years of illegal entry across the border and working in the United States. (C, CH)
- Roberto and Edwina were eventually married, with Carlos being the first of four children. As the oldest male, Carlos had a certain amount of freedom from household responsibilities and was encouraged to excel with all the opportunities he could get as an American citizen. (CH)

(continued)

Table 8-4 (*continued*)

- Growing up, Carlos was marginalized by many of his school-aged peers, who regarded him and his immigrant family as burdens on the system. (CH)
- Carlos's coming from an immigrant family has given him an appreciation for sociopolitical issues on both sides of the border. (C, SI)
- Carlos's experience of growing up was challenging through the ethnic isolation that he faced, but it helped him develop a strong Mexican cultural identity. (PS)
- He was able to see his family as a source of strength and internalize this into a sense of autonomy and personal identity. (PS)
- Carlos learned from his family and from experiences early on in school to face his critics and to speak out when he was being marginalized. (PS)
- Carlos currently manages a social service agency that addresses the needs of immigrant and illegal aliens in the community. (C, CH)
- Carlos joined the group at the suggestion of Maria, who felt that he was not contributing enough to the chores at home because of his passion for his work and his claim that he is exhausted at the end of the day. (SI)

Isaiah

- Isaiah is a 52-year-old heterosexual African American male. (A)
- Isaiah speaks English, is slightly built in stature, and is middle-class status. (A)
- Isaiah identifies as a black, African American racially and culturally. (B)
- He has lived in this country all his life, and his family has a proud tradition that traces back to their enslavement in this country. (B, CH)
- He is a U.S.citizen living on the outskirts of San Diego. (B)
- He has a high school degree and has worked in auto repair/auto parts since graduating from high school. (B)
- He and his wife, Peggy, have a rich spiritual Christian life, attending regular services at a Pentecostal church. (B, CH)
- He and his wife's income place him in a struggling middle class, similar to those who live in his surrounding area. (B, SI)
- Isaiah's ancestors were enslaved and brought to the United States in the early 1800s. His great-grandfather survived the horrors of slavery and after emancipation settled as an agricultural worker. (C, CH)
- Isaiah was a very young child when the civil rights movement took hold in the United States. (C, CH)
- Isaiah's ancestors came to the United States on slave ships generations ago. At first they worked in fields on plantations. They were not allowed to read or to get any kind of education. They drew on strong spirituality and survived the horrors of slavery. (CH)
- Eventually, one of Isaiah's great-grandfathers escaped from slavery and fought in the Union army during the Civil War. After the war, the family survived doing mostly agricultural work. (CH)
- Members of the family learned to read, and in later generations they took advantage of opportunities for education. Some of the men in the family attended college and obtained degrees in agriculture. Several of the women in the family developed careers in nursing. (CH)
- Isaiah had a tough time growing up, leaving him with some concerns about how comfortable he was interacting with other people. He grew up in a poorer section of town. (PS)
- Isaiah did not excel as his test scores would indicate. (PS)
- He took more pleasure in doing his schoolwork and keeping a low profile among his peers. He was seen as quiet by his peers and did not form many friendships but had one or two schoolmates that he depended on for friendship. (PS)

(*continued*)

Table 8-4 *(continued)*

- In order to avoid troubles in the community he grew up in, Isaiah kept to himself as a strategy for success. (PS)
- Isaiah works as a regional manager of an auto parts distributor chain. He is married to Peggy, and they have two grown children, the youngest just completing college. Both kids are now working and settling into a life financially independent from their parents. This will allow for greater financial security for Isaiah and Peggy as they approach retirement. (SI)
- Isaiah is feeling the "empty nest" with both kids being out of the house, and although he could bury himself in his work, he is wondering what retirement and life with Peggy will be like now. (SI)
- With Peggy working contract hours and her job changing, it allows her a certain amount of freedom but also creates lack of predictability in when she will be at home. Isaiah is missing the relationship with his kids and a settled relationship with his spouse. (SI)
- The men's group was suggested by a retirement planner Isaiah spoke with at his company's Employee Assistance Program. (SI)

Greg
- Greg is a 25-year-old heterosexual Caucasian male. He is middle class, tall in stature, and speaks English. (A)
  Greg claims his ethnicity to be Caucasian "American." He sees his own identity as being an "American" and does not identify with his Germanic heritage. (B)
- He holds U.S. citizenship and has lived in the United States all his life. (B)
- His family goes back many generations, working as farmers in the Midwest. (B, CH)
- He has a college degree in agribusiness and was the first person in his family to attend college. (B)
- He has worked primarily in farming until college and is now working in agribusiness in a middle-class-income job. (B)
- His family history pre–World War II is sketchy. Many of the males in the family served and lost their lives in WW II. Other family members died at a young age from childhood diseases. Because of these deaths, Greg does not know much about his family prior to the stage where the family farmed corn. (C, CH)
- Greg grew up in a very monocultural rural Midwest environment and did not have any exposure to cultural differences. Greg's father made a lot of money farming and was able to send Greg to college, where Greg studied agribusiness management. (CH)
- Greg grew up with the sense of psychological security bestowed upon him through his mother (who lavished over the kids) and a father who was always present working at the farm/home sharing the sacrifices that his parents made to make it better for him and for Greg. (PS)
- Greg went to the flagship university in his state that was a predominantly monocultural institution. Greg is a new manager in an agribusiness company and is having a hard time adjusting to the work environment. He is working with people who are older than he, from different regions and different cultures. (SI)

Don
- Don is a 35-year-old Caucasian heterosexual male. He is middle class, medium build in size, and speaks English. (A)
- Don sees himself as typical white American of European immigration origin. He holds U.S. citizenship and has a high school education. He has worked the manufacturing industry in a middle-management, middle-class position. (B)
- The men in the family had been iron workers in industry in England. The work was dangerous and injury was common. Being tough became a value among the men. (CH)

(continued)

Table 8-4   (*continued*)

- Influenced by both a religious tradition that valued reading, particularly reading the Bible, and later by the early feminist movements, the women in the family came to value education and autonomy. (CH)
- Growing up, Don and his two brothers were pretty much responsible for each other. Don's father would interact with the kids when he could, but with swing shift hours his father's time at home and awake never was in sync with the family's daily schedule. (PS)
- Don admired his father but developed a sense of security in his family through his brothers and his mother, who was the primary caretaker of the family. (PS)
- Don was well-liked by others as a child, and this helped him form good social bonds as an adult. (PS)
- He feels the pressure of changing times, the export of manufacturing, and in many ways sees himself (and his family's experience) as relics in modern America. (C, SI)
- His company has managed to stave off foreign competition and exportation of their manufacturing, but it is a constant struggle in this economy. This has led to longer hours, greater stress, and less focus on his family. (SI)
- Martha is concerned with Don's unavailability for his sons. She sees the same patterns of parenting being expressed in Don that Don knows were part of his father's patterns. Martha is concerned for Don, his job, and the welfare of the family as a whole. She recommended that Don come to the group to find alliances with other men facing similar issues. (SI)

Angelo
- Angelo is a 45-year-old heterosexual middle-class Hispanic American. He is small in stature and speaks both Spanish and English. (A)
- Angelo claims both Mexican and Spanish heritage and holds strong national affiliation to the United States through his family's historic involvement in the military. (B, CH)
- Angelo identifies himself as an American (U.S. citizen) of Hispanic descent. (B, CH)
- He holds an associate's degree from a vocational/technical college and has worked for the power company for 23 years. (B)
- His economic status is middle class, which compares equitably to the area where he resides. (B, SI)
- He is a practicing Catholic and is involved in community service through his church. (B, CH)
- Angelo's family has roots in Mexico (mother's side of family) and Arizona (father's side of family). (CH)
- Angelo's mother's family lived in Mexico many generations before some members of the family immigrated to Arizona. This branch of the family is proud of being Mexican and maintains strong ties through frequent visits to Mexico. In Arizona they experience a lot of discrimination, some of which is blatant and more of which is subtle but consistent and real. This part of the family speaks primarily Spanish. (CH)
- Angelo's father's side of the family is descended from early Spanish landholders in the Southwest. They consider themselves Spanish and not Mexican. (CH)
- Angelo has managed to blend both heritages well and has a strong sense of ethnic pride and human dignity. (PS)
- Because of the strong ethnic pride in his family, Angelo also had a good sense of psychological security. Others perceived Angelo as being a stable, well-mannered and emotionally strong child, mature beyond his age. (PS)
- With a father who had military service, Angelo learned early on that your character speaks louder (and sometimes for) your culture. His dad would refer to the military as the "great equalizer," where every culture would be treated the same. (PS)
- Angelo is the only person of Hispanic descent in his division at the power company. It is part of the company's institutional goals to provide opportunities for diverse employees at all ranks. (SI)

(*continued*)

Table 8-4   *(continued)*

- Although he is proud of his rise in the ranks to the management level, he has doubts that others he has to supervise see his advancement anything other than a minority hire. Because of this prejudice, he has a hard time garnering the respect of his work team leaders and other mid-level managers in the company. (SI)
- Angelo is feeling the stress of work and the role of being a sole minority employee and is seeking stress release. (SI)

Richard

- Richard is a 38-year-old middle-class heterosexual Caucasian male of Irish ancestry. He is medium size in stature and build and speaks only English. (A)
- Richard claims an Irish heritage but does not have a rich sense of understanding of that heritage. (B, CH)
- He has lived in the United States all his life, holds U.S. citizenship, and his family can trace itself back through multiple generations of westward U.S. settlers. (B)
- He has a college education and B.A. in marketing. He is middle class, and a nonpracticing Catholic. (B)
- Richard takes pride in his family history of westward migration in the United States when the country was expanding. He also keeps the family tradition of sacrificing for the benefit of the next generation. (C, CH)
- He has strong values of family heritage include valuing exploration and adventure, doing what you need to do to survive, and opening new frontiers. (CH)
- Richard has a strong sense of human dignity as promoted through the stories of his ancestors as settlers of the western territory. (PS)
- He has a strong work ethic, which gives him a sense of personal pride. He sees his own experience of working up through the ranks of the company as a message to others that good work ethic leads to success. (PS)
- Richard has succeeded in his job and is happy in his marriage but is beginning to be disillusioned by not facing any new challenges at work. He could look for advancement in his company, but that would require relocating, and he does not want to uproot his family for his own unhappiness. (SI)
- Richard is looking for the group to provide him with meaningful alternatives that can help his work life be more adventurous without giving up the stability he has established for himself and more importantly his family. (SI)

Exercises for Active Learning
Cultural Complexity in the Men's Group

1. Based on some of the cultural indicators, are there members in the group who might align similarly? Are there those in the group who may differ or have challenges based on a particular cultural indicator?

2. Are the members of this group so *similar* culturally that it may add to the homogeneity of the group at the risk of diverse ideas? Are the members of this group so *different* culturally that it may add to the diversity at the risk of group cohesion? Given either of these scenarios (culturally similar, culturally different) how might that impact your leadership of this group?

3. Based on the members' self-ratings on the various cultural dimensions, do you predict any possible divisions between members? Do you predict any immediate alliances? How might you work with these members to maintain a dynamic balance with the group?

4. As the leader, suggest a culturally appropriate way to have Carlos begin the group.
5. What might be good topics for the members to begin discussing?
6. Given the nature of the group, are there any special considerations or group rules that you may wish to make?
7. Think of your own development as a leader for this group:
   a. What areas of your own self-awareness would you need to address regarding being an effective leader for this group?
   b. What knowledge areas would you need to address regarding being an effective leader for this group?
   c. What culture-specific skills would you need to address regarding being an effective leader for this group?

From the exercise on complexity in a group's cultural dimensions, you can appreciate the vast complexity of cultural differences common in most any group. The number of members multiplies the potential diversity issues that one could deal with as a leader. It becomes a daunting task for any leader. If your group's focus is not specifically cultural diversity enhancement, then you want to explore cultural differences and similarities and make that part of the conversation. If your group is focused on addressing cultural differences, then you would want to spend more time and effort working through Stylistic dimensions and moving from the cultural-historical dimension through to the action stage of the scientific-ideological action dimension. You would also want members to acquire skills to effectively confront and address oppression to themselves or others.

LEADING CULTURALLY HOMOGENOUS GROUPS

Occasionally the opportunity may present itself for you to lead a group whose membership has similar ethnic/cultural heritage. Examples of such homogeneous groups are found throughout the counseling literature with guidelines suggested for the planning and execution of culturally homogeneous groups. The specifics of running such groups are too vast to cover in this text, but readers are directed to more substantive articles on working with African American groups (Pack-Brown & Fleming, 2004), Asian groups (Chung, 2004), elderly members (Gatz, 1989; Henderson & Gladding, 2004), Latino groups (Torres-Rivera, Wilber, Roberts-Wilber & Phan,1999; Torres-Rivera, 2004), Native American groups (Garrett, 1998; Garrett, 1999; Garrett & Carroll, 2000), people with disabilities (Falvo,1999; Seligman & Marshak, 2004), and sexual identity groups (Chojnacki & Gelberg, 1995; Horne & Levitt, 2004). If you work in a counseling setting that serves a primarily homogeneous population, you will more than likely be developing homogeneous groups with which to work.

Often homogeneous groups rely on common cultural elements as points of linkage for members. Using a Stylistic framework, this may mean that a support group for marginalized African American males ties the common theme of historic oppression (cultural-historical dimension) that African Americans, and in particular African American males, face in a dominant white culture. People with disabilities could have the common group bonding experience in a discussion about the ways nondisabled people interact with them and their disability. Elderly group

members may wish to address the ways in which their younger caretakers are limiting their sense of autonomy. An effective leader finds these culturally binding situations and helps members share their experience as a way to develop group cohesion prior to moving on to the working phase.

Comparing Culturally Homogeneous and Heterogeneous Groups

Homogeneous and heterogeneous groups have their inherent advantages and struggles. The wonderful symmetry of members in culturally homogenous groups can lead to members forming quick alliances based on similar cultural life experiences. Heterogeneous groups may have great struggles finding common experience but have a greater diversity of experiences by nature of the members' diverse cultures. These struggles can lead to creative solutions to the issues that the diverse membership brings to the group. We believe it is useful to consider differences between homogeneous groups and heterogeneous groups in terms of Yalom's curative factors (Yalom and Leszcz, 2005).

- **Universality.** In homogeneous groups universality may be experienced around culturally similar issues. In heterogeneous groups universality may be experienced around more global or transcultural issues.

- **Instillation of hope.** Both heterogeneous and homogeneous groups instill hope in group members. There may be cultural differences that affect the instillation of hope in certain cultures based on their level of investment in traditional treatment methods and also based on the emphasis the culture places on collective solutions to problems.

- **Group cohesiveness.** As we have suggested, group cohesiveness may develop faster in homogeneous groups as a result of fewer cultural differences that members must negotiate in bonding.

- **Catharsis.** Both group types can experience catharsis as a result of expression of feelings. The evocative response may be constrained in certain cultures, making this expression a challenge in homogeneous groups of that cultural origin.

- **Existential factors.** Existential factors are possible outcomes in both homogeneous and heterogeneous group types. Certain cultures are more open to raising questions regarding the meaning of existence and recognizing one's mortality.

- **Altruism.** Altruism is experienced in both homogeneous and heterogeneous groups. The experience of working for the common good in a collective fashion is a culturally bound variable, and the culture of origin of the member should be considered.

- **Imparting of information.** One of the most profound outcomes that both homogeneous and heterogeneous groups can experience is the imparting of information. Having members of diverse cultural backgrounds may mean that information may be less culture bound and may provide diverse solutions.

- **Developing socialization techniques.** Both heterogeneous and homogeneous groups can improve members' social skills. Heterogeneous groups may provide more opportunities for members to have experience of cross-cultural socialization.

- **Interpersonal learning.** Both group types provide members experiences from which they can learn about themselves and work through their current and past experiences with others.

■ *Recapitulating the family of origin.* The ability to share or challenge early familial conflicts is possible in both heterogeneous and homogeneous groups, but members' willingness is related to cultural mores about disclosure and family experience.

■ *Imitative behavior.* Homogenous and heterogeneous groups give members opportunities to learn healthy behavior from other members and from the leader.

Exercises for Active Learning
Selecting Members for Culturally Homogeneous Groups

Angelo (p. 179)	Isaiah (p. 176)	Red (pp. 168–169)
Anna (p. 167)	Kyle (p. 166)	Richard (p. 180)
Carlos (pp. 176–177)	Miguel (pp. 166–167)	Shana (pp. 167–168)
Don (p. 178)	Nancy (p. 168)	Tyler (p. 167)
Greg (pp. 178–179)	Ramon (pp. 165–166)	

1. Referring to the profiles of the group members previously presented in this chapter, select members (based on cultural background or life experience) who you might feel would benefit from the following groups. After each name, explain briefly why you selected this member for the group.

    A cultural-pride group for Latino clients

    _____

    _____

    _____

    A group for African American clients addressing the African American identity

    _____

    _____

    _____

    _____

    _____

    _____

    A group for married men on balancing work and family demands

    _____

    _____

    _____

_____

_____

_____

A 50-plus age group on planning for retirement

_____

_____

_____

_____

_____

2. Which of the above groups would you feel comfortable leading? What factors influenced your answer?

STUDY QUESTIONS

1. Explain each of the dimensions in the Personal Dimensions of Identity Model. How does each of these dimensions influence the other dimensions?
2. Explain each of the dimensions in the Stylistic Model of Transcultural Counseling. How does each of these dimensions influence the other dimensions?
3. What are the comparative differences between the PDI model and the Stylistic model? What aspects of cultural identity does one model address differently than the other model?
4. What are the advantages and disadvantages to group process of running culturally homogenous groups? What skills have you identified as being of importance in successfully leading culturally homogenous groups?
5. What are the advantages and disadvantages to group process of running culturally heterogeneous groups? What skills have you identified as being of importance in successfully leading culturally heterogeneous groups?

KEY CONCEPTS

"A" dimensions p. 163
"B" dimensions p. 164
"C" dimensions p. 164
cultural-historical dimension p. 171
culturally heterogeneous p. 160
culturally homogeneous p. 160

Personal Dimensions of Identity
    Model p. 163
psychosocial dimension p. 171
scientific-ideological dimension p. 172
Stylistic Model of Transcultural
    Counseling p. 170

REFERENCES

Association for Multicultural Counseling and Development. (1996). *Multicultural counseling competencies.* Alexandria, VA: American Counseling Association.

Association for Specialists in Group Work (ASGW). (1998). *Principles for Diversity-Competent Group Workers.* Retrieved August 14, 2007, from The Association for Specialists in Group Work website http://www.asgw.org.

Arredondo, P., & Glauner, T. (1992). *Personal dimensions of identity model.* Boston: Empowerment Workshops.

Carter, R. T., & Qureshi, A. (1995). A typology of philosophical assumptions in multicultural counseling and training. In J. G. Ponterotto et al., *Handbook of multicultural counseling.* Thousand Oaks, CA: Sage.

Chojnacki, J., & Gelberg, S. (1995). The facilitation of a gay/lesbian/bisexual support therapy group by heterosexual counselors. *Journal of Counseling and Development, 73,* 352–354.

Cross, W. E., Jr. (1991). *Shades of black: Diversity in African American identity.* Philadelphia: Temple University Press.

Chung, R. C. (2004). Group counseling with Asians. In J. L. DeLucia-Waack, D. A. Gerrity, C. R. Kalodner, & M. T. Riva (Eds.), *Handbook of group counseling and psychotherapy.* Thousand Oaks, CA: Sage.

D'Andrea, M. (2000). Postmodernism, social constructionism, and multiculturalism: Three forces that are shaping and expanding our thoughts about counseling. *Journal of Mental Health Counseling, 22,* 1–16.

D'Andrea, M. (2004). The impact of racial-cultural identity of group leaders and members. In J. L. DeLucia-Waack, D. A. Gerrity, C. R. Kalodner, & M. T. Riva (Eds). *Handbook of group counseling and psychotherapy.* Thousand Oaks, CA: Sage.

Falvo, D. R. (1999). *Medical and psychosocial aspects of chronic illness and disability.* Gaithersburg, MD: Aspen.

Garrett, M. T. (1998). *Walking on the wind: Cherokee teachings for harmony and balance.* Santa Fe, NM: Bear.

Garrett, M. T. (1999). Understanding the "medicine" of Native American traditional values: An integrative review. *Counseling and Values, 43,* 84–98.

Garrett, M. T., & Carroll, J. (2000). Mending the broken circle: Treatment and prevention of substance abuse among Native Americans. *Journal of Counseling and Development, 78,* 379–388.

Gatz, M. (1989). Clinical psychology and aging. In M. Storandt & G. R. VandenBos (Eds.), *The adult years: Continuity and change.* Washington, DC: American Psychological Association.

Henderson, D. A., & Gladding, S. T. (2004). Group counseling with older adults. In J. L. DeLucia-Waack, D. A. Gerrity, C. R. Kalodner, & M. T. Riva (Eds.), *Handbook of group counseling and psychotherapy.* Thousand Oaks, CA: Sage.

Horne, S. G., & Levitt, H. M. (2004). Psychoeducational and counseling groups with gay lesbian, bisexual, and transgendered clients. In J. L. DeLucia-Waack, D. A. Gerrity, C. R. Kalodner, & M. T. Riva (Eds.), *Handbook of group counseling and psychotherapy.* Thousand Oaks, CA: Sage.

McFadden, J. (Ed.). (1999). Transcultural counseling (2nd ed.). Alexandria, VA: *American Counseling Association.*

McFadden, J. (2003). Stylistic model for counseling across cultures. In F. D. Harper and J. McFadden (Ed.) *Culture and counseling: New approaches.* Boston, MA: Allyn and Bacon.

McFadden, J., Jencius, M., & Bowen, P. (2005). *An Adlerian application of the stylistic model of transcultural counseling.* Workshop presented for the North American Society of Adlerian Psychology, Tucson, AZ.

Pack-Brown, S., & Fleming, A. (2004). An Afrocentric approach to counseling groups with African Americans. In J. L. DeLucia-Waack, D. A. Gerrity, C. R. Kalodner, & M. T. Riva (Eds.), *Handbook of group counseling and psychotherapy.* Thousand Oaks, CA: Sage.

Paterson, J. (2007, April). Multicultural counseling: Not just for specialists anymore. *Counseling Today*, pp. 1, 46–47.

Seligman, M., & Marshak, L. (2004). Group approaches for persons with disabilities. In J. L. DeLucia-Waack, D. A. Gerrity, C. R. Kalodner, & M. T. Riva (Eds.), *Handbook of group counseling and psychotherapy.* Thousand Oaks, CA: Sage.

Sue, D. W., Arredondo, P., & McDavis, R. J. (1992). Multicultural counseling competencies and standards: A call to the profession. *Journal of Counseling and Development, 70,* 477–486.

Torres-Rivera, E. (2004). Psychoeducational and counseling groups with Latinos. In J. L. DeLucia-Waack, D. A. Gerrity, C. R. Kalodner, & M. T. Riva (Eds.), *Handbook of group counseling and psychotherapy.* Thousand Oaks, CA: Sage.

Torres-Rivera, E., Wilber, M. P., Roberts-Wilber, J., & Phan, L. (1999). Group work with Latino clients: A psychoeducational model. *Journal for Specialists in Group Work, 24,* 383–404.

Yalom, I. D., & Leszcz, M. (2005). *The theory and practice of group psychotherapy* (5th ed.). New York: Basic Books.

CHAPTER 9

Interventions for Critical Incidents

Learning Objectives

As a result of studying this chapter you will be able to
- Explain what is meant by a critical incident.
- Describe some problems that might develop in the first session and explain leader interventions to address the problems.
- Explain several possible reasons a member might question, confront, or attack the leader.
- Discuss possible leader interventions in conflicts between members.
- Describe some concerns about a departing member that may require leader attention or intervention.
- Discuss possible concerns of the remaining members if a member leaves the group.
- Discuss concerns of the school or agency when members depart from the group.
- Write examples of interventions that leaders could use to respond to critical incidents.
- Describe safety considerations for leading final sessions of multiple-session groups.

INTRODUCTION

We began this text by showing you the steps to start a group. Next we provided some instruction on how you could use the skills you have from individual counseling to lead groups. Then we introduced a set of basic group leader skills and went through a process for planning groups. We followed by addressing the complexities of integrating cultural considerations in group leadership. Now we turn to **critical incidents**—events that have the potential of disrupting the group's progress and therefore require an immediate response from the leader—and the more advanced skills of recognizing these events and responding to them purposefully. We include these skills in this text for beginning leaders because it has been our experience that critical incidents may occur in any group, even possibly the first group you lead. Therefore, we believe you need some skill in recognizing and addressing such incidents in order to provide a safe and productive group for members.

Definition of **critical incident**   An event whose outcome might drastically affect the process and progress of the group (Donigian & Hulse-Killacky, 1999).

Cohen and Smith (1976a, 1976b) identified 34 critical incidents in the beginning phase of groups, 14 in the middle phase of groups, and 13 in the end phase of groups. While the Cohen and Smith texts have gone out of print with the passage of time, the concept of critical incidents remains active in conceptualizations of group leadership. In this chapter we discuss five types of critical incidents and the practical leadership skills you need for responding to these incidents. (For students interested in studying this subject further, a short list of advanced readings on critical incidents in groups has been provided at the end of the chapter.) Generally, critical incidents require you to intervene actively. In some cases, if you do not address the incident or do not manage it correctly, member safety can be compromised and/or the group process and progress may decline from that point forward.

Ethics Pointer

ACA Ethics Code A.8.b requires counselors to protect clients (members) (American Counseling Association, 2005, p. 5). This code implies that you should take action to protect members during critical incidents.

CRITICAL INCIDENTS IN THE BEGINNING PHASE OF GROUPS

The first session of any group is a challenging time for the leader. Members are likely to be somewhat anxious. Even if you have carefully screened and thoughtfully prepared members for the group, going to the first session is still to some degree an appointment with the unknown. Members in the group are likely to be unknown to one another prior to the group. The group process, and more importantly what will be expected of each member personally, is only known to the degree you addressed it in the screening process. Members may be anxious about disclosing

problems, their feelings about the problems, and their feelings and self-perceptions about needing help.

Members may have different levels of readiness to work in the group. One member may have used the time between screening and the start of the group to prepare her thoughts, gather her courage, and be ready to do more intense work in the first session. She may want the relief of putting her concerns out in the open. Another member may come to the first session to test the waters, evaluate perceptions of safety, and decide if the group is right for him. While both of these members would like to be in the group, they enter the first session from different starting points. Some members may have come to the group primarily at the urging of others in their lives, or they may have been sent by principals or courts. These members may be ambivalent or negative about being in the group. What is similar about all group members is that each approaches the group from a perspective rooted in his or her personal attitudes and expectations.

You, the leader, approach the first session from a different perspective than members. You are concerned with many tasks primarily related to the formation of the group and the building of interpersonal relationships and cohesion among the members. Here are some of your tasks for the first session:

- Welcoming the members.
- Reviewing the purpose of the group.
- Setting, reviewing, or refining group norms.
- Providing some structure to help members know what to expect and thereby reduce member anxiety.
- Engaging all members—each member should begin to speak in the group and participate in activities.
- Encouraging appropriate member disclosure.
- Starting the process of building connection and cohesion among members.
- Generating an expectation of working together for change.
- Reviewing or clarifying member goals.
- Promoting the expectation that the group can help members progress toward goals.

Besides starting this long list of tasks, you must engage a range of members, some of whom will be anxious and each of whom has a different expectation about the group. You are challenged to manage time and group process so that the tasks of the group are begun. At the same time you must set a tone of caring deeply about the members (Stockton, 1992). Let's look at two types of critical incidents that commonly occur during the early phase of a group. The first occurs when a member does not participate at all, and the second occurs when a member overparticipates by going too deeply into a topic before the group is ready.

Critical Incident Type 1: A Silent Member in the First Session

A prime task in the first session is to set the norm of balanced participation. Imbalance in participation opens the way for two possible critical incidents to occur, either of which could be harmful to members or destructive to the group's process. The most common situation of imbalance in a first session is a **silent member**.

Definition of **silent member**   A group member who does not speak during the group or who does not participate.

The best way to avoid the development of one or more silent members is to make your initial request for participation nonthreatening. Consider the following contrasting examples of directions for beginning a group for prostate cancer patients:

Example 1

We are going to start by getting to know each other a little bit. I'd like you to pair off with the person next to you and share your name and a little bit about yourself.

Example 2

We are going to start by getting to know each other a little bit. I'd like you to pair off with the person next to you and share how you felt when the doctor told you that you had prostate cancer.

Starting a first session with the second of these directions makes it more difficult for hesitant members to begin participating in the group. If the member is already hesitant, it is more likely that he will develop as a silent member. In contrast, if you use the first direction, members are empowered to choose what they feel comfortable disclosing at this early point when even the names of the other members are not known.

If after several requests from the leader, a member still does not participate, and if this continues for a couple of sessions or if a member participates minimally but only with extensive encouragement from the leader each time, then the leader should address the issue more directly. For example, the leader might consider one of the following approaches:

- Ask the silent member to comment on what is hard for him.
- Ask the member to pick a specific member to talk with in the group about her silence.
- Remind the member of the commitment he made during screening to participate and to help others.
- Ask the member how he intends to contribute to the group.
- Talk with the member between sessions to see if the member wishes to continue the group participating appropriately.
- Remove the member from the group.

As a leader you need to be aware that a chronically silent member is likely to slow down the development of or decrease the level of trust in the group because the other members may not connect with or know what to make of a member who is silent or speaks minimally. The cohesion needed to promote group development just may not develop. The other members may be less willing to take risks of self-disclosure, and little progress may be made toward goals.

Critical Incident Type 2: Premature Deep Disclosure

Definition of **premature deep disclosure**   A disclosure made early in the life of the group before members know each other well and before other members are disclosing at a deep level.

Often in the introductory rounds of a first session, there is a member who wants to tell the full, detailed story of why he is in the group. This member begins to talk as part of a round and then continues to talk until or unless you intervene (Stockton, 1992). A **premature deep disclosure** can be problematic for leaders for several reasons:

- You do not know the members well and therefore cannot predict how other members might respond to the disclosure.
- You do not know the members well and therefore may be less able to make connections between the issues in the disclosure and possible similar concerns of the other members.
- Norms of the group regarding giving and receiving support or feedback may not be well established, and members may have little practice using them.
- Cohesion—the sense of belonging to the group—may not be well established.
- If members do not know the member making the disclosure, it is likely that they will simply not respond to the disclosing member, which will result in the disclosing member feeling exposed, vulnerable, and neglected rather than heard and cared about.

The following is an example of the development of a premature deep disclosure in Matt's prostate cancer group. Matt started a round in which each man was to say one thing that was hard about having cancer.

Mike: The worst thing for me is that all those exams the doctors do are very embarrassing.

Steve: It's threatening to think, what if they can't treat this?

Matt: Mmm . . .

Greg: It sure is. I wonder what will happen to me. My wife is busy checking the life insurance policy, and my uncle is telling me not to leave my wife without protection. He called up a friend of his in insurance and asked what I could get. Then my uncle called the funeral home to find out how much a funeral and a burial plot would cost. He also called the bank to find out how much money I had in my savings account. Thankfully, the banker told him . . .

In this example Greg appears to be started on a long disclosure that will continue for some time. Greg's disclosure is related to the topic of the group and even to the topic of the specific round in progress; however, the extent of the disclosure is too long and probably too deep. If you do not intervene, the focus of the group will shift entirely to Greg, and the process of the round will be lost. A goal of leaders in the first group is to promote participation of all members; therefore, leaders must cut Greg off compassionately and return to the process of the round.

Matt: Hold on a minute, Greg. This is pretty detailed, pretty deep, and it's real important. I know that your situation is a tough one and that each of you probably needs to share a great deal. Listening to and helping each other is going to be central to the process of our group. There will be a time and a place in the group to do that, but first we need to do introductions.

Greg: Mmm, home is confused right now.

Matt: Not giving you the support you need?

Greg: *[Quietly]* No.

Matt: We can give you some support here in the group, and you can give some support to the others. *[Looking at Greg and then around the group]* We can do that better if we get to know each other a little better—we'll be able to help each other if we can get acquainted first. We will come back to working with the details of each of your situations in later groups. Our task in this session is to just get to start to know each other a little bit. Can you just say in one sentence what the worst thing is?

Greg: My family is already assuming I'm going to die.

Matt: That's one possible bottom line, one of several that are possible, and the least optimistic one. I'm thinking others have had those thoughts at least fleetingly, and we will be able to talk about that a little later in the group. We are also going to consider all the possible outcomes and focus more on treatment and getting better, because that gives you more hope.

Greg: I need to have some hope.

Matt: There is some, and we'll talk more about it.

Greg: Good.

Matt: Let's go back to the introduction round now. Fred?

Matt has cut Greg off. He let Greg know that what he is sharing is important and will be worked on in the groups but not during the round. Then he framed a request that let Greg know how much he wanted him to say. The round continued. You should note that Matt needs to remember what Greg said and to follow through on his statement that Greg's concerns would be addressed in later sessions. Also, as the round comes to an end, Matt should in some way acknowledge the depth of the issues presented in the round.

Matt: So some of you are most concerned about everything—the medical treatments and family disruption—you are going through right now, and others of you are more conscious of your concern about the final outcome—the "will you get better" question—and both of these areas are huge. You have a lot on your plates, and you have the courage to seek help. It takes a lot of strength to deal with issues as big as this head-on. I'm really glad that you decided to be in the group so you can get some support. The hospital has run this type of group for years because the men in the group tell us it has provided support, accurate information, and hope. I'm confident that this group will be helpful to you—that you will be able to help each other, and I'm looking forward to working with each of you as we go along.

Now let's look at an example of someone making a disclosure, and no one responds at all. Matt has started the group for men with prostate cancer by asking members to introduce themselves and tell one thing about themselves. During this opening round, Frank makes a deep disclosure to which the group makes no response.

Daniel: I'm Daniel, and I work as a truck driver hauling material from the stone yard to construction sites.

Greg: Hi, I'm Greg. I have a wife, Marta, and a 6-year-old, Paul. I'm a traffic signal repairer for the railroad.

Ian: My name's Ian, and I'm a foreman at the bakery. My wife, Sue, is a law student.

Frank: My name's Frank, and I'm the assistant coach for track at the college. My wife is Alice. Last night was the third time she tried to hang herself, and I'm scared.

Moe: I'm Moe, and I work as meat cutter.

Ted: I'm Ted and my wife is Janet, and we both work at the hardware store.

In this example Frank's disclosure was deeper than any of the things the other men had shared. The other members did not respond to the disclosure, rather they continued with the round as if Frank had not spoken. This lack of response is not uncommon in situations in which the members are surprised by a deep disclosure from a member they do not know. Hopefully, leaders were monitoring group process and realized what had happened. If leaders do not intervene, a likely outcome is that the group will proceed with no discussion of what was disclosed.

Let's look at some possible experiences of the member related to this incident. The disclosing member may

- feel that he took a great risk in the group and received no response from the group,
- feel embarrassed at his disclosure,
- feel the group is an unsafe place, or
- not return to the group the following session.

Other group members may

- be uncertain about what types of disclosures are appropriate in the group,
- have a variety of affective responses to the disclosure including being frightened by it,
- experience the group as an unsafe place, or
- not return to the group the following session.

Let's pick up the example with Frank's disclosure and see how Matt makes an intervention to help the group.

Frank: My name's Frank, and I'm the assistant coach for track at the college. My wife is Alice. Last night was the third time she tried to hang herself, and I'm scared.

Moe: I'm Moe, and I work as meat cutter.

Ted: I'm Ted and my wife is Janet, and we both work at the hardware store.

Matt: OK, let's stop for a minute and look at what just happened here. We were going around saying a little introductory information about ourselves and Frank said something about his wife that was a much deeper disclosure than what the rest of you were doing. After Frank spoke, we just went right on with the round and nobody said anything to Frank. We finished the round, and now we need to say something to Frank. I'd like us to go around and each of us say something, a sentence or two about how you felt or what you thought when Frank made his disclosure. I'll start. *[Looking at Frank]* When you said Alice tried to hang herself,

I thought that's a lot for Frank to carry—concerns about his wife and now about his own health.

Frank: I need to be here for her.

Matt: Daniel?

Daniel: I felt really scared thinking about someone hanging.

Frank: Yeah, it's real scary for me.

Greg: I'm glad you told us. Maybe we can be a support for you.

Moe: I don't know what to say. I can tell by the tone of your voice you love her.

Frank: Yeah, I really do. I'll try any of the treatments the doctors want because Alice won't be OK without me.

Ted: I thought, I want to help him. I wish there was something specific I could do.

Frank: Thanks.

Matt: Frank, I'm wondering if you'd like to talk with me outside the group about how to get some help for Alice.

Frank: Yes, I would.

Matt: How are you feeling right now about the things the group said to you?

Frank: I feel like they understand and they care.

Matt: Mmm. . . . That understanding and caring is real, and it is there about your wife, and all of you will understand and care about each other as you deal with your cancers.

Consider how Matt helped the members respond to Frank. First of all, he stopped group process and called the disclosure and their lack of response to it to the attention of the members. Next, he directed members to make some response to Frank that focused on members' reactions to Frank and his disclosure rather than on problem solving around the disclosed issue. Then, Matt went first and modeled a type of appropriate response.

After all the members responded to Frank, Matt offered to meet with Frank outside the group to consult about help for Alice. This was an honest, direct offer of concrete help for Frank. Matt checked Frank's reactions to the members' responses to him. And finally, Matt stressed that the same caring the members had just expressed regarding Frank's wife would be central to the cancer support group. He shifted the focus from Frank and his wife to the process of caring and then generalized the focus from caring back to the cancer support group. At that point, Matt should continue with the support group as planned.

In this example and the previous example, we have shown you two possible responses to deep initial disclosures in the first session. We intentionally showed quite different approaches so that you would have alternatives from which to select when you are leading a group and need to respond to deep first-session disclosures. Both approaches provided caring and some attention to the member who made the disclosure and then returned the focus of the group to the initial round. In both cases, the leader gave some explanation why he was returning the group to work on the initial round.

Exercises for Active Learning

1. Paula and Justin are starting a group for adults in their 20s who would like to change jobs. The purpose of the group is to help the members consider the pros and cons of jobs they are considering. Justin starts the first session by inviting the members to participate in a round.

Justin: Welcome to the group. As we talked about in the screening interview, the purpose of this group is to help you examine the pros and cons of jobs you've been considering. Let's start by going around and saying your name and something about your current job.

Carla: My name's Carla, and my job now is assistant to the nurse in the surgery at the hospital.

Dominique: I'm Dominique, and I'm working cooking burgers and fries.

Carlton: I'm mowing lawns at the cemetery in the summer and shoveling roofs in the winter. My name's Carlton.

Debbie: I'm Debbie, and I'm working cleaning offices at night. Those doctors are so conceited. They call me "you" and "hey, cleaning lady" and expect me to call them "doctor" and "sir." They make late appointments well into cleaning time and then act like I'm in their way. Yesterday, one of them threw a big pile of bloody swabs on the floor and acted like I could just pick them up.

On the lines below, write an appropriate leader intervention to this disclosure.

_____

_____

_____

_____

2. Meg and Lyndon are starting a group for fourth-grade boys who live with their mother and have sporadic visits from their father. The purpose of the group is to help the boys process their feelings about their fathers and set goals for interacting with their fathers. Meg opens the first session by asking the boys to share their names and tell how often their fathers visit.

Tommy: I'm Tommy, and Dad comes to visit the first Sunday of the month.

Danny: Danny here. My daddy visits on my birthday and at Christmas. I wish he would visit more.

Alfred: He visits sometimes when he promises and sometimes if he thinks it will make Mom mad, and I'm Al.

Nicholas: My name's Nick, and Dad visits on the weekends Mom has to work at the hospital.

Meg: Jay, How about you?

Jay does not answer Meg and is looking intently at his shoes. Write a leader intervention for Lyndon or Meg to use to help Jay.

_____

_____

_____

_____

CRITICAL INCIDENTS IN THE MIDDLE PHASE OF GROUPS

Now let's look at three types of critical incidents that most commonly occur in the middle phase of groups. The first type of critical incident involves a challenge to a group leader's authority by one or more members; the second involves conflict between members; and the third occurs when a group member walks out of a session or leaves the group before the final session.

Critical Incident Type 3: Criticism of Your Leadership

When a member questions your ability to lead the group, it is a critical incident because your response influences members' perception of you and of the group. Challenges concerning your competence may range on a continuum of severity from a simple question, to a confrontation, to an attack. The questions, confrontations, or attacks often have two components: information and emotion or affect. While reasonable questions asked in a civil tone are a normal part of group process, attacks delivered in highly emotional tones should be considered critical incidents. Such attacks may evoke defensiveness from you, making it harder for you to lead effectively. An overall strategy that can be applied to attacks and confrontations has three components:

1. Do your best not to take confrontations and attacks personally.
2. Stay emotionally centered and grounded; try not to become defensive.
3. Respond to the information request contained in the confrontation or attack.

By staying centered and grounded and responding with information, you provide information useful to all members and decrease the emotional intensity.

Your experience, your counseling knowledge, or your ability to understand the group members' concerns or lives may be the subject of the question, challenge, or attack. The following examples contain member statements that challenge a leader. These examples are grouped based on the issue underlying the challenge. In the first example, the leader's competence is challenged.

Jeff: Pete, I don't understand why you're leading the group by yourself if you're an intern.

[It is important for Pete to respond to these challenges in a genuine, nondefensive, and caring manner. He should respond directly to the questions asked since these are reasonable questions.]

Pete: OK, let me talk a bit about what it means to be an intern. First of all, it means that I did all my class work successfully. That took about two years. After that, I did

practicum—working with clients at the university under supervision—and I did that well. The next step is internship, and that means working more independently in an agency as a student under supervision. Remember we talked at your screening interview, and you signed permission that the sessions would be taped and watched by my supervisor so that you get the best care, and I get ongoing instruction.

Jeff: OK. Do you have experience leading groups like this one?

Pete: I led a group on the topic during my practicum at one of the university dorms.

When members attack your competency, try to respond as Pete did by discussing your experience as it is. Use a conversational rather than a defensive tone to share your experience directly. You should be honest with the members. Credit yourself for what you have done but don't embellish it. Don't act apologetic for experience members ask about but you don't have. One way you can look on these challenges whether they are minor or major is that the challenges give you an opportunity to model being genuine in the group.

In the next example, Mike is starting a group for women at an assisted living facility. The critical incident occurs when members focus on personal characteristics of the leader.

Sally: Mike, you look young enough to be my son. I thought we'd get a leader who was our age.

Ella: Right, and I really wanted a woman for our leader.

This type of challenge often makes beginning leaders nervous because the members are focusing on a personal characteristic that cannot be changed. These challenges point out the importance of pregroup screening. If at all possible, it is desirable for you rather than an intake counselor to do the screening. Potential members would then meet you, connect with you and have the opportunity to voice any concerns prior to the group. While screening may not prevent member concerns about your age or gender from coming up in the group at a later point, screening does facilitate member–leader connection and informed consent. Continuing with the example, Mike responds openly and caringly to member challenges.

Mike: [Smiles and nods to Sally, who appears to be in her 80s] Well, I'm 27—probably I am young enough to be your son.

Sally: Grandson.

Mike: OK, grandson. And I don't know what it's like to be 80 or 90, but I want to know. I expect you have a lot of wisdom about life. I'd like to hear it, and I'd like to help you share that wisdom with each other. I'd like to help you work out ways to encourage each other so that every day here is a little more pleasant than it would have been without the group.

Gertrude: More pleasant would be a good thing.

Mike: [Looks at Ella] I know you wanted a woman, but there wasn't a woman available at the agency till after the first of the year. Certainly you can choose not to be in this group, and I won't take it personally. I'm here because I'm interested in people your age and how to make life good for you. [Mike scans the group.] Also, we wanted to

offer a group now because we are approaching the holidays, and they can be both very happy times and also times when we miss the people who used to be in our lives and aren't with us anymore. We thought maybe this was an important time for support.

Ella: OK, you seem like a nice boy, and I could use some support.

Notice that Mike was gracious and offered Ella the freedom to choose not to be in the group. He also provided encouragement and caring to which the members responded. Mike is secure in himself and interprets Ella's description of him as a "nice boy" as acceptance.

A common type of challenge focuses on the idea that you don't have experiences similar to those of the members. This lack of similar experience may raise questions in members' minds about your competence. Some possible challenges might be the following:

- We just got back from Iraq; I thought our leader would be someone who was a veteran. You don't have any idea what we've been through.
- You seem to be a nice woman, but I wonder if you have a clue what it's like to be a gay man in a conservative state.
- All of us are alcoholics; are you a recovering alcoholic, Sam?
- How are you going to be able to able to lead a group for parents of difficult foster children if you've never had any kids of your own?

You should respond to challenges like these by acknowledging the truth in the members' concerns. Then you could make some statement about your caring for the members or the members shared concern. You might also present what you will offer to the group. Let's look at some examples. André is starting a group for veterans who are returning to civilian life and have enrolled in the university. The purpose of the group is to help the veterans make a successful transition to college.

Kyle: We just got back from Iraq; I thought our leader would be someone who was a veteran. You don't have any idea what we've been through.

André: No, Kyle, I don't know what you have been through. *[André scans the group as he speaks.]* I do want you to know that I respect all of you for your service. I do know that some of you did not expect to go overseas and that for some of you it was very tough on your families. It's because you took risks and made sacrifices that I want life to be good for you now that you are home. I want to help you as you start in college. College is a different world than the army—one with different challenges—and it's one I'm familiar with. If you're willing to work with me, I'd like to know whatever you're OK sharing about what you did go through and particularly how you got through. I want to help you use your strengths to get through the first semester of college. One thing we know about college is that if you can have a good first semester, your chances of graduating are good.

Troy: My wife worked two jobs while I was gone. I'd like to learn enough to get a better job so she won't have to work as hard as we get older.

Albert: I'd like to get absorbed in school—be off to a fast start—and get my life going again.

André: I think I can lead this group so that you can help each other get your lives back again.

Zack: That would be good.

Bailey is leading a group for gay men. The men were referred to the group by their counselors, who identified them as needing better housing and medical services. The purpose of the group is to help the men explore options for better housing, improved medical services, and connections with agencies providing practical support within the community.

Alf: You seem to be a nice woman, but I wonder if you have a clue what it's like to be a gay man in a conservative state.

Bailey: *[Bailey looks at Alf.]* Well, Alf, I don't have the experience of life you do. I do have some experience leading this type of group, so what I know is from listening to gay men talk about their lives and how they negotiated for their needs to be met here in our state. *[Bailey scans the group as she speaks.]* As a woman, I do know what it's like to have people who don't know me judge me as incompetent or talk down to me as if I had problems understanding them. I know the hurt that causes me, and I expect that some of the experiences you've had are painful too. Perhaps because I know what it feels like for me to be on the receiving end of prejudice, I'm very committed to social justice. I'm the one in this agency who focuses most on helping people get access to practical things—housing, food, transportation, and medical care—that they need for a better daily life. As we talked about during screening, your counselors referred you to the group because each of you had some area where the counselors thought you could be helped to get better services. I'd like to help you with that, and I'm hoping you'd be willing to work with me.

Pratt: Give her a chance.

Donald: Yeah, we'll take a chance on you. *[Several members nod.]*

Bailey: Thanks, I'll work hard to help you.

Exercises for Active Learning

1. Althea and Sam are starting a group for adults over the age of 40 who have serious drinking problems. Early in the group, members ask about the leaders' experience with alcohol. Althea is 33. During her college years she drank some, but rarely drinks at this time. Alcohol has not caused problems in her life. Sam is 35. After an arrest for driving under the influence, he went to counseling and stopped drinking. He considers himself someone who had some problems drinking but was not an alcoholic. As you write responses for Sam and Althea, remember to keep the focus on how they can contribute as group leaders rather than on their personal stories.

Tonya: All of us are alcoholics; are you a recovering alcoholic, Sam?

Sam:

_____

_____

_____

_____

_____

Susan: Althea, you told me before that you rarely drink. I keep wondering, how are you going to be able to help us? Are you going to judge us because most of have been to counseling before and we still have drinking problems?

Althea:

_____

_____

_____

_____

2. Sarah is leading a group for foster parents who are parenting children with severe mental health issues. She is 31 years old and does not have any children of her own. Prior to going to graduate school, Sarah worked for three years as an elementary school teacher. This is the first time Sarah has led a group for foster parents.

Anna: How are you going to be able to able to lead a group for parents of difficult foster children if you've never had any kids of your own?

Sarah:

_____

_____

_____

_____

3. Sarah is leading a similar group four years later. During those years, Sarah and her husband, Dave, have tried unsuccessfully to have a child. Although Sarah and Dave are now trying to adopt a child, Sarah is still upset that she cannot have her own child. Sarah has led a group for foster parents six times in the last four years. Overall, the foster parents have rated her groups as "very helpful" and described her help as "reality based." Up to this point, the current group has been working productively. This challenge has a distinct tone of attack and occurs in the fourth session of the group. Write a response for Sarah to answer Ed's challenge. Remember not to react to an attack with an attack. Reply thoughtfully and intentionally. Finally, keep in mind that while Sarah's history related to wanting her own children may influence her leadership of the group, it is not necessary and it may not be wise for her to disclose her entire history to the group.

Ed: Last night that kid spit in my face and yelled, "You're definitely not my dad and never will be." *[Ed looks at Sarah.]* These things you've had us do aren't helping me at all. I don't know why I expected that they would since you don't have any kids. Can't we get somebody different to run this group?

Sarah:

_____

_____

_____

_____

Critical Incident Type 4: Harmful Conflict Between Members

Definition of **conflict between members**   A verbal argument between members.

Conflicts between members occur in groups as part of the normal group process. These conflicts require skilled leadership because they have direct potential to become critical incidents in which members may be harmed. This potential for harm is greatest in incidents in which one member physically or verbally attacks another member or two or more members get into a heated argument. Psychological harm to the members involved is likely to be the result (Lieberman, Yalom, and Miles, 1973).

The long-term effect of a conflict on the group may depend on how cohesive the group was before the conflict, how well the conflict was processed, and whether or not you were able to turn the processing of the conflict into an opportunity to teach all the members some point related to the purpose of the group. Even when the processing has gone well, you should not be surprised if a major conflict in the group has one or more of the following effects on group process:

- Increased distance between some members of the group.
- Changes in group cohesion.
- A lowering of trust among members or a recycling of trust issues previously addressed in the group.

At such times you will need to be patient with members and may need to normalize their concerns. Express your confidence in the members and your hope in the group process.

Ethics Pointer

The ACA Ethics Code states that one of a leader's main ethical responsibilities is to provide for the safety of members (American Counseling Association, 2005). An effective leader monitors conflicts between members and intervenes as needed to cut off members attacking other group members and clarify or reinforce group norms. A member who persists in attacking other members should be removed from the group.

Minimizing the Possibility of Conflict

While conflict between members might happen in any group, a vague plan for a group and/or passive leadership may invite unpredicted member-to-member interactions. One of the reasons that good planning and active leadership are so important

is that they help to prevent conflict in a group. Consider the following questions about your own leadership style:

- To what degree do you plan your groups?
- How actively do you facilitate group process?

Keep in mind that while overplanning and overactive facilitation help to prevent conflict, they may also prevent active participation and growth among the group members. An effective leader therefore seeks a balance between too much and too little planning and facilitation. Indeed, experienced leaders often welcome a conflict in a group as an opportunity to increase the range of issues or depth of an issue related to the purpose of the group. However, most new leaders need more practice before they are ready to turn such negative events into meaningful positive events. Therefore, you should consider if a specific conflict is actually an opportunity for the group, and balance that consideration with your level of confidence in your leadership skills. The time remaining in the session should also influence the time you put into addressing the conflict, because it is best not to leave conflicts unresolved when the session is over. At the very least, you should intervene to bring any combative behavior to a halt, and remind members of the group norms and ask or direct them to follow the norms.

Leading During Conflict

Your ability to lead during conflict has much to do with your personal characteristics, leadership style, and level of confidence. Consider the following questions:

- How able are you to observe interpersonal interactions of members and anticipate sources of conflict?
- How comfortable are you with intense emotion in the group?
- How comfortable are you with conflict?
- How confident are you in intervening in conflicts?

While all member conflicts require your careful monitoring, physical or verbal attacks by members on other members require you to intervene actively and intentionally. It is important for you to stay calm and centered if the group becomes emotionally intense. It is also important to intervene immediately to prevent a verbal attack from escalating into a physical attack. While you may monitor your own levels of comfort or discomfort with the group interaction, you should not allow your anxiety to paralyze you into passivity. Not making a leadership intervention is a choice you remain responsible for should members be harmed by your failure to intervene. On the other hand, you should not intervene based on your own anxiety but rather from a position of purposeful leadership. While you may be concerned that the member making the attack will not like being cut off, your leadership role in the group makes it your responsibility to cut off any members who attack others.

When one or more members attack another member, it is important to be conscious of the reactions of the members not involved in the conflict. These members may have the following reactions:

- Be frightened by the conflict and withdraw emotionally or possibly physically (move their chairs back out of the circle).
- Take sides and expand the conflict.
- Focus on you to see how you respond to the conflict.
- Focus on you to see how you provide for member safety.

Often the remaining members will take cues from you on how to respond to conflict situations.

Intervening When Conflict Becomes Too Heated

A useful strategy in dealing with member conflicts and attacks parallels the strategy suggested for dealing with questions, conflicts, and attacks on leaders in which we focused on responding to the informational content rather than the emotional content. When we intervene in conflicts among members or attacks on members, we deal first with reestablishing physical safety. We separate fighting members and move them to seats on opposite sides of the circle or, if necessary, remove one or more of them from the group. Next we focus on group norms and information rather than emotion to move the interactions among group members out of the range of attacks and heated conflicts and back into the range of appropriate member interactions. At least initially, it may be wise for you to intervene in a stepwise manner with the following sequence:

- Reestablish physical safety immediately—separate fighting members—seek help from security personnel or other adults as needed.
- Intervene to stop any attacking or derogatory statements.
- Clarify group norms.
- Process the nature of the conflict with the members having the conflict.

    1. Cut off inappropriate comments and inaccurate information.
    2. Clarify information and/or interpersonal feedback.
    3. Check out the accuracy of the information and/or interpersonal feedback with the group.

- Process the experience of the remaining members.

Examples of leaders following these steps will be presented shortly.

Conflicts force you to reflect on what has happened in the group up to the point of the conflict at the same time you are making initial interventions to decrease the intensity or potential explosiveness of the conflict. The following questions may be useful to you, since the answers to the questions may influence how you process the conflict with the members.

- Why has the conflict developed at this time?
- Is this conflict related to a breach in confidentiality?
- Is there a reason to cut off one or both members at this time?
- How related is the conflict to the purpose of the group?
- Can you generalize the issues in the conflict to issues that can be discussed by the whole group?

Now let's look at a pair of conflicts and see how leaders address the conflicts.

Example 1: Breaking Up an Angry Argument Between Members

Ned and Zack are leading a group for men ages 20 to 30 who have recently experienced the death of their fathers. The purpose of the group is to help the men process their loss and to help them identify and focus on positive memories of their fathers. Each session is set up as a two-hour session with a 15-minute break for refreshments at the end of the first hour. The group is in the fourth session and has been working well. As the men return from break, Ned becomes aware of sharp voice tones between two of the members.

Ralph: *[Addressing Lloyd and moving toward him]* I just can't believe you did that. How could you give birth control pills to a 13-year-old?

[Ned sees that both men look angry. Ned intervenes in a voice carrying a tone of command.]

Ned: Ralph, Lloyd, both of you back up and go sit down on the sides of the circle where you are now—opposite each other. *[In a softer tone]* The rest of you get your coffee and sit down too.

Lloyd: I'm her father, and . . .

[Ned holds out a hand toward each of the men in a blocking motion.]

Ned: No more! Both of you be quiet and listen to what I'm going to say. *[Ned's coleader, Zack, has switched seats in order to sit between Lloyd and Ralph. Ned scans the group as he talks.]* Birth control is a hot topic and one on which people have widely differing opinions. It is not a topic we are going to get into here in this group because it's not related to the purpose of our group. We are going to focus on grief and loss and capturing important memories about your fathers. Now let's get back on and stay on that topic. And remember, no matter what we discuss in here, I expect you to treat each other and talk to each other with respect. *[Ned looks at Ralph and Lloyd who nod in agreement, then he nods to Zack to proceed.]*

Zack: OK, let's go around and show and talk about the photograph you brought—the one showing a good time with you and your dad together. Allen, we'll start with you.

In this example, Ned verbally blocked discussion of the topic causing the conflict, because it was not related to the purpose of the group and was likely to be explosive. As he did so, his coleader physically blocked the conflict by sitting between the two members involved in the conflict. Ned then revisited the purpose of the group and the norm of respect, and Zack redirected the group to its task.

Example 2: Stopping a Physical Attack

Ellen and Nancy are counselors at a middle school in a suburban area. They are leading a group for eighth-grade girls who identified themselves as having drinking problems or were referred by their parents for help stopping drinking. The group meets during second period every Tuesday, and in general members have been quite supportive

of each other. The group meets in a square room under the landing of a staircase in an old building. The girls generally come in the room and cross through the circle to a seat of their choice. When the conflict occurs, half the group is in the room and seated. Jenna enters, circles behind the chairs, and punches Emily soundly between the shoulder blades. As Emily stands to retaliate, Ellen grabs Emily's clenched fist.

Ellen: No fighting in group—ever.

Nancy: Not for any reason. Jenna, come here and sit next to me.

Kaitlyn: Send her to the principal.

Nancy: *[To Kaitlyn]* Not right now. Jenna, come sit right here next to me. Mabel, you move over one chair.

Ellen: Emily, you and I are sitting over here. *[Ellen releases her grip on Emily's arm after Emily sits where she was told to sit. This release of grip is Emily's reward for following Ellen's instructions.]*

Nancy: OK, I want to hear from you two what's going on, and I don't want any of the rest of you to interrupt.

Jenna: She told everyone in English class what I said in group last week.

Emily: She stole my boyfriend, and I hate her.

Ellen: So you broke Emily's confidence and the confidence of the whole group to get even with her.

Jenna: You bet.

Nancy: Jenna, revenge is not OK. You not only hurt Emily but you essentially told everybody what this group is about, and you agreed before you came in the group not to do that.

Grace: Kick her out of the group.

Ellen: I'm thinking about that. First I want to go around and have each of you say two sentences about how Jenna's breach of confidentiality is likely to affect you. And then the second time around I want each of you to say two sentences about what Jenna could do to earn back your trust and be part of the group. We're going to take three minutes to think quietly and then we will start with you, Claire. Jenna, while they are talking I want you to listen, and I don't want you to say anything.

Nancy and Ellen have broken up the fight and moved the fighting members apart. They identified the source of the conflict and set into motion a round involving feedback from each member to Jenna. It is likely that the leaders will have to help members in this feedback process. At the end of the round, it will be clearer how members feel about Jenna's behavior, and the members will have taken some responsibility for helping Jenna understand how she could begin to repair her relationship with them. After the round, leaders will have to decide how to proceed both with Jenna and the group. Note two things: First, this method of processing is possible because the conflict happened early in the session. And second, while leaders engaged the group in a feedback and clarification process, leaders retained for themselves the power to make the decision about Jenna's removal from or retention in the group. Jenna's attention to what the group says to her and any response leaders solicit after the rounds may strongly influence leaders' decisions regarding Jenna's continued membership.

Table 9-1   Leadership Steps to Consider When Members Fight

Step 1.   Stop the fight. Intervene physically if it is necessary and safe to do so.

Step 2.   Reestablish physical safety by moving members apart or by removing one or more members from the group.

Step 3.   Silence the members and then give clear directions about how the group will proceed.

Step 4.   Clarify the root of the conflict.

Step 5.   Make a statement clarifying the relationship or lack thereof between the conflict and the purpose of the group and/or group norms.

Step 6.   Direct the group regarding the procedures to follow if you decide to pursue the issue raised in the conflict, or clearly indicate that the group will not pursue the topic.

Table 9-1 summarizes some steps for you to consider when members fight in a group. While most member conflicts in groups do not take the form of a physical fight, a fight or some form of hitting may occur as it did in this group. In this example Ellen restrained Jenna from punching Emily a second time. After this intervention, both Jenna and Emily followed the leaders' verbal directions.

In general you should screen out of groups members who have a history of physically hitting or attacking others. However, if you work in sites where you may have to physically restrain clients, you should take steps related to your own safety and to promote your professional and ethical practice. Here are some practice considerations related to leaders restraining clients in groups:

■   Practice only within your area of professional competence.

■   Practice under the ongoing and regular clinical direction of a supervisor experienced with the client group.

■   Review professional ethical codes with your clinical supervisor, and discuss implications of the codes related to restraining clients in groups.

■   Receive training in mental health client rights in your state and update your training annually.

■   Receive training in a recognized system of client restraint legal in your state and endorsed by your school or agency.

■   Study and implement school or agency safety and security procedures.

■   Maintain your own individual professional liability insurance. At the time you apply for professional liability insurance and at each annual renewal, indicate clearly on your application that you may have to restrain clients and what system you use. Keep a photocopy of your application for your records.

■   Each time you have to restrain a client, write a complete report of the incident and place it in the client's file before you leave the school or agency for the day.

■   Each time you have to restrain a client, contact your supervisor as soon as possible but definitely before leaving the school or agency for the day. The nature of the contact (supervision, consultation, or notification) as well the timing of the contact (immediate, during the event, after the client is safe, or at the end of the day) may vary depending on the type of restraint used, your site, your experience, your licensure level, and your supervisor's schedule. Enter a note regarding

contact with your supervisor and any directions from the supervisor into the record before leaving your school or agency for the day.

■   Review each restraint event at your next clinical supervision, and document that review as part of supervision documentation.

Above and beyond these considerations, it is important that you regularly review how you are affected by restraining clients and whether or not you wish to continue employment at sites where you may be called upon to restrain clients.

Exercises for Active Learning

Norton and Larry are leading a group for fifth-grade students who are upset about the death of their grandparents. The purpose of the group is to help the members talk about how they miss their grandparents and process their loss. This is the third session, and so far the group has been working well. Larry divided the 15-member-group into three subgroups of five members each. The subgroups were to discuss how they remembered their grandparents at the last family holiday the grandparent had been alive. Each group was to have a leader, a writer, and a speaker. In one of the subgroups, members began to argue over their roles.

Shelly: I don't want to be the writer. My writing's no good.

Tracey: Well, it's your turn, and I'm not doing it again.

Kyle: I want to be the speaker.

Steve: It's my turn to be the leader and Debbie's turn to be speaker.

Tracey: [To Shelly] You have to be the writer because it's your turn.

Debbie: Well, I don't ever want to be speaker, and I don't think we all have to take equal turns.

Norton notices that Debbie's voice tone is now the loudest in the room. He moves a chair into the subgroup to help the group work through the conflict. On the lines below list three steps you think Norton could take in helping this subgroup.

1. _____

2. _____

3. _____

Write exactly what Norton should say to the group for each of the steps you listed.

1. _____

_____

_____

2. _____

_____

_____

3. _____

_____

_____

Critical Incident Type 5: A Member Leaves the Group

During the screening process, you should include open discussions of the importance of attendance at all group sessions and obtain commitment from members to complete the group. Even when this is done, members may temporarily or permanently leave the group, and their departure may occur during a session or between sessions. Such departures are critical incidents in group process.

Departure of a Member from a Session

Members might leave the room for unexpected reasons that may or may not be obvious to you at the time. For example, a member might feel ill and leave the group. At the time she may or may not say something, so you may not understand what is happening. If one or more members make comments with a critical or attacking tone to another member and the recipient of the comments gets up and heads for the door, you should be aware of what is happening and stop the member from leaving by using your skills for dealing with conflicts between members. A member might also become emotionally upset by the content of the group discussion when the content reminds the member of a past loss or hurt. Even in cases where the interpersonal group process is appropriate, it may bring forth emotionally loaded memories or concerns from a member's past or present. Whether or not you can anticipate members' reactions to specific group content depends primarily on how well you know the members and how well you monitor and interpret any nonverbal signs of discomfort that might precede a member's exit. The sooner you anticipate the problem, the better you can deal with it and prevent the leave-taking.

When the problem is not anticipated and a member leaves in the middle of a session, you have a clear and immediate responsibility to provide for that member's safety. Tailor your intervention based on your assessment of the situation. If the members are adults, it may be OK to ask another member to check on that member. Another option is for you to follow the member just outside the door to ask the member what is going on, if he wants help from you or another member, and whether he is planning to return to the session or to leave the area. You should be mindful that all children and some adults require direct supervision at all times and should therefore offer the member who left the group only appropriate alternatives. Sometimes you must call parents to pick up children who want or need to leave the group.

One huge advantage of coleading groups is that in situations where a member exits a session, one leader can attend to the member who left the group room while the other leader remains with the rest of the members and attends to their needs. If you lead alone, you are forced to make a judgment about whether the health or safety of the departing member is at immediate risk and whether or not you should pursue the member. Some schools or agencies may have intercoms or phones you

could use to summon another adult. In that case you should clarify the assistance being requested. For example, if a third grader runs out of the group because he is ill and wants to go to the bathroom, it may be fine to ask the secretary who answers the intercom to check on the child. On the other hand, if a third grader who has made suicide attempts in the past runs from the group, you may need to go after the child, leaving another adult with the remainder of the group or sending the members back to their classroom teachers.

Ethics Pointer

ACA Ethics Codes B.1.b and B.1.c indicate that clients (members) have rights to privacy and confidentiality (American Counseling Association, 2005, p. 7). As a leader you may have learned a great deal of information about some of your members in the screening process; however, members have the right to decide what they will share with the group.

When a member leaves a group, you must be judicious in what you say to the remaining members. For example, it may be all right to say, "[Name of group member] is OK and will be back in a few minutes," or "[Name of group member] has gone home." However, it may not be appropriate to share the details of why the member exited the session. Consider a situation in which a member, Suzie, remembered she had failed to take medication. Telling the other members specifics of Suzie's medical condition without Suzie's permission would be a breach of Suzie's confidentiality. Similarly, if a departing member leaves because the group discussion brings back memories of childhood sexual abuse, you have no right to share that information with the remaining members without specific permission.

Departure of a Member from the Group

Members who leave the group permanently may do so in some of the following ways:

- Announcing their departure during a group session,
- Telling you after the close of a session that they are not coming back to the group,
- Calling you or members between sessions or leaving a message on voice mail that they are not coming back to group.
- Leaving with no warning or further contact with you or with members.

The departure of a member between sessions forces you to make several assessments often complicated by limited information. If possible, you must make a judgment about the cause of the departure. Is the departure due primarily to interpersonal interaction in the group that upset the member, or is it an intrapersonal reaction to the content of the group? Is the reason for the departure a family event—for example, the illness of a child or an unexpected change in family vacation plans—or is it unknown?

You must also assess the likely condition of the departed member. Is there any reason to think that the member might engage in self-injuring or suicidal behavior?

Is there any reason to think that the member might harm others? Is there any reason to think that the member might have lost contact with reality and thereby be in danger? If safety concerns exist, you must address these concerns immediately by following the law in your state and the policies of your school or agency. Note your actions in the case record.

The best thing to do about members leaving the group permanently is to work hard to prevent this occurrence. Dates and times of the group should be made clear when you advertise the group. One focus of your pregroup screening should be obtaining a commitment from each member to attend all sessions. The commitment to attend all sessions and to keep confidentiality after the group ends (including circumstances in which the member leaves the group before it ends) could be included in a contract signed by each member during prescreening.

Ethics Pointer

During the screening process you should inform prospective members of the information specified in ACA Ethics Code A.2.b. One way to document that you have provided this information—as well as to document other aspects related to group process and members' commitments to the group—is to employ a signed group contract.

When a member announces her intention to leave the group near the end of a session, you could offer the departing member the opportunity to say a few words of appreciation for the other members. Members might also be offered the chance to say a few words of appreciation for the departing member. You should note that these directions request positive statements only and do not open the opportunity for either the departing member or the remaining members to express negative feelings or to make outright attacks. In this way you can provide at least an element of processing and closure in a safe manner.

If members notify you of their intended departure in person after the close of a group or call or leave messages, you should make efforts to follow up with the departed member. These follow-up attempts should be clearly noted in the member's record. When you are successful reaching the departed member, you should accomplish the following:

■   Try to determine why the member left the group.
■   Address any safety issues.
■   Express appreciation for the member.
■   Determine if the member desires further counseling and provide referrals as appropriate.
■   Indicate that the member's group case record will be closed.
■   Provide appropriate hotline phone numbers.

After the follow-up contact, you should note the follow-up contact in the member's file and close the case. Unless it is clear that a member's departure has nothing to

do with the member's experience in the group, a member who departs mid-group may be considered a group failure—that is, for some reason the group was not helpful to the person. Therefore, you should seek specific clinical supervision regarding each person who departs. During supervision, you and your supervisor should try to figure out why the group did not work for the person who departed. Sometimes there will be a clear answer to this question, and other times reasons for departure won't be clear.

Ethics Pointer

> ACA Ethics Code A.1.b indicates that counselors must maintain records of counseling services (American Counseling Association, 2005, p. 4). Since one reason a member might leave a group is that the member was harmed in some way during the group, it is important for you to make careful records regarding member's who depart from the group. The record should include information about (a) how the member left the group, (b) what is known about why the member left the group, and (c) how the leader provided or attempted to provide follow up, processing, and closure with the member.

Regardless of the cause of a departure, when a member leaves a group, the remaining members may respond to the departure in a number of ways. The members may

- be upset,
- wonder if they caused the member to leave,
- have genuine concern about the departing member,
- provide information useful to leaders in assessing the situation,
- be concerned that the departing member will break confidentiality,
- watch to see if leaders act to provide for the safety of the departing member, and/or
- be less trusting of other members.

A group from which a member leaves may process this event over the next several sessions. You should help the remaining members process their feelings about the member who left, the way the departure occurred, and the effects of the departure on the group. It is important that you reassure the members that the group can continue to help those who stay in the group. If the group had been working on deep affective issues prior to the departure of the member, it may need to return to a more cognitive and less affective focus for a time. Members may need time for trust to grow again and for them to be willing to take risks again. If there are only a few sessions left before a group is scheduled to end, the group may not have the time to recover from a member's departure and return to the level of work being done prior to the departure of the member. In this case you should try not to be discouraged by this recycling of the group to an earlier phase but rather work to make the group as useful as possible to the members who remain for the time they have left together.

Exercises for Active Learning

1. On the lines below, draft statements that you could include in a contract that explain the members' expected commitment to attendance and to confidentiality.

_____

_____

_____

_____

_____

_____

2. You are leading a group for women who lost their jobs when a vacuum cleaner manufacturing plant closed and moved production to Mexico. The purpose of the group is to help the women process their feelings regarding the job loss and to develop plans for future employment. During the screening process, members signed an agreement to attend all five sessions and to complete a "reemployment" plan. Members paid $100 for the group in advance. The contract clearly states no refunds will be given. The group has been working well processing feelings and giving support around job loss. Members will start the development of their reemployment plan during the third session. At the mid-session break in the third session, Verna tells you privately that she is not attending sessions four and five because her husband wants her to go with him on vacation for the next two weeks. She requests a refund for the final two sessions.

   a. On the lines below, write out how you would explain to Verna why you would like her to tell the group members about her impending departure.

_____

_____

_____

_____

_____

   b. Write what you will say to Verna about her request for a refund.

_____

_____

_____

_____

c. Verna refuses to talk with the group about her plan to leave. What will you say to the group at the start of the next session when Verna does not appear?

_____

_____

_____

_____

d. On the lines below write your note to go in Verna's case file to close her case. The date of the third session was 11/6/07.

_____

_____

_____

_____

_____

_____

3. You are leading a group for men who have been diagnosed as having an alcohol abuse problem. The group is in the ninth week, and all members have attended each session. During the week between the ninth and tenth sessions, one of the members, Jaime, leaves a message on your voice mail that he is quitting the group because it is too hard. In your opinion Jaime sounded intoxicated.

a. List three concerns you have about Jaime.

1. _____

2. _____

3. _____

b. What actions might you take to help Jaime?

_____

_____

_____

c. Write what you will tell the other group members when Jaime does not appear for the next group session.

_____

_____

_____

d. On the lines below write your note to go in Jaime's case file to close his case. The date of the voice mail was 11/21/07.

_____

_____

_____

_____

_____

_____

A CRITICAL INCIDENT AT THE END OF THE GROUP

As the group nears the final session, you should shift the focus of the group to processing members' experiences in the group and preparing for closure. The final session may focus only on closure. The number of sessions given to final processing and closure may vary depending on such factors as the overall length of the group and the type of group. For example, longer groups that are more counseling and therapy focused may require more processing at the end than brief, psychoeducational groups. Useful goals for the final processing and closure of groups might include some of the following (Stockton, 1992):

- Discussing what members learned about the problem or issue that was the central focus of the group.
- Discussing what members learned about how they related to others.
- Discussing what members learned about themselves.
- Planning for using what they learned to help them in their lives after the group.
- Setting short-term goals for future growth.
- Expressing appreciation for other members.
- Saying good-bye to other members.

These goals focus on integrating and applying learnings and closing the group. Except for expressing feelings related to the process of closure, emotional intensity is minimized. The work of the group is mostly cognitive—reflection and planning.

Critical Incident Type 6: Deep Disclosure at the End of the Group

Definition of deep disclosure at the end of the group   A **disclosure** whose timing makes it difficult to adequately process its content and that has the potential to disrupt the end of group processing and closure.

Occasionally, in the final session a member will try to make a deep disclosure— one that has potential to raise emotional reactions and may require a great deal of time to process. For example, members who disclose drug addiction in a final session are attempting to open a serious topic that the group has no hope of giving proper attention to in the short time remaining. This type of disclosure is a critical incident because

it makes it difficult for you to proceed with the planned process of the group. The other members recognize the depth of the issue disclosed and the very real need of the member for assistance. However, at this point in the group, if you change focus to address the disclosed topic, you would have to do so instead of leading an appropriate processing and closure for the rest of the group members. You are challenged to maintain the focus on processing and closure so that members may consolidate and use their gains. To hold focus, you will need to cut off the disclosing member in a kind but firm way.

Minimizing the Possibility of Deep Disclosure at the End of the Group

The best approach to dealing with deep disclosures at the end of the group is prevention. During each session you can remind members of the number of planned sessions and how many sessions are left. They can be reminded that no new topics will be introduced in the final session and encouraged to begin working on their issues at a more appropriate time. The leader in Example 1 demonstrates how these reminders might be phrased.

Example 1:

Nigel is leading a group on friendship skills for sixth-grade students. The group is planned for eight sessions, and Nigel is talking to the group during the closing of the third session.

Nigel: You all did a nice job on today's work. Before we leave I want to remind you that we have four more sessions and the final pizza lunch left, so if there's something important to you that you want to bring up, I'll remind you to start with that at the beginning of next week's group. Be thinking during the week about what you really need to talk about.

Nigel is addressing the subject again at the start of the sixth session.

Nigel: Good, everybody is here. As we start today, I want to show you the calendar. *[Nigel points to the calendar on the wall as he speaks.]* OK, today is November twenty-fourth, next week is the first of December, and the week after that is December eighth. On the eighth we are going to have the pizza party, so that means on the first we will talk about what we have learned and how we can use it and then I want you to say some appreciations to each other. We will not start any new discussions next week. That means that if you have something important you want to work on in this group that we haven't done yet, we need to do it today. I want you to give me the thumbs-up sign if what I'm saying is clear to you. *[All members give him the thumbs-up sign.]* Good. I want you to put your heads down on your desk and think quietly for three minutes about if there is anything else you want to bring up in this group, and after the three minutes, we will do a round to see what you thought.

A second approach to preventing deep disclosures in the final session is to start thinking early about members' post-group counseling needs. In a longer group you can close a session three or four sessions before the final session by asking members to reflect on their gains in the group and their possible counseling needs after the group.

You then have time to assist members with referrals for post-group counseling before the final session of the group. This timing gives members a chance to decide if they have further need for counseling.

Example 2:

Eva is leading a group for firefighters who are returning from fighting brush fires in the southwest. The firefighters witnessed widespread destruction of homes. One firefighter in their unit was badly burned when the wind shifted unexpectedly. The group is scheduled for six sessions, and while most of the firefighters in the unit appear to have made progress on processing their experience, two or three of them have remained quite quiet. It is the end of the third session, and Eva is addressing the group.

Eva: We are about to close for tonight but before we do, I'd like to talk with you about how you are doing. We are at the end of the third session or about half way in the group, and most of you are talking about your experience in the fire and the feelings and thoughts you have about it. The county runs a group like this every time you come back from a major fire, and most of the time for most of you it is enough processing to be helpful and to help you support each other long after the group is done and the counselor is gone. Most of you have been in these groups before and know how they work. *[Most of the firefighters nod.]* At the same time we know that it is normal that sometimes one or more of you need a little more counseling after the group. This week between sessions I want each of you to think of what else you need to talk about in the next two sessions—the last session is processing only with no new topics—and if you think you might still want some individual counseling after the group ends. I'll ask each of you next week so that if you might want more counseling, it can be all set up before the group ends. You will know who your counselor will be after the group, so as we end the group, it will be easier for you to close with the group knowing you will get the care you need and deserve. For anyone who doesn't want more counseling, I will give you another copy of those hotline numbers that are especially for firefighters.

Handling Deep Disclosure at the End of the Group

If you take preventative approaches and members still try to introduce deep issues in the final session, you may need to do referrals after the group, but you may feel more confident in redirecting the group to a processing and closure focus during the final session. While the member making the disclosure may be upset that you did not focus on it, both you and the other members will know that you provided opportunities for members to discuss their issues or seek extended counseling prior to the final session. Your leadership was caring, ethical, and professional.

Example 3:

Wilhelm is leading a group for probationary teachers in a large suburban school district. The purpose of the group is to help the teachers meet the district's requirements for becoming a tenured teacher. Wilhelm has kept the group posted on time until the end of the group and encouraged members to share issues of importance

to them early in the life of the group. Last week he provided post-group counseling referral for all members who requested it. Halfway through the final session Margot begins to introduce a new issue.

Margot: This group has been real helpful, particularly about how to talk with parents. I . . . I just don't know what to do, because last month my principal told me I would have to pass the Spanish fluency test to be tenured, and I don't think I can do it.

Wilhelm: That's a big issue, Margot. I wish you had brought this up before now—two or three sessions ago when we would have had time to help you and anyone else that has this concern. I can talk with you for 15 minutes or so after the group to set up an appointment when we can do a referral. If you want to set up a time to do a referral, talk with me right after the group. Right now we need to finish processing our last session so that the group closes well. Let's go back to the round we were doing. Dianna, you go next.

As you plan a final session there are several things you may wish to consider that will make the process of leading the final group and finishing with the paperwork and supervision of the group easier:

- Engage the members in activities that will help them process the group. For example, working in subgroups to identify learnings, writing letters to themselves about future goals, or writing appreciations for other members on index cards and then giving the index cards to the members.
- If you do not have a coleader, try to arrange for a backup counselor in case a member needs one during the final session.
- If your members have anger issues, schedule the final session (and perhaps all sessions) when security personnel are on duty, and talk to the security personnel about the location of your group and procedures for both helping you if you call them and for summoning further help if needed.
- Leave the hour after the final session open in your schedule in case you do need to be available for an individual member.
- Complete your case files on the group within 24 hours of closing the group, noting the progress of members identified during the group and in the final processing of the group.
- Schedule the final clinical supervision for your work with the group within one week of closing the group.

A READING LIST FOR ADVANCED STUDY OF CRITICAL INCIDENTS

Cohen, A. M., & Smith, R. D. (1976a). *The critical incident in growth groups: A manual for group leaders.* La Jolla, CA: University Associates Inc. and Cohen, A. M., & Smith, R. D. (1976b). *The critical incident in growth groups: Theory and technique.* La Jolla, CA: University Associates Inc.

As mentioned at the beginning of the chapter, in these classic texts the authors identify some 51 critical incidents in groups. They then offer a theory concerning the best ways to intervene in critical incidents.

Donigian, J., & Hulse-Killacky, D. (1999). *Critical incidents in group therapy* (2nd ed.). Belmont, CA: Wadsworth.

> This is the most prominent current text focusing on critical incidents. The text briefly reviews twelve theories and then focuses on responding to six critical incidents from different theoretical perspectives.

Kottler, J. A. (1994). *Advanced group leadership.* Pacific Grove, CA: Brooks/Cole.

> This text on advanced group leadership includes a chapter on critical incidents, which the author describes as nine types of problem member behavior.

STUDY QUESTIONS

1. What is meant by a critical incident?
2. What are some of the tasks for leaders in the first session?
3. What are some reasons a member might attack a leader?
4. Why is conflict between members a critical incident?
5. How can leaders intervene in conflicts between members?
6. What are some examples of different kinds of situations in which members might leave the group?
7. What are some concerns about the departing member that may require leader attention or intervention?
8. What are some possible concerns of the remaining group members when a member leaves the group?
9. What are some possible effects of a member's departure on group process?
10. What are some possible concerns of the school or agency when members depart from the group?
11. What should be the focus of work for the last session of a group?
12. Why is it not appropriate for members to make deep disclosures at the end of a group?
13. What are some possible leader interventions aimed at preventing deep disclosures at the end of a group?
14. What are some safety considerations for leading the final session of multiple-session groups?

KEY CONCEPTS

conflict between members p. 201	premature deep disclosure p. 191
critical incident p. 188	silent member p. 189
deep disclosure at the end of the group p. 214	

REFERENCES

American Counseling Association (2005). *ACA code of ethics.* Alexandria, VA: Author.

Cohen, A. M., & Smith, R. D. (1976a). *The critical incident in growth groups: A manual for group leaders.* La Jolla, CA: University Associates Inc.

Cohen, A. M., & Smith, R. D. (1976b). *The critical incident in growth groups: Theory and technique.* La Jolla, CA: University Associates Inc.

Donigian, J., & Hulse-Killacky, D. (1999). *Critical incidents in group therapy* (2nd ed.). Belmont, CA: Wadsworth.

Kottler, J. A. (1994). *Advanced group leadership.* Pacific Grove, CA: Brooks/Cole.

Lieberman, M. A., Yalom, I. D., & Miles, M. B. (1973). *Encounter groups: First facts.* New York: Basic Books.

Stockton, R. (Presenter). (1992). Association for Specialists in Group Work (Producer). Developmental aspects of group counseling [Videotape]. (Available from the American Counseling Association, Alexandria, VA)

CHAPTER 10

Leading Psychotherapy Groups

Learning Objectives

After reading this chapter you should be able to
- Describe sources of information encoded in a diagnosis.
- Explain the relationship between diagnosis and treatment.
- Discuss different types of psychotherapy groups and how the goals of the groups might contribute to a treatment plan.
- Discuss screening for diagnosis-focused groups.
- Discuss the influence of diagnosis on member participation.

INTRODUCTION

In this chapter we address two general types of psychotherapy groups. The first type of group is formed to address a particular diagnosis, for example, depression or conduct disorder. The second type of group involves general issues faced by clients with mental health diagnoses; for example, medication compliance or employment problems. The chapter is divided into the following sections: leading diagnosis-based groups, groups addressing the psychosocial and environmental problems of clients, the influence of diagnosis on group participation, and mental health groups in schools.

LEADING DIAGNOSIS-BASED GROUPS

The privilege of doing a mental health **diagnosis** of a client is generally granted by professional licensure boards only to those specifically trained in this process. However, if you are not licensed to do diagnoses, you may still lead or colead groups that contribute to the treatment of clinically diagnosable disorders. In order to plan such groups, you must understand the connections between the members' diagnoses and the group's goals.

***Definition of* symptom**   A feeling or behavior that indicates a potential physical or mental health concern.

***Definition of* diagnosis**   A coded summary of a client's symptoms and functioning based on the five "axes" specified in the diagnostic manual of the American Psychiatric Association.

A counselor, mental health professional, or physician considers the following types of information in determining a diagnosis for a client:

- History.
- Diagnostic interview.
- Test results from clinical instruments, both screening instruments and diagnostic-specific instruments.
- Mental health records.
- Medical assessment.
- Substance use/abuse screening.
- Medication list.
- Safety assessment.

Using the American Psychiatric Association's (2000) *Diagnostic and Statistical Manual of Mental Disorders, fourth edition, text revision* (DSM-IV-TR), the diagnosing professional codes the information from multiple sources on five axes:

- Axis I: Clinical Disorders.
- Axis II: Personality Disorders and/or Mental Retardation.
- Axis III: General Medical Conditions related to Axis I or II Disorders.
- Axis IV: Psychosocial and Environmental Problems.
- Axis V: General Assessment of Functioning (DSM-IV-TR, 2000, p. 36).

Each of the first four axes describes one area of client functioning. Axis V provides a code number between 1 and 100 that rates the client's overall functioning.

Table 10-1 lists general types of group goals related to each of the first four axes. Possible groups range from therapy groups aimed at modifying problematic personality patterns to groups addressing educational, occupational, or social support issues. The commonality of the groups is that they each directly address one or more of the **symptoms** on Axis I, II, or III that resulted in the client receiving the diagnosis. Any time you plan a group for members who share a particular diagnosis, you should be able to tie the purpose of the group to one or more symptoms listed on the five axis diagnosis. Axis IV allows the counselor to code client's psychosocial and environmental problems: for example, problems with support, family, housing, education, employment, the law, or any other similar concern. Groups that focus on one of these Axis IV issues might include members with different diagnoses or a mix of members with diagnoses and those who do not have a diagnosis.

***Definition of* treatment plan**   A comprehensive plan for a client's care aimed at decreasing the number and intensity of symptoms, improving client functioning, and sustaining improved functioning.

You should know what role your group plays and how it fits into the overall **treatment plan** for each member.

Table 10-1   Possible Group Goals for Axis I–IV

Axis I: Clinical Disorders

- Decrease symptoms specific to the diagnosed disorder.
- Increase functional behaviors, thoughts, and feelings.
- Understand action of psychotropic medications and/or promote medication compliance.

Axis II: Personality Disorders and/or Mental Retardation

- Decrease symptoms specific to the diagnosed disorder.
- Increase functional behaviors, thoughts, and feelings.
- Moderate problematic personality patterns.
- Understand action of psychotropic medications and promote medication compliance.

Axis III: General Medical Conditions Related to Axis I or II Disorders

- Understand medical condition and its interaction with mental health concerns.
- Understand action of medications, and promote medication compliance.

Axis IV: Psychosocial and Environmental Problems

- Improve social support.
- Address problems related to social environment.
- Address educational problems.
- Address occupational problems.
- Address housing problems.
- Improve access to health care services.
- Address problems related to legal system or criminal behavior.

Source: Adapted from DSM-IV-TR, 2000, p. 32.

Table 10-2   Individual Treatment Plan for Midge

Diagnosis	Treatment Plan Components
Axis I—Mild Depression • Depressed Mood	Brief group (4 sessions) to decrease depressive symptoms
• Decreased interest and participation in activities	Individual work with a counselor at a local community college to develop and implement a coordinated educational/employment plan
• Insomnia	
• Fatigue	
• Sense of worthlessness	
Axis II—No Diagnosis	
Axis III—No Diagnosis	
Axis IV • Job loss—Poor attendance at job when working—High school graduate but most local jobs require an associate's degree	
• Decreasing social support as she withdraws from previous activities	

Table 10-2 shows the overall treatment plan for a client named Midge who is experiencing mild depression. Her treatment plan has two parts:

1. A brief, four-session group with the purpose of decreasing the depressive symptoms that contributed to her Axis I diagnosis of mild depression.
2. Individual counseling to address educational and employment issues noted on Axis IV.

In Midge's case you might lead the four-session group for her and other members with similar types and levels of symptoms, while another counselor might work individually with Midge. One thing you should note is that the counseling done to help Midge address the issues coded on Axis IV also helps to address her Axis I diagnosis. One way you can think about how this works is to think about the feelings people typically have after losing a job—sadness and discouragement. Midge may have lost her job after she felt depressed, or the feelings of depression may have made it more difficult for Midge to function normally in terms of getting to work. Either way, if she is able to get a new job that she likes, or even engage in a plan that will lead toward a new job, it is likely that Midge will feel less depressed and more encouraged rather than discouraged. In other words her Axis I symptoms will lessen.

Anytime aspects of a treatment plan are delivered by different professionals, whether or not they consider themselves officially a treatment team, someone should be designated as the supervisor of the treatment or the leader of the treatment team. This person must be licensed in your state with a **scope of practice** that includes diagnosis and treatment of mental and emotional disorders. If you live in a state that has a supervisor license or endorsement, you will need to consider that license

and its scope of practice when you decide who supervises the treatment team. The coordination provided by the supervisor should result in all aspects of the plan working together and effective treatment being provided.

***Definition of* scope of practice**   The range and types of care a counselor is licensed or certified to provide.

What is important for you as counselor and as a leader is to be clear what part of the treatment you are delivering in your group and how it fits into the overall plan for client care. You should also be sure that you know who is the supervisor or the lead counselor and how you will connect or interface with that supervisor. For example, you might be expected to attend treatment team meetings, to provide clinical notes and file them in a particular part of the client's file, or to meet regularly with the client and the supervisor.

Ethics Pointer

ACA Ethics Code C.2.a indicates that counselors work only within the boundaries of their competence (American Counseling Association, 2005). ACA Ethics Code B.3.b indicates that clients should be informed of the existence and composition of treatment teams. Further, clients should be told what information will be shared and the purpose for which the information is shared (American Counseling Association, 2005).

Screening and Composition of Diagnosis-Based Groups

Now let's consider how to select members and compose groups when you want to form a group focused on symptom reduction. For our example we have used members with depressive symptoms. We intentionally focused on depression, because clients (potential group members) who have depressive symptoms frequently seek help at community agencies. They seek counseling in order to get relief from the unpleasant feelings of sadness, hopelessness, and worthlessness commonly experienced as part of depression.

Table 10-3 lists five potential members for a group with the purpose of reducing depressive symptoms. If a potential member has or is experiencing one of the symptoms listed in the left-hand column as part of his depression, this is indicated by one or more Xs in the column under the client's name. The more Xs in the column, the more serious or prominent that symptom is for the client. In this example, as we would expect in practice, the types of symptoms present and the severity of the symptoms vary among clients even though all of them are seeking treatment for depression.

Let's consider what you might learn from this type of chart. First of all, Deter appears to be more severely depressed than any of the other members. He has or is experiencing all the symptoms of the list. He experiences more frequent or severe depressed mood, diminished interest in activities, weight loss, and worthlessness or guilt than some of the other members. In addition, he is the only client on the list

Table 10-3   Symptoms of Potential Members

Symptoms (DSMIV-TR, 2000)	Ed	Norla	Deter	Karen	Kurt
Depressed Mood	X	X	XXX	XX	X
Diminished interest in activities	X	X	XX		
Weight loss or gain			XX	X(Gain)	X
Insomnia or hypersomnia	X	X	X	X(Hyper)	X
Psychomotor agitation or retardation			X		
Fatigue/energy loss	XX	X	X	XXX	
Worthlessness or guilt			XX	X	X
Thinking/concentration	X	X	X		
Suicide thoughts, plans, or attempts			2 attempts	thoughts	thoughts

to have made actual suicide attempts. You might ask if you should screen Deter out of the group if his symptoms are more severe. You might consider one of these options:

- Seek a group for Deter in which the other members had symptom patterns and severity similar to his.
- Refer Deter for individual counseling, and include him in a group after he begins to experience some reduction in symptoms and after he has refrained from suicide or other self-injurious behavior for a period of time.
- Include Deter in the group you are forming, and arrange for concurrent care including individual counseling focusing on both symptom reduction and client safety.

You should note that if you choose to keep Deter in the group without concurrent individual counseling, his progress may be slower than that of the other members. Also, you will be responsible for his safety plan, and you may need to see him individually and possibly arrange for safety monitoring. Further, since Deter has made two suicide attempts, you will want to have him evaluated to see if medication should be prescribed to lessen his symptoms.

Karen appears to be experiencing atypical depression. She is gaining rather than losing weight, and she is not experiencing the restlessness and insomnia the other group members are experiencing. We would suggest you look for another potential member who also has atypical symptoms. This is likely to help Karen feel that she is like other members in the group.

Particularly when you lead limited-session groups, you may not be able to address all symptoms or to give equal amounts of attention to each symptom on which you choose to focus. Suppose you decide to include in your group all five members from Table 10-3. The patterns of symptoms shown in the box may provide information about focus points that are likely to produce some benefit for the most members. All of the members are experiencing symptoms of depressed mood and sleep irregularities, and everyone except Karen is experiencing problems with fatigue or energy loss. Therefore, you may want to focus one or more sessions on

addressing these symptoms in some way. Three of your members are experiencing feelings of worthlessness or guilt, and these same three members report suicidal thoughts or actions. You will want to address this topic to improve member safety. In contrast, only Deter has psychomotor symptoms. If overall group time is limited, you may choose not to address this symptom as a working focus of a session. In groups with more total time, you may choose to address psychomotor issues in a later rather than an earlier session.

Exercises for Active Learning
Acute Stress Disorder Group

Your agency has asked you to consider forming a group for clients experiencing acute stress. Descriptions of five possible clients/members are given below. Read the descriptions and chart the clients' symptoms in Table 10.4 using a system similar to the one shown in Table 10-3.

Melvin

Melvin is a 27-year-old man who sells welding rods and welding equipment for a living. Three weeks ago Melvin was driving to a sales appointment when he was involved in a seven-car pileup on an icy bridge span. Melvin was trapped in his car for about half an hour before rescue workers were able to free him; however, Melvin does not remember anything about the time he was trapped. Since the accident, Melvin has flashbacks of his car sliding into the pileup and of the sound of metal crunching. He avoids busy bridges and icy roads. If driving conditions are bad, he cancels his sales calls. Melvin has to file a report on his sales every two weeks. When Melvin's supervisor saw the report of decreased sales, he put Melvin on probation.

François

François is a 20-year-old college student. He works as a currier in downtown Chicago. He rides his bike from building to building in the loop area delivering documents between businesses. A week ago he was struck by a pickup truck when the driver made a left-hand turn from the wrong lane. The accident was witnessed by a city traffic aide, who filed papers indicating that François was not at fault. François lay in the street for about 10 minutes before the ambulance came. He was in a daze and felt like he was above the scene looking down at himself lying in the street. Since the accident, he has repeated thoughts and images of the truck coming straight at him. When François sees a bicycle, he begins to shake. He has nightly dreams of standing in traffic with vehicles coming at him and brakes screeching. François is frightened by these symptoms. He is anxious and concerned he is going crazy. While François has continued to work as a currier, he is hypervigilant at all times.

Mave

Mave is a 59-year-old retired postal clerk. When she retired, Mave received a one-time payment of $50,000, which is about a third of the overall retirement money she expects. Mave invested this money in an annuity strong in international investments—oil fields and refineries—recommended by a friend. Last week the government of one of the countries in which a major field and refinery complex was located nationalized these assets and refused to pay anything to the internationally based oil company that had

been operating them. The value of Mave's annuity fell 50 percent. Mave is anxious and sad. She fears for her future. She has had several dreams that she is falling through purple black clouds. She wakes up just before she hits the ground covered with sweat and with her heart beating rapidly. Last week when her retirement check was due, she took a chair and sat on the side of the road by the mailbox all morning waiting for the mail because she was afraid someone would steal her check.

Geno

Geno is 43 years old. He is an airplane mechanic who works on planes for international flights. Sometimes his company sends him to Europe to assist with repairs on that end of the flight plan. Last week when Geno was in England, the police uncovered a plot that would have placed a bomb aboard one of the planes he was repairing. The day this happened, it was raining heavily. Now Geno cannot get the idea out of his head that a plane might blow up while he is repairing it. He is on constant alert and challenges anyone who comes to service any aspect of the plane or baggage. He refuses to work on days it rains heavily because he says he can see a picture of a clock in his mind, and it's ticking down to zero and an explosion. Yesterday he was working inside the cabin of one of the planes when a crew member dropped a coffee pot and broke it. Gino jumped three feet sideways. Gino spends a lot of time on his cell phone getting his family to reassure him.

Sue

Sue is a 37-year-old farrier. Three days ago a tractor backfired while she was shoeing a Belgian. The huge draft horse kicked her in the abdomen, knocking her about six feet down the aisle of the barn into a metal stall gate. Sue does not remember anything about the incident itself. She is distressed that she is black and blue. Now she begins to shake when she sees a draft horse. When she shoes other horses, her concentration is poor. She used to talk with the horse owners as she shoed the horses, but now she is nervous and doesn't talk. Several of them asked her if she was mad at them.

Table 10-4 Symptoms of Potential Members of the Anxiety Group

Symptoms list based on DSM-IV-TR (2000, p. 472)	Melvin	François	Mave	Geno	Sue
Dissociative symptoms: numbing, detachment, in a daze, derealization, depersonalization, amnesia					
Reexperiencing: images, thoughts, flashbacks, reliving event					
Avoidance of people, places, or events that bring back memories of trauma					
Symptoms of anxiety or arousal: poor sleep or concentration, anxiety, startle responses, hypervigilance					
Distress or impairment					

Respond to the questions on group composition and session focus using the data in Table 10-4 to help you.

1. If you were to create a group of four members, whom would you include?

_____

List two symptom areas you might make a priority to address in the group.

2. (a) _____ (b) _____

3. Whom did you screen out of the group? _____

_____

What care does this client need?

_____

GROUPS ADDRESSING PSYCHOSOCIAL AND ENVIRONMENTAL PROBLEMS

As you may recall, Midge's treatment plan included individual work with a counselor to deal with her educational and employment issues. However, she might also have benefited from counseling in a group setting, if an appropriate group were available. In that kind of group, members might have different mental health problems, but the common denominator would be the need for help dealing with the educational or economic problems that often result from mental health problems. In this section of the chapter, we will discuss the types of groups that address DSM Axis IV issues.

In Table 10-5 we show the treatment plan for Carl, a machine operator in a steel mill who began experiencing a depressive type of schizoaffective disorder about a year ago. His treatment plan has multiple parts:

1. Medications—both an antipsychotic and an antidepressant.
2. A medication compliance group.
3. A cognitive therapy group to address depressive symptoms.
4. A teaching session with Carl's wife about his symptoms.
5. A collaborative meeting with Carl's union representative.
6. A planning meeting with a bank representative.

You might be involved with Carl's treatment plan as a leader of the medication compliance group, the cognitive therapy group, or both of these groups. We have listed medicating Carl and enrolling him in the medication compliance group first, because Carl's ability to participate in any other aspect of his treatment may be directly decreased if he continues to have delusions and hallucinations, as these symptoms interfere with his ability to focus and stay focused on the therapy. Another way you could think about this is to consider that to the extent Carl is focused on delusions and hallucinations, he is not focused or he may not be able to hold focus on other therapeutic work. Thus he needs to become stable on his medications before other parts of the treatment plan proceed.

Table 10-5   Individual Treatment Plan for Carl

Diagnosis	Treatment Plan Components
Axis I: Schizoaffective Disorder Depressive Type	
• Predominantly sad affect	• Antipsychotic medication
• Insomnia	• Antidepressant medication
• Weight loss without dieting	• Medication compliance group—weekly for the first month and biweekly thereafter
• Suicidal thoughts	
• Poor concentration	• Weekly cognitive therapy group to decrease depressive symptoms
• Fatigue	
• Hallucinations	
• Disorganized speech	
• Delusions	
Axis II: No diagnosis	N/a
Axis III: No diagnosis	N/a
Axis IV:	
• Problems with Primary Support Group—wife is tired of his sad mood and "irresponsible behaviors"	• Counselor will meet with wife to explain the nonvoluntary nature of delusions and hallucinations.
• Occupational Problems— on probation at work (steel mill) due to unsafe behavior—also fined for behavior at work as part of probation	• Carl and counselor will meet with union advocate to discuss and further assess how mental health policies at work apply in Carl's situation.
• Economic Problems—missed mortgage payment resulted in additional financial penalties from bank—fine at work strained finances	• Carl and his wife will meet with customer service representative at the bank to develop a repayment plan.

Note that Carl's treatment plan provides an example in which parts of the treatment plan are sequenced with one part of the plan beginning and then either proceeding to a predetermined point or finishing before other parts of the plan are begun. For other clients and treatment plans the parts of the plan may be done concurrently. Both the components of the plan and the timing of the parts are important to providing effective care.

You might wonder how a symptom-focused group and a medication compliance group would differ, particularly if you were to lead both groups. To help you see the difference in focus for the two kinds of groups, here are the purpose statement and goals for each of the two groups that Carl will attend.

Example 1: Medication Compliance Group
The purpose of this group is to improve member consistency in taking prescribed medications.

Goals
Members will

- Understand their diagnoses and how the medications should affect symptoms.
- Understand the name of their medications and the amounts and schedule for taking medications.
- Understand possible side effects of medications, and identify those that make them hesitant to take their medications.
- Identify other issues (for example, shortage of money) that interfere with them consistently taking their medications.
- Develop and implement strategies that overcome obstacles to taking medications.

Example 2: Cognitive Therapy Group to Decrease Depressive Symptoms
The purpose of this group is to decrease depressive symptoms using cognitive therapy.

Goals
Members will

- Identify depressive, self-defeating thoughts and modify them.
- Chart sleep schedule and modify behavior to promote better sleep and decrease insomnia.
- Chart eating habits and modify to provide proper nutrition.

The symptom reduction and medication compliance groups are similar in that each of them directly addresses Carl's diagnosis. They are different from the perspective of group composition. In screening members into the cognitive therapy group to decrease depressive symptoms, you would choose members who have been diagnosed with depressive symptoms. In contrast, the common denominator grouping screening for the medication compliance group is that each member has one or more medications that need to be taken consistently. The actual diagnosis of the members might vary—for some it might be depression, for others it might be anxiety, and so forth.

Leading Medication Compliance Groups

If you are to lead a group with members who take medications for their diagnosed disorder, you should accept the responsibility of learning about the medications your members take. There are a number of books that describe medications, including their names, purposes, appropriate dose, half-lives, and side effects. The books vary in size, complexity, and organization. We suggest that you consult your clinical supervisor about which type of book and which specific book would best serve you considering your

- Current knowledge level.
- Typical clientele.
- Typical medications you are likely to encounter in your practice.

Besides the specific nature of members' medications, there are some other pieces of practical information that you will want to get from the members either as part of the screening process or perhaps during the first session. This information includes the following:

- What are the members' medication lists?

- What are the names and contact information of prescribing physicians? (In most situations you may need to ask members to sign release forms for exchange of information with the physicians in the screening process.)
- Are members scheduled for regular visits with prescribing physicians for medication checkups, or how are medications being monitored?

You will also want to learn other information in the early sessions of the group:

- Source of medications; for example, are members getting their medications at a local pharmacy, or are they ordering 90 days at a time through the mail?
- Members' plan to pay for their medications and whether their plans are working.
- Members' process for integrating the taking of medications into their daily routine.

Ethics Pointer

> Counselors should obtain signed client consent before requesting information about the client from other professionals. In addition, ACA Ethics Code B.3.e indicates counselors should take steps to ensure confidentiality of information transmitted by verbal, written, or electronic means (American Counseling Association, 2005). This code has implications for privacy of office space in which phone conversations are held; for controlling access to voicemail, answering machines, computers, and servers; and for encryption of computer records and electronic transmissions. ACA Ethics Code B.3.c indicates that counselors discuss client information "only in settings in which they can reasonably insure client privacy" (American Counseling Association, 2005, p. 8).

INFLUENCE OF DIAGNOSIS ON GROUP PARTICIPATION

In this section we will consider how diagnosis might influence member participation. The ideas in this section would apply to members in groups focused on symptom reduction and medication compliance discussed in the last section. However, this discussion about member participation should be considered anytime you have a member in a group who has a mental health diagnosis. An example of this would be if you are leading a group in a community agency on menopause, and in that group are members who are depressed. Their participation in the menopause group will be influenced by their diagnosis even though the purpose of the group is not focused on addressing their diagnosis. You could reasonably anticipate that they might show behavioral and emotional symptoms of depression during the group. Their emotional tone may well effect the overall emotional tone of the group, since they would be more likely than other members to be depressed rather than optimistic about menopause. You should anticipate that you will need to work hard as a leader to keep the tone of the group positive.

In a similar way, if you are conducting a men's group and one of the members has a diagnosis of conduct disorder, you should expect that he may do some of the behaviors in the group that resulted in his receiving the diagnosis. In this situation you will need to be mindful of the safety of the other members and possibly of your own safety. You should be very clear with the member about expected behavior in the group with other members and at the physical site—the agency, practice, or school—at which the group is conducted.

While your initial reaction may be to consider screening clients with a diagnosis out of non-diagnosis-focused groups, that may be an overreaction. Many clients with mental health diagnoses may benefit from and contribute to a broad range of groups. If you are aware of and ready to respond to these clients in an appropriate way, they may receive a double benefit from being a member of your group. First, they do productive work regarding the purpose of the group, and second, they learn to interact appropriately and productively in the group.

LEADING MENTAL HEALTH GROUPS IN SCHOOLS

Our observation is that the role of school counselors varies greatly among school districts and often from school to school within the same district. Some schools direct counselors to focus almost exclusively on programs designed to support improved achievement test scores. Other schools want counselors to focus a great deal on social and emotional needs of students. If student behavior becomes repeatedly disruptive or dangerous to self or other students, it is likely that school counselors will be sought out by the administration to resolve these issues regardless of the school's initial position on counselor role. Groups may be proposed as a method to address problematic concerns. For example, the principal may ask you to conduct a group for students whose diagnosis is attention deficit hyperactivity disorder (ADHD). It is our advice that you give such a proposal thoughtful consideration before committing to lead such a group.

Ethics Pointer

ACA Ethics Code C.2.a indicates that counselors practice only within the boundaries of their competence (American Counseling Association, 2005). Some state laws may describe the boundaries of counselor's range of practice as the permitted "scope of practice."

When diagnosis-focused groups are proposed at school, some of the first things you should consider are staying within your scope of practice as defined by the law in your state and staying with the areas of counseling for which you have been trained. It is our observation that such courses as psychopathology, diagnosis, and treatment of those with mental health diagnoses are often optional courses in school counseling programs. Courses on counseling children and adolescents range from focusing primarily on developmental counseling to focusing primarily on treatment. Before you take on a particular diagnosis-focused group, ask yourself honestly if you have the training and experience to lead the group. Depending on your training and the group suggested, some of you may be ready to lead the group immediately after your graduation, while others of you may develop the needed knowledge and skills over time.

Another issue you should consider is the possibility that some of the children proposed as members may already be receiving group or individual counseling in the community. If so, you should (with signed release forms in hand) consult with parents and the agency counselor about the role of the intended group in the child's overall treatment and whether or not the group might add to or interfere with current treatment.

While we encourage you to use your abilities to help your students, we also caution you to keep the clinical difficulty of your groups reasonable considering the clinical supervision and on-call and referral sources available to you. As an example, let's consider a type of proposal we often receive as a group proposal in university group work class—a proposal to conduct a group at middle school level for students (often girls) with eating disorders, bulimia, and/or anorexia. It is true that some students at the middle-school level have eating disorders, some of which are serious enough that they could be or have been diagnosed. We find that our graduate students often don't know or fail to consider that there is a fatality rate associated with anorexia. They also don't think about lack of supervision. If after graduation, your only supervisor is a school administrator who has no clinical training (a situation unfortunately all too common), you should refrain from leading groups for students with disorders with fatality rates or with high rates of self-injurious or suicidal behavior. Even when you have training, experience, and quality clinical supervision, you should consider if the level of medical, psychiatric, and crisis resources available for your potential members supports the level of group you wish to lead.

Ethics Pointer

ACA Ethics Code A.8.b requires counselors (group leaders) to take precautions to protect clients (members) (American Counseling Association, 2005). It is wise to consider both your skills and the complexity (and possible danger) of client concerns before agreeing to lead a group.

INTEGRATIVE CASE EXAMPLE: LIVING IN THE GROUP HOME

Anaya and Frank are two counselors who work 7:00 PM to midnight at a small group home for men with various mental health problems. The group home is situated in a neighborhood of small homes in a midsized city in the northeast. Four men live at the home and work at carefully chosen jobs in the community. The men travel to and from work on a bus that also serves three other group homes.

The home, which the men have named "Sunshine," is staffed to provide minimal but adequate support. "Cookie" arrives at 6:00, wakes the men and cooks hot breakfast while the men shower, dress, and clean their rooms. Cookie also packs lunches and puts them in backpacks for each man to take to work. The men eat breakfast at 7:00 and get on the bus about 7:30. After the men leave, Cookie stacks the dishes and does bookkeeping and any paperwork needed by the agency that provides partial funding for the group home. Cookie goes home at noon.

The men return from work about 4:30. They relax or do needed work on the yard until 6:00. For dinner they microwave their choice of dinner and have fruit or ice cream for dessert. They usually watch the evening news during dinner. After dinner and before 7:30, they do the daily dishes and laundry. These jobs are done on a rotation.

Anaya and Frank arrive at 7:00. At 7:30 they lead a 30- to 45-minute group to help the men process the events of their day. Anaya typically stays until about 9:00 when

the men start to go to bed. Frank is on duty until midnight when he is relieved by one of several graduate students who serve as fire watch during the night. The men have little interaction with the graduate students and call them all simply "Fire Chief."

It is the intention of the group home's funding agency that the home should be both homelike and therapeutic for the men. Maintaining employment in the community, getting along with others in the home, and maintaining the home are all viewed as therapeutic. The group sessions Anaya and Frank lead are intended to promote these goals. The group focuses on helping the men live and appreciate everyday life. The leaders work to activate Yalom's therapeutic factors, particularly cohesion, universality, interpersonal learning, and altruism. They help the members learn how to function in spite of their mental health problems. In the following series of sessions, the group addresses three situations: a dispute around chores, an emergency, and the possible departure of a member.

Living in the Group Home: First Friday in March

Frank: Anaya and I noticed that some of you seemed upset when we got here this evening. Would someone like to tell us what's been happening? *[Drawing out]*

Al: Yup. This all started at breakfast.

Anaya: Mmm.

Austi: Jim started yelling at Quentin and then he banged his fist on the table and upset Cookie and yelled at her. *[Austi is addressing Jim and points at him.]* If Cookie doesn't come back, it's going to be your fault.

Anaya: Austi, let's not point at people. *[Cutting off]* I can tell you're upset, but let's slow down so Frank and I can understand what happened.

Jim: Every time it's my turn to do dishes Cookie makes French toast, and Quentin puts so much maple syrup on his that a whale could swim in it to get to the toast.

Frank: So you think that Cookie intentionally picks your day for French toast.

Quentin: That's what he said that upset her. He said, "You always pick on me for the gooey French toast, and it's messy doing the dishes."

Anaya: Well, maple syrup is hard to wash off the dishes. If Cookie was targeting your day for French toast and if Quentin was adding extra syrup just to make it hard for you, then I could see why you might be upset.

Jim: You wouldn't like that either.

Anaya begins to work with Jim with two goals in mind: she uses a cognitive approach to help examine the truth of Jim's perceptions, and at the same time she is working with Jim to help him have more insight into his symptoms and how they affect his perceptions and interpersonal behaviors.

Anaya: No, if it were true, I wouldn't like it, but let's look at the true part. Jim, you know how we've talked about how sometimes when you think people are picking on you what is really happening is your symptoms are showing up. *[Teaching]*

Jim: Uhmm . . .

Anaya: . . . and sometimes it really is somebody picking on you.

Jim:	Sometimes they do . . .
Anaya:	Sometimes they do and sometimes you pick on them.
Jim:	Sometimes . . .
Frank:	Let's first look at the part about Cookie picking on you. Al, can you tell me about the breakfast schedule? About how often does Cookie make French toast?
	[Here Frank engages the group. He solicits information from a specific group member to clarify the facts of the story given by Jim.]
Al:	Almost every Friday unless we don't have any cinnamon bread left.
Frank:	And how often does Jim get to do the dishes?
Al:	There's four of us so every fourth day. Dishes are always a little messy on Fridays.
Anaya:	But Jim doesn't always do dishes on Fridays?
Quentin:	No more than the rest of us.
Austi:	Cookie was upset because when she started here about a month ago, she asked us what we wanted for breakfast, and all of us said French toast, and now you blew up at her about French toast.
Jim:	Yeah, I remember that. So OK, I guess she wasn't trying to get me.
Al:	No, just trying to make us happy.
Jim:	I should apologize? *[Jim expresses a degree of insight and follows by proposing a behavior change related to his insight.]*
Anaya:	Yes, Jim, you should apologize. *[Anaya reaffirms that apologizing is an appropriate behavior. For Jim it is therapeutic to learn how to repair interpersonal relationships since this is crucial to getting along with others in the world and specifically with others in the group home.]*
Quentin:	And I should rinse off my plate better before I put it in the sink. *[Quentin also gains some insight into how his own behavior affects others. He comes to this insight on his own and proposes an appropriate behavior change.]*
	[The other three men all nod.]
Frank:	That would help everybody.
Austi:	We're all in this together, and we have to make it work.
Anaya:	Yes, Austi, you are all in this together, and this is a nice home for all of you, so it's worth the effort. *[Universality]*
Al:	It's good for me because I don't see real good and I can take the bus. And if I want to go for a walk or to the store, you guys check on me but you don't try to boss me around or treat me like I was a baby.
	[All four men nod.]
Anaya:	It's good for each of you in your own way. *[Anaya generalizes from Al's statement to the group. This generalization promotes universality and cohesion.]*
Frank:	It is good for each of you in your own way. This is a comfortable home with a pleasant yard, and you are located where you can walk to the shopping center and several other things you like. One of the things that you do well is to use this group

to help you live together well and have a pleasant future. [**YTF Reminder:** Instillation of hope]

[There are more nods from the group.]

Living in the Group Home: Fourth Monday in March

Anaya: Fire Chief called Frank and me and told us that the fire alarm went off in the middle of the night last night and that you were pretty upset. He thought all of you might need to talk about it tonight.

Anaya opens the group by letting the members know that she and Frank know what happened. She then invites discussion. If there is a particular event that you as leader want the group to discuss, it is wise to open the session with a straightforward statement that invites the group to focus on the event, as Anaya did here.

Al: He was right. It was terrifying to be woken up by the smoke detector.

Frank: How about if each of you tells us what happened and then we'll go around and talk about how you felt then and how you feel now. *[Drawing out] [Structuring a round]*

Frank provides some structure, so members know they will all be heard. He also set up a process that gets the facts of what happened first since this will help Anaya and him respond realistically to the members. He lets members know from the start that they will have a chance to focus on their feelings after the story of the events has been told.

Al: Austi should talk because he was the first one that figured out what was going on.

[The other members nod.]

Frank: Austi, can you tell us how it started?

Austi: About two o'clock the smoke alarm screeched.

Quentin: And then there was a big bang out on the street, and the lights went out.

Austi: I could hear Fire Chief. He was saying, "We're OK; the fire is next door. We need to go down in the yard like we do in a fire drill."

Anaya: And what were other people doing? *[Draws out other members reports of what happened]*

Al: I heard Fire Chief say, "Fire drill," but I could smell smoke, and the lights were out. And I was scared and knocked my glasses off my nightstand and couldn't find them in the dark.

Jim: The smoke was thick, and at first I thought we were being bombed.

Quentin: There were two more big bangs. And smoke was coming in the window at the end of the hall.

Jim: I said, "We're being bombed!" and Quentin said, "No, no, there's a fire next door, and we have to do a fire drill."

Anaya: So you woke up in the darkness to smoke, and you heard explosions, and, Al, you couldn't see correctly because you lost your glasses. And then the power was out, so you couldn't put the lights on. All those things together made a pretty scary situation. Quentin kept his cool, and he helped you and you listened to him. *[Summarizes]*

Jim: You helped me a lot because you listened to Fire Chief and then I listen to him too.

Austi: Fire Chief was the only one with a flashlight, so I said, "Jim, get behind Fire Chief, then Quentin, then Al, and me last, and we will all go down together," and that's what we did.

Quentin: The fire trucks arrived about the time we got down on the porch. The neighbors' kitchen burned, and we learned that the bottles of propane for their stove were what made the explosions and took down the electric wires.

Frank: There are two things that I want to point out that you all did really well. First of all, you kept your heads and thought before you acted—you problem-solved together. Second, you followed the drill that you practice for this situation, particularly listening to Fire Chief and remembering to go down together. *[Teaching]*

Frank reaffirms their thoughtful, cohesive problem solving. He also reinforces them for following the directions of the staff person on fire watch.

Al: All of us and the neighbors and their two boys slept in our living room last night. And this morning when it got light, I found my glasses.

Jim: None of us were hurt, and Sunshine is OK.

Frank: Can you say something about feelings? *[Drawing out]*

Jim: Last night I was scared, and now I'm relieved.

Austi: Yeah, scared and now glad it wasn't our home that was damaged.

Al: Scared and grateful for Fire Chief. He helped us a lot.

            [Everyone nodded.]

Anaya: Did anyone tell him that?

Austi: We sure did.

Frank: Quentin, how were you feeling? *[Drawing out]*

Quentin: I was scared and now I'm exhausted.

Frank: You've been through a lot together. What did you learn from this? *[Drawing out]*

Jim: I learned when there's an emergency, I should listen to the other guys and not to my fears. I learned to remember what we practice. *[Self-understanding]*

Anaya: That's an important insight for you. Say that again.

Jim: When there's an emergency, I should listen to the other guys and not to my fears.

Quentin: I learned that even though I haven't lived here as long as the other guys, you guys and our home are really important to me. [**YTF Reminder:** Cohesion] And I learned we all need to have our own flashlight, so we walked to the store together before dinner and each bought one.

Al: I learned how important it was to look out for each other in an emergency and how important you guys are to me. *[Cohesion]*

Quentin: I learned that sometimes I can do what I need to do even if I feel a little scared. *[Self-understanding]*

Austi: I agree with all of that, and I learned it felt good to help the neighbors, that we could help the neighbors 'cause usually they help us. [**YTF Reminder:** Altruism]

Frank: Those neighbors are very kind and make you feel welcome in the neighborhood.

Jim: And we invited them to dinner for the next two nights so they could get their kitchen fixed.

Anaya: That was very kind. Do you have a plan for doing those dinners?

Quentin: Tonight we are going to order pizza delivered, and tomorrow we are going to barbeque chicken on the outdoor grill. Al will buy the chicken because he gets home the earliest and has time to go to the grocery store.

Anaya: That works. When Frank and I come in tomorrow night, we will bring a cake that you can share with the neighbors for dessert. [**YTF Reminder:** Cohesion and Universality.] *[By contributing to the meal, the coleaders express their connection to the group.]*

Anaya is working to encourage social interest and altruism. This is important because some of the neighbors wish the group home was not in their neighborhood. It is important that the members of the home are good neighbors to others.

Frank: *[Scanning the group]* I'm noticing that some of you are starting to look tired.

Austi: We didn't get that much sleep last night, and it was emotionally exhausting. Maybe we could go to bed now. *[Others nodded.]*

Anaya: Good night, sleep well.

Living in the Group Home: Fourth Thursday in June
Anaya and Frank arrive in the evening as usual. To their knowledge the day has gone well and was uneventful. Frank starts the group warm-up with a round.

Frank: Let's start with a check-in round. Give us a number one to ten about how your day went. Al, can you get us started?

Al: It's a seven—pretty ordinary.

Jim: Me too—a seven—work was OK and dinner was good.

Quentin: Maybe a four. *[Quentin looks down like he is uncomfortable.]*

Anaya: For me a nine—I'm looking forward to my vacation next week. Remember we discussed last week that Frank will be here and do the groups, and Chuck, the redheaded Fire Chief, will be here with him to learn to do groups for his college class.

Al: He will be all right.

Frank: I think so. Austi, how would you rate your day? *[Drawing out]*

Austi: I'd say a nine. I stitched enough shoes today to finally earn my bonus for the month. My boss told me I did a good job.

Anaya: So this is a lot better than last month when you expected a bonus and then didn't get one.

usti: It's lots better.

Frank: Sounds like you all had a pretty good day except for Quentin. Quentin, could you say a little bit about that? *[Drawing out]*

Frank draws Quentin out because his number response raised a question about how his day went.

Jim:	He got a letter from his sister, and he won't tell us what's in it.
	[Anaya motions with her hand for Jim to be quiet.] [Cutting off]
Anaya:	Quentin can talk if he wants to.
Quentin:	I got a letter from my sister, and she wants me to come live with her.
	Frank is scanning the group. From the looks on the faces of the other members, Quentin's news is a surprise to them.
Frank:	Say a little more Quentin.
Quentin:	She's about 10 years younger than I am. She asked me to go live with her once before I came here, when I was in the other group home.
Anaya:	But you didn't go.
Quentin:	Her husband was in the military. He flew helicopters, and they moved a lot, and I . . . I was scared of the moving part.
Anaya:	You didn't know if they would move someplace you didn't like?
Quentin:	Mmm.
Anaya:	But now you are thinking about going to live with her?
Quentin:	Yes. She said she won't move anymore. Her husband's helicopter was shot down and he was killed in January. She says she would still like me to go to her house.
Al:	Do you like her?
Quentin:	Yes, but I like you guys too, and it's a long way.
Jim:	Where does she live?
Quentin:	On the west coast up by Seattle. I went there once for the holidays.
Austi:	Did you like it?
	Notice that Anaya and Frank are letting the other members work with Quentin, and since they are doing a good job, the leaders are monitoring but not actively intervening.
Quentin:	It's a small farm by a nice lake. She has some horses and some goats and woods where I can take walks.
Jim:	You going to have a job?
Quentin:	She asked if I could help feed the horses and the goats. That would be fun. I'd need a heavy jacket for winter, but that would be OK.
	This all sounds quite positive, but Anaya senses Quentin is quite hesitant and draws him out about his hesitations.
Anaya:	That sounds pretty good, Quentin, and yet the look on your face says something is making you hesitate. What's hard?
Quentin:	Feelings.
Anaya:	Feelings about?
Quentin:	These guys. *[Quentin looks around the group.]*
Anaya:	There's something you want to say to the guys that's hard.
Frank:	These guys mean a lot to you. It's OK to tell them that. *[Frank is trying to get Quentin to express the feelings he is holding in. This might activate the therapeutic-factor catharsis.]*

Quentin:	*[Speaking in a warm and genuine tone, although some of his body language shows a bit of discomfort.]* You guys are very special. I feel like we are all part of a family here, and I never felt that way since I was little until I came here. I probably will go to my sisters now because it will put me back with my relatives, and that would be good for her and me for a long time. But I want you to know that I love you guys like you will always be my brothers. *[Quentin has tears in his eyes as he talks.]*
Jim:	You know we care about you too.
Frank:	Good, I'm wondering if any of you would say something to Quentin—something about your feelings or your hopes for him.
Jim:	I'm gonna miss you a lot. I'll never forget that you helped me the night the fire alarm went off. I hope it's good for you at your sister's, but maybe you could call us once in a while.
Austi:	I feel very proud of you that you have the courage to make a change. Some people would be too scared. I hope you enjoy the horses and maybe, maybe somehow we could come visit you.
Al:	I feel like you're one of my brothers, and I'd like to write once in a while if that's OK. *[Quentin nods.]*
Al:	My hopes for you, mmm, I hope you enjoy every day.

Frank now moves to helping Quentin bridge what he has learned in the group home to living in his sister's home.

Frank:	Seems like you've learned a lot since you've been here. Are there a couple of things you learned here that you want to remember because they will help you get along with your sister and help you have a happy future there?
Quentin:	*[Nods and thinks for a minute.]* Well, I should remember if I have fears to think before I do anything.
Jim:	Yup.
Quentin:	And to listen if I'm scared. If I have fears, I should listen to my sister. *[Everyone is nodding.]*
Al:	And you should remember that you and your sister are going to be in it—in life—together now.
Quentin:	Like we were all in it together here.
Al:	Right.

Notice that Al has made a great intervention. Such an intervention might have been made by one of the leaders, but Quentin easily accepts Al's point.

STUDY QUESTIONS

1. Discuss some types of information considered in making a diagnosis.
2. How is the diagnosis used in constructing a treatment plan?
3. Discuss different types of groups and how the goals of the groups might contribute to a treatment plan.
4. Discuss screening for diagnosis-focused groups.

5. How can you use information about the type and severity of members' symptoms to help you think about selecting members for a group?
6. How can you use information about the type and severity of members' symptoms to help you think about goals for sessions of the group?
7. Discuss the influence of diagnosis on member participation.

KEY CONCEPTS

diagnosis p. 222   scope of practice p. 225
symptom p. 222   treatment plan p. 223

REFERENCES

American Counseling Association (2005). *ACA code of ethics.* Alexandria, VA: Author.

American Psychiatric Association (2000). *Diagnostic and statistical manual of mental disorders, fourth edition, text revision.* Washington, DC: American Psychiatric Association.

CHAPTER 11
Moving Toward Professional Practice

Learning Objectives

After reading this final chapter you will be ready to

- Explore your own future professional development needs as a practicing group leader.
- Identify continuing-education opportunities for professional development.
- Describe methods to network with other group workers.
- Discuss the importance of supervision of your group work.
- Explain the value of joining professional associations.

THE MYTH OF THE NEXT "BEST" TECHNIQUE TO LEARN

Often, new counselors think that they are just one more technique away from being a better counselor. They are excited about learning new approaches and becoming better equipped as a counselor to work with clients. While learning new approaches and new techniques gives you a wider range of possibilities with a group, we know that the main influence on success in leading a group is your ability to form effective relationships between yourself and members and among members in the group.

As a counselor in individual counseling you have the luxury of focusing on developing one relationship between you and the client. With individual counseling you do not have to take into consideration any other person in the room. Neither do you have to consider relationships between other clients, because with individual counseling the only immediate relationship concern is you and the client. Even with couples or family counseling, you might have multiple counseling relationships to form, but the clients (couple or family members) already have a relationship with one another. The couple or family members are not complete strangers (as members most likely are in groups), so you do not have to work to acquaint family members as you do in other groups. With couple or family work you can focus on developing a relationship with each member of the family to move toward effectively working with them through their family issues.

Problem emphasis is also an important skill that is challenged in a different way with groups. Leaders have to learn the technique of juggling multiple members' various problems. Skilled leaders need to be able to select, combine, and orchestrate multiple members for the group. In individual counseling, your clients bring you their significant problems, and they set the goals with little interference from outside agendas. In groups, the leader must respond to many goals, and the true skill lies in being able to work with the group as a whole while addressing concerns and goals of individual members. We would encourage you for your next step of professional development to get ongoing experience as a leader.

Exercises for Active Learning

1. Reflect on the method you have used to form relationships in the groups in which you have been a member or leader. What do you perceive as your current strengths in forming relationships with members? In what ways can you improve your skills in forming relationships with members? How might you implement these new skills in the next group you participate in?

2. Reflect on how you manage multiple concerns in groups. What are your strengths in handling individual member goals while working with a group? In what ways can you improve on handling this complex group process? How might you take a next step toward improving on handling multiple group concerns in the next group in which you're involved?

CONTINUING YOUR PROFESSIONAL DEVELOPMENT

If you have progressed through the text to this point, you have learned and practiced in class beginning leader skills that will serve you well as you lead groups. So what do you do to continue your growth as a leader? We would encourage you to take some planned steps that strengthen your commitment and continue your development as a leader. Here are a few ideas for building on the beginning of your professional career as a group leader.

Receive More Training as a Group Leader

The Association for Specialists in Group Work (ASGW) (2000) provides Professional Standards for the Training of Group Workers, which designates core training in group work and specialized training in group work. Core training in group work consists of a minimum of 10 clock hours supervised practice (with 20 hours recommended) and content knowledge training in group dynamics, theories of group counseling, group work methods, leadership styles, skills used in group work, and approaches used in a variety of group types. Core training is standard training received by masters counseling students who are in a program accredited by the Council for Accreditation of Counseling and Related Educational Programs (CACREP, 2001).

Specialized training in group work allows for training institutions to develop their training in accordance with ASGW training standards, including emphasis on task group facilitation, group psychoeducation, group counseling, or group psychotherapy. Each group specialization has its own particular literature, and those attempting specialization training should become acquainted with the literature as well as already having completed core training standards. Clinical instruction for specialized training varies with group specialty areas. For Task Group Facilitation and Group Psychoeducation specialization, a minimum of 30 hours of experience, with 45 hours recommended. For Group Counseling and Group Psychotherapy, 45 minimum experience hours, with 60 hours recommended.

Other opportunities for training in group leadership exist outside of a formal degree-granting program. A good source of leadership training is with national associations. The Professional Development Committee of the Association for Specialists in Group Work (ASGW, 2000) has as its purpose to "mobilize the training resources of ASGW and activate professional training." The committee organizes association workshops, group training workshops, and a keynote speaker's bureau. Association workshops focus on the three main ASGW training and standards documents: the Professional Standards for Training of Group Workers (ASGW, 2000), the Best Practices in Group Work (ASGW, 1998), and the Principles of Diversity Competent Group Workers (ASGW, 1998).

ASGW's National Group Conference provides an opportunity in a friendly environment to connect with many of the leaders in the group counseling field. The annual ASGW conference has a series of workshops covering specialized topics. The conference also has a track of training for those who wish to gain a foundational understanding in group work. Attending a national conference for training

purposes not only advances your leadership training but also starts you along the path of networking professionally with other leaders.

You can also find additional professional training opportunities in your community. Look for practitioners who have been specially trained in group techniques and offer training groups either as course work through a university or as part of their private practice. These experiences are available for you as you enrich your experience. The challenge for the newly trained leader is doing the professional networking to find these training experiences.

Exercises for Active Learning

1. If you are currently in a counseling, social work, human services, or psychology training program, compare your training standards for group work to those established by the Association for Specialists in Group Work. How do they compare? When you consider the training standards and your current level of knowledge and experience, what might be the next step for you to seek out training?

2. Explore local, state, regional, and national resources (Association websites, publications, and conference information) for opportunities to expand your group leadership training. List one resource of each type that you feel will be helpful to you.

Website
Organization

_____

Web address

_____

Book
Author or Authors

_____

Title

_____

Journal article
Authors

_____

Title

_____

Conference
Sponsoring organization

_____

Dates and location

_____

Get More Experience as a Group Leader

Of course we would also support new leaders getting more experience in coleading and leading groups. Now that you have an understanding of the basic skills needed to plan and lead groups, like any newly acquired skill you will need to practice these skills in order for them to become more integrated as part of your counseling repertoire. The closer you can tie the learning experience of this text, and perhaps the class associated with it, to the practice and demonstration of skills in actual group work, the greater advancement you will have toward your capacity as a group leader. You will get the greatest impact of this text by the immediacy that you can begin using these leadership skills. Use the skills now, and they more easily move into your leadership repertoire; use them later, and the learning transfer of skills is protracted.

In your training setting or in your new clinical setting, work with others who are well trained and experienced in group leadership. Finding like-minded others who have similar interest or greater experience in groups can be a great asset to your own development as a leader. Once you have found that individual, spend some time sharing your experience and interest in group work. You will more than likely find similar interests and have similar ideas about how groups could be applied to your current setting. In CACREP accredited counselor education programs, your training expectations include a portion of group leadership in practicum and internship, so finding application for groups in your setting can help you achieve those requirements. Once you have ideas for groups in your setting, getting administrative approval to start the group is the first necessary step. After approval, spend a judicious amount of time planning for the group and selecting and screening participants. We would encourage you to use coleaders with your beginning attempts at groups. Coleadership early on increases the likelihood that your group will be a success and gives you someone that you can process group activity with and make necessary adjustments to the group.

Getting Experience in School-Based Settings

The American School Counselor Association (ASCA) National Model provides a structure to support groups in the schools as part of a comprehensive school guidance program (ASCA, 2003). If you are working in a school, following the ASCA National Model gives you a rationale and precedent to infuse groups through your setting. An integral part of the ASCA National Model delivery system is group counseling provided in three components: school guidance, individual student planning, and responsive services. The *school guidance component* is designed to facilitate the

delivery of school guidance programs that address developmental needs in academic achievement, career guidance, and personal social issues. Typical group activities under this arena include large classroom guidance lessons, which could incorporate your group leadership skills. *Individual student planning* involves appraisal and advisement in career and personal/social issues. The ASCA National Model suggests that these can be accomplished in small groups. *Responsive services* involve school counselors addressing immediate personal social concerns of the student body. The group counselor's role in responsive services could range from early intervention to a crisis response. Activities could be engaging small groups of students to address the death of a classmate or working with groups of students to normalize the school setting after a hurricane. Each component of delivery system in the ASCA National Model provides you with a new opportunity to develop your leadership skills.

Getting Experience in Agency-Based Settings

In agency-based settings the opportunity arises for you to develop and run groups to address particular needs of the population served by your agency. Many agencies often have ongoing topic or support groups. As a new leader, coleading an established group with a more experienced leader will be a good bridge to developing and running your own groups for the agency. If the agency or clinic addresses a particular mental health problem (addiction, eating disorders, depression, hospice), over time you will see common issues that your clients in individual counseling bring to you (anger management, self-esteem, social skills). These common issues can be addressed with topic-focused groups for clients. The most valuable knowledge component for running new groups is to know your clients and know their needs.

Exercises for Active Learning

1. Imagine you are working in the counseling setting of your dreams (or perhaps you already are!). You have the opportunity to develop and run groups. What questions would you have for supervisors and colleagues about groups in this setting? Before initiating a new group in this setting, what kinds of things would you need to know?
2. If you work in a school, review the American School Counselor Association National Model (ASCA, 2003).
   - What types of groups would you need to plan for your school if you were the elementary school counselor?

   _____

   - What types of groups would you need to plan for your school if you were the middle school counselor?

   _____

   - What types of groups would you need to plan for your school if you were the high school counselor?

   _____

3. If you work in an agency, think about the problem areas that your agency addresses with clients. What might be some associated groups you would plan for your clients?

Get More Experience as a Group Member

One experience that will prepare you for being a leader is being involved in a group as a member. Therefore, we would recommend that you not only continue your professional training as a leader but also continue your professional personal growth by being a member of a group. The experience of being a member puts you in your client's shoes. Being a member of a group and participating under another's leadership gives you a visceral experience that cannot be experienced by only running groups. The fact is we have learned some of our best leadership skills from having multiple experiences as members. Many of the examples in this text emerged from our experiences as leaders *and* as members. There is nothing like being a member of a well-run group. You have the luxury as a member to savor the experience without having to focus on the process and content as you do in the leader role.

Many opportunities to be involved in groups will come to you as part of your professional development; you just have to be open to them. For example, you may be the member of an ongoing, task-oriented group of professionals who meet regularly to plan a counseling conference. The group would develop through phases and settle into accomplishing the task, planning the conference. As part of that conference you may attend a workshop where someone gives a presentation on Gestalt groups. This professional contact might provide you with a professional contact who offers Gestalt group experiences for your own personal growth. During the Gestalt group experience you might get in touch with your unfinished business regarding the loss of a parent. At the end of the Gestalt group experience, your professional contact might suggest a psychodrama group you can become involved in to address some of these personal-loss issues.

This example gives you three levels at which you can become involved as a group member. The example presents membership opportunities that range from less personal engagement (task-oriented group) to more personal engagement (group psychotherapy). As a new leader you can learn more about group process by being a member at any level of personal involvement. Being a member also offers you the opportunity to use your leader skills while you are a member of a group. For example, if as a member you feel a connection with another member, you could make a statement directly to that member, expressing your experience of connection. Doing so models for other members how to link with those with whom they feel a similarity.

So we would recommend that you pay attention for opportunities to become a group member as they present themselves throughout your professional career. Your personal experiences in groups can lead you to pursue advanced training in a particular type of group (task group facilitation, psychoeducational groups, group counseling, or group psychotherapy) and particular style of group (Gestalt, Encounter, Psychomotor, Psychodrama, etc.).

Exercises for Active Learning

Consider learning about group leadership by being a member of a group. Pick a specific type of group (task/work, psychoeducational, counseling, or psychotherapy). Look within the type of group you picked to find a specific group that interests you. Set a concrete goal to become a member of that group to learn about the group and to observe the leaders at work.

Infuse Group Leadership into Your Work Setting

Another method to develop your skills is to use the leadership skills you've learned in this book in nonclinical settings where you have to work in groups, like team meetings or problem-solving sessions. The skills that you learned in the book can apply effectively to various settings where you are dealing with a group of people. We are not suggesting that you attempt to do therapeutic groups in a work setting but simply use the skills you have learned in relationship to leadership with groups you commonly come in contact with.

For example, you might put on your leadership lenses next time you are in a meeting. Observe how the person responsible for running the meeting affects the group process. Observe how the leader and the members use or fail to use communication skills. Notice how the meeting leader handles differences in opinion between meeting members. Does the meeting leader use methods to focus the meeting? Given the opportunity to ask questions, what kinds of questions are being asked by members of the group? Are there leadership techniques such as linking and drawing out being used by the meeting leader? Does the leader use rounds for coming to group consensus for a decision?

Arrange for Supervision of Your Group Work

Ongoing supervision of your counseling, whether it be individual, family, or in groups, is essential for the welfare of you and your members. Supervision helps you make the transition from training to practice. Supervision is one of the best ways to keep your skills sharp, enhance your growth as a leader, and ensure a professional practice. Unfortunately supervision of groups is not as available as it should be. We are supportive of live supervision of group leadership at all levels of professional development but particularly early in your career.

DeLucia-Waack and Fauth (2004) summarize some of the issues unique to group work supervision. They support the necessity of supervision on the basis of the complicated multiple relationships that develop between leader and members, leader and subgroups of members, and between members. Supervision issues common for individual counselors (performance anxiety, parallel process, and countertransference) are greatly magnified for group leaders in the complexities of a group. DeLucia-Waack and Fauth further discuss types of supervision that should be available for new group leaders: individual supervision of group work; dyadic, triadic, and group supervision of group work. We would encourage you to make sufficient supervision of your group work an expectation for your ethical practice.

Exercises for Active Learning

Consider your current skills and activity related to group work. What kinds of professional development issues might you look for assistance with through group work supervision? How could a group work supervisor assist you with this?

Join Professional Associations

Joining professional associations related to counseling and group work is a significant means to continuing your education as a leader. Professional organizations provide multiple opportunities for you to experience and become further trained in groups. Professional associations assist in the continuing development of their members by providing professional journals, providing conference opportunities, supporting specialized training, and creating an available resource network.

The Association for Specialists in Group Work's (ASGW) *Journal for Specialists in Group Work*, is a quarterly journal aimed at group work practitioners and group educators. The journal's emphasis is on related theory, practice, interventions, research, and current issues. As a professional, receiving *Journal for Specialists in Group Work* keeps you up to date with current theory and practice in the field of groups. ASGW has an annual conference specifically focused on group work and brings together some of the top educators and practitioners in group work for an intimate conference related to sharing knowledge and enhancing skills. In addition, as a division of the American Counseling Association, ASGW also has a presence at ACA's annual conference. Attending conferences of professional organizations puts you in the presence of many great professional resources. There is often the availability through professional associations to receive specialized training. ASGW also has the ASGW Board Approved Speaker's Project, which is a listing of board-approved speakers on various group and leadership topics. These contacts are available for specialized training and continuing education as affiliated with the professional association.

The greatest impact of being part of a professional association is networking. Group work professionals have a collective personality type that makes them want to engage new leaders in the process. These professionals model inclusion in their professional organization and are extremely welcoming to newly trained group leaders. We both feel that we have a community we can network with each time we go to an ASGW conference. Relationships forged years ago and separated by miles and time are automatically renewed when professional colleagues meet at conferences. The networking available for you at conferences is the first step in your lifelong professional development.

We are pleased that you are looking at further extending your professional training as a group leader. It is a fulfilling journey, and we are glad that this text was one of the steps along your path. To some, you may have already started the journey, and this text has been a refresher of skills or a reaffirmation of what you are already doing. To others just beginning the journey as a group leader, we are excited about what group work holds for your future.

REFERENCES

American School Counselor Association. (2003). *The ASCA national model: A framework for school counseling programs.* Alexandria, VA: Author.

Association for Specialists in Group Work (ASGW). (1998). *Association for Specialists in Group Work Best Practice Guidelines.* Retrieved July 20, 2006, from *ASGW website*: http://www.asgw.org/best.htm.

Association for Specialists in Group Work (ASGW). (1998). *Association for Specialists in Group Work Principles for Diversity-Competent Group Workers.* Retrieved July 20, 2006, from ASGW website: http://www.asgw.org/diversity.htm.

Association for Specialists in Group Work (ASGW). (2000). *Professional Standards for the Training of Group Workers.* Retrieved July 20, 2006, from ASGW website: http://www.asgw.org/training_standards.htm.

Council for Accreditation of Counseling and Related Educational Programs (CACREP). (2001). *2001 Standards.* Retrieved August 2, 2006, from CACREP website: http://www.cacrep.org/2001Standards.html.

DeLucia-Waack, J. L. & Fauth, J. (2004). Effective supervision of group leaders: Current theory, research, and implications for practice. In J. L. DeLucia-Waack, D. A. Gerrity, C. R. Kalodner, & M. T. Riva (Eds.), *Handbook of group counseling and psychotherapy.* Thousand Oaks, CA: Sage.

INDEX